INEFFECTIVE POLICIES

Causes and Consequences of Bad Policy Choices

Edited by
Ian Roberge, Heather McKeen-Edwards,
and Malcolm Campbell-Verduyn

P

First published in Great Britain in 2025 by

Policy Press, an imprint of
Bristol University Press
University of Bristol
1–9 Old Park Hill
Bristol
BS2 8BB
UK
t: +44 (0)117 374 6645
e: bup-info@bristol.ac.uk

Details of international sales and distribution partners are available at policy.bristoluniversitypress.co.uk

British Library Cataloguing in Publication Data
A catalogue record for this book is available from the British Library

ISBN 978-1-4473-7155-7 paperback
ISBN 978-1-4473-7157-1 ePub
ISBN 978-1-4473-7156-4 ePdf

Cover design: Liam Roberts
Front cover image: iStock/Sergei Chuyko
Bristol University Press and Policy Press use environmentally responsible print partners.
Printed and bound in Great Britain by CPI Group (UK) Ltd, Croydon, CR0 4YY

Contents

List of figures and tables

Figures

Tables

Notes on contributors

Alberto Asquer is Reader in Public Policy and Management, SOAS University of London, UK.

Malcolm Campbell-Verduyn is Senior Lecturer in International Political Economy in the Department of International Relations and International Organization, University of Groningen, The Netherlands.

Thomas Greitens is Professor of Public Administration in the School of Politics, Society, Justice, and Public Service at Central Michigan University, USA.

Blayne Haggart is Associate Professor of Political Science at Brock University, Canada.

Jacob Hasselbalch is Associate Professor at the Copenhagen Business School, Denmark.

David Jesuit is Professor of Political Science in the School of Politics, Society, Justice, and Public Service at Central Michigan University, USA.

Matthias Kranke is a Fellow within the Young Academy for Sustainability Research (YAS) at the Freiburg Institute for Advanced Studies (FRIAS), University of Freiburg, Germany.

Erin Lockwood is Assistant Professor in the Department of Political Science, University of California, Irvine, USA.

Heather McKeen-Edwards is Associate Professor in the Department of Politics and International Studies, Bishop's University, Canada.

Ian Roberge is Professor in the School of Public Policy and Administration, York University, Canada.

Madison Stirling is Master in Environmental Studies (MES) Planning Student, Faculty of Environmental and Urban Change, York University, Canada.

Natasha Tusikov is Associate Professor in the Department of Social Science, York University, Canada.

Mariëlle Wijermars is Assistant Professor in Cyber-Security and Politics at Maastricht University, The Netherlands.

Mark Winfield is Professor in the Faculty of Environmental and Urban Change (EUC) and Coordinator of the Master of Environmental Studies and MES/Juris Doctor programs at York University, Canada.

Acknowledgment

We are grateful to Dr Tony Porter (McMaster University) who served for each of us as our PhD dissertation supervisor and intellectual guide. He gave us the freedom to experiment with new concepts and inspired us to explore off-the-beaten-track ideas such as that of bad policy. Tony, we thank you for all that you have done for us.

Ineffective policies: causes and consequences of bad policy decisions

Ian Roberge, Heather McKeen-Edwards, and Malcolm Campbell-Verduyn

Introduction

It is hard to miss references to bad and ineffective policy in everyday media stories and general conversations – and for good reason. The climate emergency is real, and yet government responses have come up short for decades. The 2007–08 global financial crisis brought the world economy to a standstill; the decade of reform that followed resulted mostly in marginal policy adjustments and the entrenchment of many of the same bad policies and regulatory practices that led to the crisis in the first place. The rapid application of emerging technologies is reshaping the way we work, live, and play as governments seem at a loss about how to steer these developments. These fields and many others have been shaped by ineffective (if not outright undesirable) and bad policy.

But what exactly is a bad or ineffective policy? Given the ubiquity of this analytical framing and the importance of the policy challenges citizens around the world are facing, it is important to scrutinize ineffective policy to generate better (if not outright good) and effective policy. We know increasingly more about successful policies: those that work best or are bound to be effective. Yet, there are no easy definitions or simple fixes to ineffective policy: hence this book, which we intend not merely as an academic exercise in conceptual refinement but also to help overcome governments' inability to address environmental, financial, technological, and other types of problems. At a fundamental level, the lack of progress in addressing serious problems, and even the tendency of policy to *worsen* rather than to improve them for citizens worldwide, deepens perceptions that government is not working. The decline in trust in government and search for easy answers by populist movements can be countered; however, for that to happen, this volume argues that it is necessary to clarify what makes for ineffective policy and to identify where governments are falling short to develop, in turn, policies that meaningfully address the problems with which we are collectively confronted.

This volume is concerned with policy that is developed, adopted, and/or sustained despite being shown as ineffective/ineffectual and generating undesirable and/or unanticipated negative outcomes. Such policies are by their very nature ineffective. This definition grounds research in empirical cases of how and why governments develop and pursue ineffective policy. Such a position draws from the American political scientist Harold Lasswell, who helped found the field of policy studies. He argued that policy work ought to be multidisciplinary, focused on problem solving, and explicitly normative (Torgerson, 1985). Taking their cue from these principles, contributors to this book sought to identify ineffective policies and to lay the foundations for citizens, scholars, and policy makers alike to tackle them in more comprehensive ways that account for government deficiencies without seeking to undermine their work. Hailing from a broad range of disciplinary backgrounds and methodological approaches, contributors to this book share a commitment to improving trust in governments and to the development and implementation of the policies necessary to tackle problems in and across the diverse fields of environment, finance, and technology.

Part of this framing is an acceptance that research on ineffective policy requires an explicitly normative approach that recognizes there are good and desirable policies, as well as bad and undesirable policies. Not shying away from using such words allow scholars and policy makers alike possibilities to consider the substantive questions openly and honestly about the type of policies that societies need and ought to favor, as well as those that governments ought *not* to adopt and implement. Being explicitly normative in identifying and advancing solutions to serious societal problems has its place in policy studies. Doing so in no way removes the rigor and systematic research upon which the policy assessments and recommendations provided in this volume rely. All research and policy analyses are subject to biases which we argue need to be explicitly acknowledged. Identifying ineffective policies as not meeting outcomes, failing to produce expected outputs, having implementation issues, generating unexpected effects, and/or having outright failed all ultimately requires judgment underlined by normative stances. Referencing effective policy as good and desirable, and ineffective policy as bad and undesirable, in short, helps engage in more foundational debates while maintaining a focus on much-needed policy improvement. It also allows the connection with language used in everyday framing of policy, opening important spaces for communication beyond the ivory tower/academic world.

Ineffective policies in Europe and North America are identified in this book across three fields that are core to societal well-being in the 21st century. These policy fields have been selected, in fact, because of their significance for the future well-being of populations around the globe.

Environmental policy is a clear case where bad decision-making in advance industrialized countries over decades is having substantive consequences that are felt around the world daily. Similarly, financial policy steers a sector whose services underpin the world economy, yet has become increasingly volatile and disconnected from everyday economic production and exchange and more central to the lives of increasingly indebted populations. Finally, current policies towards emergent technologies have widespread present and long-lasting consequences for societal well-being. What is needed for achieving a brighter future is getting policy in these fields right, which this book argues involves explicitly identifying and labelling ineffective policies where bad decision-making is holding back progress towards better paths forward.

The rest of this introductory chapter proceeds in four sections. First, we substantiate just how widespread the use of bad policy and ineffective policy references are in policy literatures drawing on a bibliometric analysis while highlighting that their conceptual consideration is often lax and superficial. Second, we provide our conceptualization of ineffective policy as the initial foundation for further refinement and application of the term. Third, we situate the distinct contributions of this book. Fourth, we lay out the organization of the book and address practical limitations.

Bad and ineffective policy: widely but loosely used terms of trade

Invoked widely in popular culture, references to ineffective and bad policy are also common in scholarship. Our bibliometric analysis indicates just how widely these terms are used across academic disciplines drawing on the JSTOR and Portico databases. Through its 'data for research tool' Constellate, JSTOR provides access to scholarship in 75 disciplines, covering its 2,800 academic journals as well as Portico, a preservation archive that works with 1,288 libraries and 1,076 publishers, and covers just over 38,000 ejournal titles (Portico, n.d.). These two datasets created were explicitly limited to research articles published in the past 25 years (between 1998 and 2023) to catch modern usage of these terms.

In the first dataset the term 'bad policy' was identified in 2,577 articles, appearing 21 times in titles and six times in keywords.[1] This large number of references is a clear indication of the widespread use of 'bad policy' within scholarship. Figure 1.1 shows that use of the phrase is found in economics, business, or development journals (543 references), law (488), science/ medicine/psychology (254), and anthropology/criminology/sociology (190). Tellingly, however, one fifth (20 percent) of articles over the period hail from political science, public policy, and administration (329 articles), and international relations and security studies journals (191 articles).

Figure 1.1: Articles utilizing 'bad policy' by journal subject focus (n = 2,577)

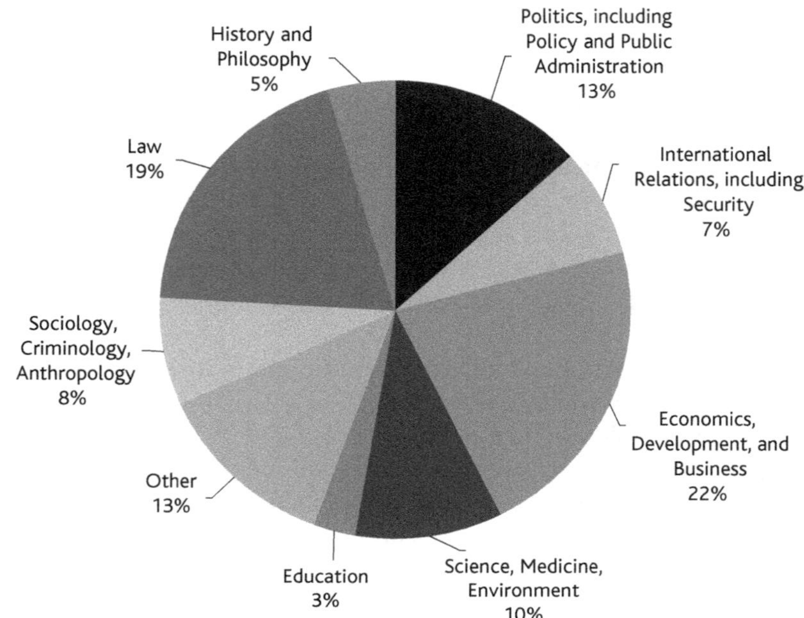

Meanwhile the term 'ineffective policy' was identified in 545 articles and books (see Figure 1.2). One hundred of these references are in the fields of political science, public policy, and administration, and another 25 are in the field of international relations. While clearly this phrasing is less prominent then 'bad policy', it is also apparent that references to ineffectiveness are still used in a limited number of policy studies publications (twice used in titles).

These bibliometric analyses demonstrate the ubiquitousness of 'bad' and 'ineffective' as descriptors of policy, as well as the extent to which these terms are invoked liberally and usually without much conceptual depth or empirical operationalization. In short, there is a need to give serious thought to the application of these terms that are used widely and to consider what exactly makes something an ineffective or bad policy. We fill this gap by beginning to deepen our conceptual understanding of these terms and providing empirical applications in the pages that follow.

Some conceptual refinement

We start by referencing ineffective policies as 'those developed, adopted and/ or sustained even though they can be shown to be ineffectual and generate undesirable and/or unanticipated negative outcomes', which provides for

Figure 1.2: Books and articles utilizing 'ineffective policy' by subject focus (n = 545)

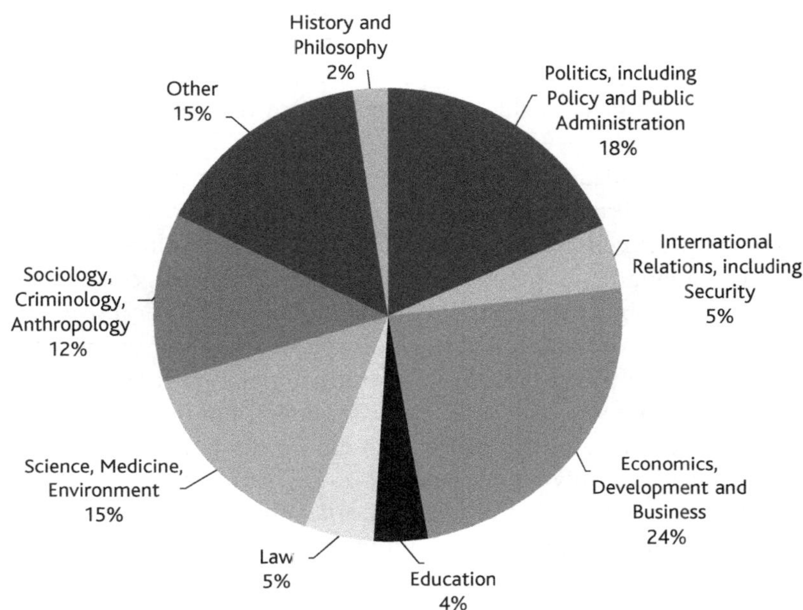

a two-pronged approach to the study of the concept. First, the definition considers processes of policy development emphasizing the determination of the objectives and goals to be attained. Are policy goals normatively undesirable, if not in some cases outright objectionable? Was it known and apparent before adoption that the policy could not and would not meet its objectives, could not work and was bound to fail? While policy makers may not necessarily aim for unwarranted objectives on purpose – decision makers make legitimate errors – decisions can still be made with intent to pursue directions that ought not to be taken. This definition allows for such normative assessment to be made in exploring the initial development of ineffective policies, with a view of proposing alternative goals and objectives that are less objectionable.

The second part of the definition emphasizes policy impacts. This brings into consideration questions of undesirable and/or unanticipated outcomes. The word ineffective is used loosely in general discussion to highlight something that does not have a significant impact. In this book, however, a policy is considered ineffectual because it does not work and/or because the outcomes and impacts are detrimental – the policy's effects are significant because of their undesirableness. The policy may even be harmful, and in some cases lead to unexpected and seriously detrimental outcomes for society at large. Harm may not be intended, here as well, yet still be one of the policy's main outcomes. Is a policy pursued even when such harm comes to light? Plenty is of course known about path dependency phenomena; less is known about whether paths are maintained in the face of knowledge about considerable harm.

Bringing these parts of our definition together points to policies as ineffective either (1) right from a problematic onset stemming from the development of objectionable goals; or (2) from the effects of otherwise desirable goals whose effects due to poor formulation, problems of implementation, inadequate collaboration and sheepish regulation and management are distinctly negative for society. Although our presentation of policy ineffectiveness bears a resemblance to policy failures, it remains distinct in that our definition of ineffective policy acknowledges that a policy can still meet its objectives, and thus be deemed successful because it met its goals, irrespective of the fact that these objectives are objectionable and/or that the policy's impact is harmful. The study of policy failures is anchored in the idea that a policy has not met its objectives, but most often it does not 'judge' the nature of the impact or consider the policy's desirableness something that can only be done with a more normative approach, such as that which we take in this book. Both pathways to ineffectiveness are fluid and unfold along a continuum of policy (un)desirability and (in)effectiveness, which we break down into four sections (see Figure 1.3). At the far-left end of the continuum are the most effective policies solving crucial societal issues through positive outcomes or limited negative externalities. Then, moving to the right on our spectrum, there are moderately effective policies that address the problem that was meant to be tackled, with some deficiencies and the possibility of negative externalities. Broadly speaking, policies in our second category can be fixed – these policies are mostly effective and can conceivably be repaired. As we move to the ineffective side of the continuum, there are moderately ineffective policies that fail to address problems meaningfully, and/or have a greater risk of negative externalities. This third category of policies may be salvageable, though properly addressing the policy problem or minimizing risks requires serious policy corrections. The fourth and final category is that of ineffective or bad policies that fail to address the policy problem or make it worse, and/or can demonstrably be shown to have serious negative externalities, including possible harm. A policy that meets its stated outcomes can still fall into this ineffective category if the negative externalities clearly outweigh the positive results, requiring a readjustment of priorities.

Importantly, most policies likely fall within the moderately effective to moderately ineffective categories. The good news, therefore, is that most policies are not inherently bad *and* even those that are ineffective can be overcome: that is, they are not doomed to failure. Ineffective policies, however, do require serious attention as this book provides with a view of suggesting pathways to turn 'bad into good'. In other words, our conceptualization opens the possibility of identifying and repairing cases of

Figure 1.3: Continuum of policy (ineffectiveness)

Effective Policy/Good/Desirable

Effective Policy Problem successfully addressed Positive externalities/ no negative externalities	Moderately Effective Policy Problem addressed Low-risk negative externalities		
		Moderately Ineffective Policy Problem not well addressed High risk of negative externalities	Ineffective Policy Problem unaddressed/ made worse Substantive negative externalities/harm

Ineffective Policy/Bad/Undesirable

ineffective policy. The remaining chapters in this book serve to operationalize this definition of ineffective policy through detailed case analysis.

Situating the book

This book was not written in a vacuum. It reflects the editors' preference for returning to the roots of policy studies and its emphasis on problem–solving, and for bringing together scholars that work across different social science disciplines including political science, environmental studies, international political economy, and policy studies. Keeping this observation in mind, this book builds on, while remaining distinct from, and extends research in the fields of policy studies and policy analysis, including on policy successes and failures. We reference some of this important literature further on, and detail our own approach and contribution.

Substantive efforts have been made to reflect on policy successes and failures over the last 15 years or so (Marsh and McConnell, 2010; McConnell, 2010; Peters, 2015; Bovens and 't Hart, 2016; Lindquist et al, 2022; Begley et al, 2019; Luetjens et al, 2019; 't Hart and Compton, 2019). For its part, the literature on policy failures will, at times, describe a policy as bad (Arlow, 2019) though the focus solely relates to the policy's results. More broadly, there is also a notable literature that focuses on government mistakes, usually thought of as policy with unintended and negative consequences (Hampshire, 2018). There are also scholars who work with concepts like policy catastrophes (Moran, 2001); policy fiascos (Opperman and Spencer, 2016; Whiteford, 2021); policy disasters (Grossman, 2013); policy messes (Roe, 2016); governmental blunders (King and Crewe, 2013; Jennings et al, 2018); and policy overreactions (Hafsi and Baba, 2022). Elements of these works are also useful. Catastrophes, fiascos, and blunders represent extreme forms of policy failures where the emphasis lies on explaining the failings of government (Gaskell et al, 2020), whereas policy overreactions emphasize bad policy decisions, especially when made under duress.

As observed in the bibliometric analysis, scholars have not shied away from referring to bad and ineffective policy. Within the context of the American federal system, Shipan and Volden (2021) explore, for instance, why bad policy spreads, and good ones do not. The focus of their work is on policy learning across US states. Saldin (2017) explores bad policy as a design choice wherein policy makers view a bad policy as better than no policy with the expectation that the policy can be amended later on.

Accounting for the rich heritage discussed, this volume makes three distinct contributions in refining ineffective policy. First, the book explicitly identifies and labels policies as ineffective, bad, and undesirable. For each of the case studies, contributors explicitly note that the policy under consideration is ineffective, then present an explanation based on rigorous analysis, and consider better policy alternatives. Chapter 4, in particular, goes further, developing a typology of good, symbolic, bad, and perverse policies from which he draws a 3×3 matrix with nine different possibilities for policy options. Much of this book, as such, is about explicitly labelling ineffective policy and working to systemically understand how it emerged and its implications. The objective in each chapter and across policies is to determine what makes a policy ineffective and when and where the problems emerge: from inception, in design, in implementation or in outcomes. This is an important first step in taking ownership of the widely used but rarely conceptualized policy frame. As noted earlier, this is not done with the intent of critiquing governments per se, rather it serves as the basis for working towards having fewer ineffective policies and the development of better policy options, if not outright good policy. It takes the first step for ineffective and bad policies to potentially evolve into effective ones by acknowledging and understanding their flaws.

The second contribution of this book is that it is explicit about its use of normative considerations. The literature on policy successes acknowledges key normative considerations in determining whether a policy is a success or not ('t Hart and Compton, 2019) though it does not fully assume the different layers of subjective analyses and choices that sustain many of the cases that it presents. Policy successes are also often a matter of perception. This book's embrace of a more normative conception of policy studies is most evident in the chapters that openly contest a policy's goals and objectives. The policy in these chapters is ineffective and bad because what it tries to accomplish is undesirable. Policy decisions invariably include tradeoffs and value judgments; however, they are not random and unpredictable. Policy making requires multiple decisions during all phases of the policy cycle, and these decisions reflect intent. As knowledge and science evolve, and as understanding changes over time, recommendations regarding effective and ineffective policy may also change. Scholars can use their knowledge and understanding to challenge this intent and put forward better alternatives. Since policy making in and of itself is value-laden, it means that its study where these decisions are analyzed, admittedly or not, also reflects value considerations. While this recognition of normativity carries with it risks, it is important to restate that public policy has traditionally been about solving real-world problems. While wicked policy problems may not have easy answers (Head, 2022), and it is not the contention of this book that they do, we believe there are bound to be solutions that are more effective, and others that are less so, and that they can be identified. If the goal of policy is to make things better, scholars, we argue, have the distinct responsibility to denote policies that either do not accomplish that goal, or possibly make things worse.

Third, we argue throughout the book that the consequences of ineffective policy are serious and must be part of the conversation about democratic regression. Although it is possible to debate the extent to which this regression is happening (Diamond, 2021), the increasing lack of trust in governments and institutions as referenced in Chapter 12 is more easily measured and significant. When the policies of governments are ineffective, the case that government works and that it works in the interest of the majority gets harder to make. Ineffective policy fuels cynicism, creating openings for more extreme politics. While this book is unlikely to counter this trend on its own, we can certainly make the argument that the quest for better and more effective policy is a worthwhile effort. This volume, therefore, advances the idea that the study of ineffective policy is not only useful, but also necessary.

The structure and organization of the book

This book presents 11 cases of policies that are mostly ineffective to completely ineffective and, despite not being 'right' in the normative sense, are all on the right-hand side of the spectrum outlined in the previous section. These policies have been developed by public authorities in North America and Europe and, therefore, are primarily situated in Western democracies that exclude, for instance, policy making in autocratic states. Policies in this book examine those governing three fields: environmental policy, financial services sector policy, and new and emerging technologies. While these each run through the 'slow burning' climate crisis as well as the 'fast burning' financial crises of 2007–08, the focus is on policy making that is not developed under extreme duress such as during times of war. As far as the past decades can be considered 'normal', the focus of this book is on regular, everyday policy making.

The three-part organization of the book builds on the conceptualization of ineffective policy to firmly consider, first, the desirability of the policy, second, its concrete impacts and, third, the wider consequences of undesirable and bad policy making.

Before shifting into the case studies, Ian Roberge and Mariëlle Wijermars consider more explicitly the relationship between ineffective policy and democratic regression in Chapter 2. This chapter, which builds on the introduction, is an important first step in the discussion of ineffective policy as it brings into context a larger philosophical discussion about the consequences of ineffective policy making, highlighting that beyond the direct policy implications, they also relate to the quality of democratic practices themselves.

Part I focuses on *contested goals* in the development of ineffective policy. These five chapters present cases that consider policies where the concern stems from their inception, foundation, and core purposes, whether that be purely normative, for policies with objectives that should not be pursued, or empirical, where the goals may be desirable yet the policy from the start is doomed to fail.

In Chapter 3, Matthias Kranke examines the contested role of economic growth in environmental policy within the broader context of whether economic growth is good or bad. Focusing on the German Federal Ministry for Economic Affairs and Climate Action (BMWK), his analysis looks at whether vibrant academic debate about post-growth, or the related policy arguments, have made any inroads into the ministry and whether the BMWK has remained focused on propagating discourses of green and inclusive growth without considering the concerns of these approaches.

In Chapter 4, Alberto Asquer focuses on the policy development process around wind farms in Italy and understanding how ineffective policy is integrated into the perspectives of both target groups and other stakeholder groups when considering policies. In the process, he provides insight into how bad policies fit into a larger scale of options, spanning from ideal policies to disastrous ones, based on their perceived effectiveness and desirability, as well as the importance of understanding this nuance for policy makers and stakeholders participating in the policy discourse.

Chapter 5 shifts the focus away from the environmental sector, as Malcolm Campbell-Verduyn provides a comprehensive examination of the policies around cryptocurrency in the United States. In its first decade, US policy in this area was torn between two policy goals, one which highlighted harm in the context of national security and another which downplayed harm to promote Bitcoin's underlying blockchain technology. He argues that this tension created a 'bad policy start' that has limited the effectiveness of newer US policies in the area and has also led to ad hoc enforcement and belated reactions in the face of rapid developments.

In Chapter 6, Natasha Tusikov looks at Google's failed attempt to develop a smart city in Toronto when it was awarded the Quayside land development contract despite having little urban development expertise. The chapter shows the disproportionate benefits and power that would have been granted to commercial interests through data control and intellectual property rights ownership had this bad policy come to fruition.

In Chapter 7, Blayne Haggart focuses on the development of Canada's COVID Alert app. The detailed analysis not only reveals why the app was ineffective in fulfilling its objectives, but also how this outcome can be traced to the beginning of the policy design phase as dataism and technological solutionism reshaped the policy problem to make it fit a predetermined solution.

The four chapters in Part II of the book focus on the undesirable and/or unanticipated *negative outcomes* of policy. To start off this section of the book, Jacob Hasselbalch's chapter traces how the Plastics Strategy in the EU evolved over time and shifted its focus from addressing externalities of plastics to considering the plastic as part of a circular economy. It argues that this shift has had real negative consequences for the future as it normalizes a situation of 'toxic growth' in global plastic production.

Following this, in Chapter 9 Mark Winfield and Madison Stirling examine the Fall 2022 package of land-use and planning reforms adopted in the province of Ontario developed to address concerns about affordable housing. They show how there are not only doubts about the enacted reforms' ability to address the housing crisis, but also that additional environmental and social harms were created through the weakening of pre-existing protections for agricultural and natural heritage lands, the limiting wider public participation in the planning process, and the constraining future local government capacity to address climate change.

In Chapter 10, the focus shifts again to the financial sector as Erin Lockwood analyzes the Volker Rule, the centerpiece of the 2010 Dodd-Frank Wall Street Reform Act and a landmark regulatory policy aimed at substantively changing the US universal banking model. She highlights how core provisions of the rule have been substantially undermined over time because its many definitional ambiguities weakened its impact and gave fuel to its opponents, and how this has allowed the disproportionate privilege and influence of private financial actors in the policy field to remain largely unchanged.

Heather McKeen-Edwards brings the individual case studies to a close in Chapter 11 with her research focusing on consumer finance, particularly the regulation of payday loans to individuals in Canada and the US. She argues that this policy can be seen as ineffective because of the inconsistency in the application of regulatory tools, the regulatory arbitrage that occurs because it is governed at the subnational level, and the lack of policy emphasis on encouraging more socially beneficial alternatives. This ineffectiveness has meant that the policy has not been able to fully or consistently address the harms caused by this form of lending, which is particularly problematic for individuals with lower incomes or those subject to greater financial exclusion.

Part III wraps up the book with two chapters considering the impact of ineffective policy. In Chapter 12, David Jesuit and Thomas Greitens provide a comparative perspective on how bad policy generates an erosion of public trust. Utilizing the 2016 International Social Survey Program's (ISSP) series on the 'Role of Government' to test the relationship between policy and trust from the perspective of individuals, their analysis suggests that the public's trust in government and their perceptions of bureaucratic fairness decline when they perceive policy ineffectiveness, reinforcing some of the concerns raised in previous chapters.

In Chapter 13, the concluding chapter, Ian Roberge returns to look at the larger overall findings and common themes that have emerged across the chapters and to propose further refinement of this book's initial catalyst of a research programme on ineffective policy. Most importantly, he directly addresses the question of policy makers' intent and why and under what circumstances they prefer ineffective policy over better options.

This book represents an exploratory effort that seeks to open the door for scholars, policy makers, and citizens alike to have honest conversations about policies that exist, those that ought to be reversed as well as those that we collectively need. As with all first steps, this book has some limitations in what it can achieve and there are three important caveats to address. First, this book considers, as was just noted, ineffective/bad/undesirable policy within the context of the regular policy making process. The focus is on policy making in 'normal times' and avoids analysis of policies made under extreme duress including, for instance, during times of war. Emergencies and crises affect policy making in many ways and although they could lead to ineffective policy, they ought to be considered separately and on their own. Second, the book's chapters offer cases of ineffective policy in North America and Europe; our analyses are, therefore, primarily situated in Western democracies and exclude, for instance, policy making in other regions of the globe where political systems may differ. For instance, we account for relatively resilient institutions even in the face of democratic backsliding. Again, there would be great value in considering ineffective policy in other parts of the world, but that is beyond the scope of this project. Future work surmounting these limitations will be invaluable for extending and nuancing our understanding of ineffective policy. Finally, in encouraging methodological diversity there are small variations in how different chapters have framed their discussions. We believe that this is an acceptable trade-off for an edited book like this, particularly given the stated purpose of starting conversations and encouraging more rigor in the use of the ineffective and bad policy concepts. Despite these minor differences we believe that there are important common threads that speak across chapters that are considered more systematically in the conclusion.

With this acknowledged, we proceed to the fuller analysis of ineffective policy in the fields of environment policy, finance, and emerging technology.

Acknowledgments

The editors would like to thank Tanya Lee and Regan Simpson for their assistance in the production of this edited volume. They would also like to thank the thoughtful feedback during the conceptualization of this book from Professor Charles Conteh and the anonymous reviewers. The editors would like to acknowledge the financial support of Bishop's University, York University, and the Rudolf Agricola School for Sustainable Development, University of Groningen making it possible to publish this volume open access.

Note

[1] JSTOR search initially suggested 3,979 possible sources. These were reviewed to remove duplication, as well as book reviews, opinions, and index pages. Sources that were not addressing policy or governance in a broad sense – for example articles focused on literature and the visual arts – were also removed.

References

Arlow, J. (2019) 'A JobBridge to nowhere: the national internship scheme as fast policy leading to bad policy', *Administration*, 67(2): 71–93.

Begley, P., Bochel, C., Bochel, H., Defty, A., Gordon, J., Hinkkainen, K. et al (2019) 'Assessing policy success and failure: targets, aims and processes', *Policy Studies*, 40(2): 188–204.

Bovens, M. and 't Hart, P. (2016) 'Revisiting the study of policy failures', *Journal of European Public Policy*, 23(5): 653–66.

Diamond, L. (2021) 'Democratic regression in comparative perspective: scope, methods, and causes', *Democratization*, 28(1): 22–42.

Gaskell, J., Stoker, G., Jennings, W., and Devine, D. (2020) 'Covid-19 and the blunders of our governments: long-run system failings aggravated by political choices', *The Political Quarterly*, 91(3): 523–33.

Grossman, R.S. (2013) *Wrong: Nine Economic Policy Disasters and What We Can Learn From Them*, Oxford: Oxford University Press.

Hafsi, T. and Baba, S. (2022) 'Exploring the process of policy overreaction: the COVID-19 lockdown decisions', *Journal of Management Inquiry*, March: 1–22.

Hampshire, J. (2018) 'On the indeterminacy of policy mistakes: lessons from British immigration policy', in A. Kruck, K. Oppermann, and A. Spencer (eds) *Policy Mistakes and Policy Failures in International Relations*, London: Palgrave Macmillan, pp 285–304.

Head, B.W. (2022) *Wicked Problems in Public Policy: Understanding and Responding to Complex Challenges*, Cham: Springer Nature.

Jennings, W., Lodge, M., and Ryan, M. (2018) 'Comparing blunders in government', *European Journal of Political Research*, 57(1): 238–58.

King, A. and Crewe, I. (2013) *The Blunders of Our Governments*, London: Oneworld.

Lindquist, E., Howlett, M., Skogstad, G., Tellier, G., and 't Hart, P. (eds) (2022) *Policy Success in Canada: Cases, Lessons, Challenges*, Oxford: Oxford University Press.

Luetjens, J., Mintrom, M., and t'Hart, P. (2019) *Successful Public Policy: Lessons from Australia and New Zealand*, Canberra: ANU Press.

Marsh, D. and McConnell, A. (2010) 'Towards a framework for establishing policy success', *Public Administration*, 88(2): 564–83.

McConnell, A. (2010) 'Policy success, policy failure and gray areas in-between', *Journal of Public Policy*, 30(3): 345–62.

Moran, M. (2001) 'Not steering but drowning: policy catastrophes and the regulatory state', *The Political Quarterly*, 72(4): 414–27.

Oppermann, K. and Spencer, A. (2016) 'Studying fiascos: bringing public and foreign policy together', *Journal of European Public Policy*, 23(5): 643–52.

Peters, G.P. (2015) 'State failure, governance failure and policy failure: exploring the linkages', *Public Policy and Administration*, 30(3–4): 261–76.

Portico (n.d.) 'Facts and figures' [online], Available from: https://www.port ico.org/coverage/facts-and-figures/

Roe, E. (2016) 'Policy messes and their management', *Policy Sciences*, 49: 351–72.

Saldin, R.P. (2017) *When Bad Policy Makes Good Politics: Running the Numbers on Health Reform*, New York: Oxford University Press.

Shipan, C.R. and Volden, C. (2021) *Why Bad Policies Spread (And Good Ones Don't)*, Cambridge: Cambridge University Press.

't Hart, P. and Compton M. (eds) (2019) *Great Policy Successes*, Oxford: Oxford University Press.

Torgerson, D. (1985) 'Contextual orientation in policy analysis: the contribution of Harold D. Lasswell', *Policy Sciences*, 18(3): 241–61.

Whiteford, P. (2021) 'Debt by design: the anatomy of a social policy fiasco – or was it something worse?', *Australian Journal of Public Administration*, 80(2): 340–60.

2

Giving serious thought to bad policy and the state of democracy

Ian Roberge and Mariëlle Wijermars

Effective and ineffective policies are endogenous to policy making and to politics within a democratic environment. Governments make both sound and informed policy choices, but they also put forth and implement unwise policies. The premise of this chapter (and of this book) is that Western democracies are facing serious challenges including the environmental crisis, massive economic transformations, immense societal pressures resulting from new and developing technologies, grave threats to geopolitical stability, and so on. The return of nativism, nationalism, and populism is putting on greater pressure, possibly further undermining democratic practices. While governments and public institutions have proven to be resilient to some extent, serious concerns persist regarding their ability to address 'wicked' policy problems. This chapter aims to make explicit what is at stake when ineffective policy emerges. It situates ineffective policy within the workings of Western democratic systems and outlines to what extent and how the effects of such policies may extend beyond the sole remit of these policies and onto the quality of democratic systems themselves.

To conceptualize the relationship between ineffective policy and democracy in the settings of democratic failings, we draw upon research on (the patterns of) democratic backsliding, such as the 'state-led debilitation or elimination of any of the political institutions that sustain an existing democracy' (Bermeo, 2016, pp 5–6). The chapter's central research question is: do weakened democracies explain ineffective policy, or does ineffective policy lead to democratic failings? While scholars debate the extent and speed of the current global democratic decline, focusing on the methodological issues related to subjective and objective measurements of democratic backsliding (Knutsen et al, 2023; Little and Meng, 2023), evidence abounds of the weakening of democratic safeguards, such as independent courts, as well as of state-led attacks on these safeguards (Maerz et al, 2023; Wiebrecht et al, 2023). Research on populism also shows how, after coming to power, populists can 'use and transform state bureaucracies in order to advance their illiberal goals' (Bauer, 2023). Addressing this research question provides an opportunity to explore the relationship between ineffective policy and the state of democracy, as well as to reflect on the risk of a downward spiral where the two reinforce each other, making it increasingly challenging to meaningfully address society's various political, economic, and social ills via policies.

We argue that ineffective policy is necessarily *relational* to the democratic environment within which it emerges. Policy can be empirically studied to determine its effectiveness, but ultimately is subject to interpretation. What is desirable or undesirable, 'effective' or 'ineffective', cannot be separated from the broader environment from which policy emanates. Ineffective policy, we argue, both weakens democracy, yet also reflects a weakened democratic space. The weakening of democratic safeguards, in turn, can generate space for (further) ineffective policy to flourish. Recognizing this through more explicitly normative analysis is a first step towards better protecting democratic institutions against their potential negative effects. Ineffective policy is neither the root nor the cause of democratic backsliding, yet we believe it is a significant contributing factor that requires careful consideration. By interpreting ineffective policy in light of the strength of, and/or attacks on democratic safeguards, this chapter contributes towards a better understanding of when and why ineffective policy occurs, as well as the damages it may inflict beyond the scope of the policy itself.

We structure our argument about the relationality of ineffective policy to democratic regression around three vectors: the role of interests, ideas, and values in policy making; institutional contexts; and temporality. The latter stresses how democratic backsliding should be understood as a process, rather than an event (Wunsch and Blanchard, 2023), in which ineffective policy can, under certain conditions, play a role. The first vector – the role of interests, ideas, and values – is well-known to public policy scholars. It investigates the gray area between politics and ineffective policy, where (supposedly) fact-based decision making gives way to (more overtly) value-based assessments. The second vector – institutional contexts – examines how particular institutional configurations may enable or inhibit the adoption or abolishment of ineffective policies. Finally, the third vector – temporality – investigates how a policy can 'turn bad', for example resulting from shifting perceptions of the aptness of that policy (that is, a value-based assessment), from a change in its impact as circumstances develop over time, or because of weakened democratic safeguards.

Democratic backsliding: vertical, diagonal, and horizontal democratic safeguards

Before proceeding, it is necessary to address the prospects of democratic backsliding and the safeguards that exist, particularly when considering the relationality of ineffective policy to democratic backsliding. Following

Wunsch and Blanchard (2023), this chapter differentiates between three types of democratic safeguards against executive expansion that can play a role in democratic backsliding. Firstly, vertical safeguards 'relate to the formal electoral process and electoral turnout'. Secondly, diagonal safeguards 'comprise freedom of expression and association, and free media' as mechanisms of political contestation. Lastly, horizontal safeguards refer to an independent parliament and judiciary (Wunsch and Blanchard, 2023, p 279). Based on a sequence analysis of patterns of democratic backsliding in so-called third-wave democracies (referring to the 79 countries that experienced a democratic transition from 1974 onwards), Wunsch and Blanchard demonstrate how diagonal safeguards play a key role in democratic backsliding. While exact patterns differ, 'diagonal safeguards are most susceptible to erosion and remain vulnerable, even where they were strongly present over a longer period'. On the other hand, they find that horizontal safeguards 'appear more resilient in general but, when dismantled, coincide more readily with a full democratic reversal extending to the vertical dimension and the electoral process itself' (Wunsch and Blanchard, 2023, p 295). Even if, overall, established democracies have proven resilient to democratic decline, the weakening of democratic safeguards and how this may interact with ineffective policy should be of high concern, since comparative research shows that 'once autocratization begins, only one in five democracies manage to avert breakdown' (Boese et al, 2021).

The analysis for this chapter is structured around the role of interests, ideas, and values in policy making, institutional contexts, and temporality rather than the sets of democratic safeguards mentioned earlier. This approach allows for a more comprehensive exploration of the relationship between ineffective policy, on one hand, and democracy and its (potential) decline, on the other. However, we come back throughout the chapter to the various ways ineffective policy undermines and threatens the existing democratic safeguards. Our focus centers on theoretical explanations of ineffective policy, supplemented with policy examples when needed to clarify key parts of the argument.

Interests, ideas, and values in policy making

Ineffective policy, good politics

The three 'I's of traditional public policy analysis – interests, ideas, and institutions – offer a fruitful starting point for understanding ineffective policy and its relationship to democracy. This section focuses on the role of interests – especially in politics – including how bad ideas support the development and the adoption of ineffective policy. The role of political systems and institutions is addressed separately in the subsequent section of the chapter. The broad argument in this section is that ineffective policy is most easily explained by the old axiom of 'bad policy as good politics' (Greer, 2018) – policy making as subject first and foremost to political realities.

The policy process is inherently political. The politicized and conflictual nature of policy making is broadly acknowledged and central to the argument of this chapter. Politics and policy are naturally intertwined; political considerations are inexorably built in to the policy process. At its most basic, the timing of a new policy or reform reflects political calculations. There is, for instance, a broad literature on public policy making, especially budgets, and the electoral cycle. Strobl et al (2021) refer to the strategic timing of austerity measures in Western Europe in light of the electoral cycle. In the US, Straka and Straka (2020), among many, highlight the policy dysfunction that results from partisan politics.

There are three possible explanations to ineffective policy in considering the political nature of the policy process. The first holds that policy makers may genuinely believe they are adopting the right policy because they believe the policy will work and they adhere to its objectives. Faced with the multiple challenges associated with making policy decisions, policy makers balance multiple interests to attain their desired objectives. If the policy turns out to be ineffective, this is something that is discovered over time possibly due to a policy evaluation; the policy cycle, after all, provides a feedback loop by which corrective measures can be taken. Strong diagonal safeguards, such as free media, not only bolster such discoveries but can also generate momentum for corrective measures when the ineffectiveness of policy has become apparent, alongside a strong parliament.

The second and more interesting set of explanations contends that policy makers know or ought to know that a policy is undesirable, yet they choose to pursue its adoption and implementation irrespectively. Whiteford (2021), for instance, refers to an Australian government's policy to recover social security overpayments through an automated system as a policy fiasco, though one which is distinguishable because the failure was predictable and not the result of poor design or implementation. In other words, the government should have known, yet still went ahead with its initiative. Therefore, the question is why policy makers prefer bad policy – or policy that they know or ought to know is ineffective – over better policy options. This issue is to be discussed later in this chapter and addressed more fully in the conclusion.

There are many reasons why policy makers may prefer or support ineffective policy. They may view said policy, for whatever reason, as politically advantageous. There are policies that are popular even though they are not desirable. Partisan politics, in some cases, lead to the adoption of ineffective policy (Laing and Walter, 2020). This type of policy allows policy makers to score political points or puts their opponents in a bind. Policy makers may erroneously lead citizens toward a bad policy or follow a policy that has broad support across society even when that policy is not desirable, or its outcomes are outright harmful. Of note, policy makers may hold on to a bad policy on the premise that it is a political winner when there may, in fact, be little evidence to that effect. Brexit provides a good example of a policy with largely known negative impacts, yet policy makers carried through with its adoption and implementation (Baines, Brewer and Kay, 2020). As an alternate consideration, the reverse is also a possibility, which is to say that an ineffective policy may be politically costly. This raises the issue of when these costs are sufficient to prompt the termination of the policy and its subsequent replacement. Separately, there are exceptional circumstances in which a policy fails when assessing it against its stated objectives but is perceived as useful for meeting other goals. De Lint and Kassa (2015) argue that US counterterrorism policies have failed in deterring terrorism, yet they have been useful to obtain public support for the government's security apparatus. In such a scenario, policy makers weigh the varying effects and externalities of the policy under consideration.

Third, policy makers may simply not understand the policy that they are supporting, they may be misled, or they may feel compelled to support a bad idea. Policy makers for ideological reasons and/or out of sheer certainty may genuinely believe that a policy is desirable, even though it is bad, and its impact will be detrimental. Matthijs and Blyth (2017) suggest that policy makers can learn the wrong lessons from prior policies leading them to adopt irrational policies; Dunlop (2017) also considers the dimensions and intersections between policy learning and policy failures. Policy makers may in some cases be indifferent to the 'truth' about a policy; Perl et al (2018) ask whether policy models can cope with politicized evidence and willful ignorance. Policy myopia (Nair and Howlett, 2016) can lead to policy failures. Broome et al (2018) refer to the indirect power of global benchmarking as bad science in leading governments to adopt ineffective policy. In all three sets of explanations, democratic checks and balances are important for ensuring the possibility of evaluating the acceptability of harms, or of how ineffective policy disproportionately affects particular groups in society, and for ensuring the possibility of pushing for reform.

These considerations presuppose that policy makers may make errors, but they are assumed to have good intentions. There are, obviously, more nefarious possibilities whereby policy makers consciously intend to adopt an undesirable policy. This question is, again, explored in more depth in the concluding chapter of this volume, though a shortened version of the argument is provided here. For instance, policy makers may be captured and/or subject to pressure favoring the adoption and maintenance of an ineffective policy (OECD, 2017). Policy automatically generates winners and losers, and those who benefit from the policy certainly have a clear stake in making sure the government continues with said policy. Furthermore, politicians may be corrupt and favor a policy from which they benefit.

Weakened diagonal and horizontal safeguards, for example, when the independence of the judiciary has been undermined, heighten the risk of ineffective policy in such cases. Indeed, this is also the scenario in which one may expect to encounter attacks on, for example, media or judges involved in uncovering and assessing misconduct. Policy and regulatory capture, along with corruption, increase the likelihood of ineffective policy, although it should be noted that they do not automatically lead to such an outcome. For example, nepotism is generally undesirable, yet the problem is most acute if it is tied to incompetence which will seriously hamper quality policy making.

On a more meta level, the role of ideas in supporting ineffective policy is worth considering (Hopkin and Rosamond, 2018; Oren and Blyth, 2019). There are numerous ways in which ideas promote and sustain public policies. Most prominently, the role of paradigms (Hall, 1993) as the backdrop of policy preferences and for the selection of policy objectives and instruments, are well documented. Paradigms lay out the problems that are deemed legitimate, the policy objectives that ought to be pursued, and the instruments available. Policy makers work within the paradigm which can lead them to favor ineffective policy, even in the face of contrary evidence. After all, policies that fall astray from conventional wisdom are simply not considered. Naturally, a paradigm shift can open up the possibility of new policies. Paradigms, however, tend to exist over the long term; serious discrepancies are required for them to be questioned. The persistence, for instance, of neoliberalism and managerialism underpin the preference for addressing select policy problems, the objectives to be pursued, and the instruments by which to attain them. Hopkin and Rosamond (2018) consider post-truth politics and what they refer to as the United Kingdom's 'fetish' on deficits. Similarly, governments' unfettered beliefs in markets and their unwillingness to properly regulate financial markets before the global financial crisis also represent an example of ineffective policy with significant consequences (Blankenburg and Palma, 2009). Restrictions on diagonal democratic safeguards such as freedom of expression, media freedom, and freedom of association, which weaken democratic space, may hinder the potential for paradigm change. Bad ideas that are dominant or unchallenged are likely to lead to ineffective policy and to create circumstances for them to be more enduring.

Institutional contexts

The role of institutions – our second vector of relationality – is well-established in the study of public policy. As we discussed in the introduction, institutions are also where processes of democratic erosion play out. Beyond the broad use of institutionalist theories to study ineffective policy, two major avenues are of particular interest. From a more rational choice perspective, political systems dictate the rules of the game by which actors make public policy: constitutional obligations and conventions; the relationship among the three branches of government; how political leaders are elected and selected, among others. All significantly impact how policies are formulated and implemented. Some of the built-in dysfunctions of the US's system of checks and balances are well known. As an example, Saldin (2017) uses the vocabulary of bad policy in presenting the adoption of the CLASS Act in the US and the way it addresses problems relating to long-term care. Saldin argues that due to institutional constraints, the long-term care policy was purposely designed as ineffective; proponents knew the policy to be bad, but they also knew that this was the policy they could get through the legislative process. They also believed that an ineffective policy was preferable to no policy, especially as the policy window was about to close unless action was immediate. In these circumstances, proponents expect that once the policy is implemented, they will have the opportunity to address its problems later and that the policy's dysfunctions may in fact generate demand for a better policy. In the meantime, proponents are willing to accept and live with an ineffective policy, especially if some of the worst effects are only to be felt years later. Within such a scenario, the adoption of an ineffective policy may even represent a political victory for its proponents. There is no guarantee, however, that a new policy window will open in the near term to allow for corrective measures to be taken. If the window for reform does not open, the ineffective policy is institutionalized and is likely to persist over time. Saldin's explanation of the CLASS Act provides a prescient example of the institutionalized constraints of the legislative process made worse due to partisanship.

There are many other institutional features that affect the policy process, in ways germane to the study of ineffectiveness. The federal or unitary nature of a state is a classic example of how political organization impacts public policy. Do federal systems lead to better policy or instead do such systems generate more ineffective policy? Several considerations related to this question are relevant for our aims in this chapter. Federalism may lead to opportunities for coordination and collaboration, policy experimentation, policy learning, policy transfer and diffusion, as well as duplication, overlap, and policy redundancies or gaps. Federalism enables cooperation across various levels of authority and can enhance accountability and transparency. Nevertheless, it can also lead to the opposite outcome when one level of government blames another for policy shortcomings. Shipan and Volden (2021) focus on the workings of federalism in the US and consider why bad policies spread across states, and good policy does not. They argue that states fail to learn from each other because policies are difficult to adapt, that the political contexts across states differ, and that governing institutions do not always foster expertise.

The second area where consideration of institutional contexts in the study of ineffective policy may be particularly useful is when explicitly considering policy 'stickiness', as well as policy reversal, or policy change. Classic theories such as public choice from a rational perspective or historical institutionalism including its focus on path dependency help explain why change is often resisted, slow, and incremental. Many examples can be used to highlight policy stickiness as it relates to ineffective policy. For instance, as is well documented, the development of new technology can embed biases and prejudices whereas change becomes quite difficult once these systems are adopted and in use. Campbell-Verduyn and Hütten (2022) emphasize that when an organization like the Organisation for Economic Co-operation and Development considers techno-futures, it does so within a very specific frame of reference – managerialism – making it difficult to consider better alternatives. Diagonal safeguards and an independent parliament should play a role in creating political opportunities for policy adjustments, yet the concept of stickiness itself speaks to the limits of these safeguards. Whether ineffective policy is more 'sticky' than good public policy, and to what extent we can observe differences for 'wicked' policy problems, is a question worthy of further study.

Focusing on institutional contexts as a vector of the relationality of ineffective policy can also assist in identifying paths to overcome the 'stickiness' mentioned earlier and generate a policy change or reversal. How are entrenched interests to be overcome? When are the incentives sufficiently high to warrant addressing an ineffective policy? The most obvious way by which ineffective policy can be challenged is via the courts, which stresses the importance of this horizontal democratic safeguard. While the courts may in some instances sustain ineffective policy due to legal precedents, as well as constitutional and institutional constraints, they may also provide an avenue for policy change and innovation. For example, in a climate case brought against the State of the Netherlands by the Urgenda Foundation, The Hague District Court ruled in 2015 that the greenhouse gas emissions in the Netherlands must be reduced by 25 percent by the end of 2020, compared to 1990 levels (Leijten, 2019). The verdict was later confirmed by the Court of Appeal in The Hague and the Supreme Court. The dialogue between the legislative, the executive, and the judiciary can mitigate the effects of ineffective policy, or force policy change. Given how courts have long been at the forefront of progressive change, government-led attacks against judicial independence, and the weakening of the courts as a democratic safeguard as part of democratic backsliding processes is particularly worrying.

The time factor

The third and final vector to be considered is change over time, or temporality. The main interest lies in analyzing how policy can become (or come to be seen as) ineffective due to shifting perceptions as beliefs and values evolve, because of the development of negative impacts, or because of weakened democratic safeguards.

Before addressing these considerations, it is worthwhile pointing out that ineffective policy can also be the result of inaction, whereby policy makers choose to not (yet) act regarding emerging, or even long-standing policy problems. As previously discussed, many reasons explain the reluctance to act, including political preferences, failing to understand, or misunderstanding the problem, or a lack of institutional capacity. Whereas some policy problems may disappear on their own – maybe inaction was warranted – there is also the distinct possibility that problems will remain or worsen if left unaddressed. Li (2021) refers to 'media policy silence' to consider failures to address 'the elephant in the room', un-decisions, and considered silence in referencing policy makers' preference for not addressing an issue. The absence of policy as ineffective policy is easy to imagine across various fields. The most obvious example from the perspective of this book relates to the environment and the climate crisis. Governments' timidity and reluctance to act over the long term have worsened the policy problem. Eastwood's (2019) in-depth description of the United Nations' environmental policy-making process showcases the organization's inability, states' reluctance, institutional constraints, and entrenched interests that make actions so difficult. Many chapters in this book provide salient examples of ineffective environmental policy. Weakened diagonal safeguards or a weakened parliament can serve as an additional enabling factor for inaction. Failure, reluctance, and the inability to act or to properly recognize that a situation has changed, can have grave consequences.

When first adopted, policy can be considered good, reasonable, and fair. Policy makers sought to address a particular policy problem in good faith. Over time, though, that same policy can be judged as bad or wrong, ineffectual, and causing (disproportionate) harm. Policy can and does become bad or ineffective over time. For example, and while they recently were or are about to be overturned, policies that prevented gay men from donating blood for decades across many countries fall into this category (Orsini, 2002; Lake, 2010). Though the discrimination may have been acceptable when the policy was first approved under the guise that it helped preserve the safety of the blood supply, it has long ceased to be. From remaining prejudices to institutional sclerosis, and despite at times acute needs within the health system for the product, blood services most often failed to reform. In other words, this is a policy that has been known for decades to be ineffective, to be discriminatory in a way that could no longer be justified, yet change across countries is only now being implemented. The argument is not about rewriting history or post-facto analysis; rather, new knowledge becomes available, perceptions, beliefs, and values change, and policy needs to be flexible and account for these transformations.

Yet, policy may also 'turn bad' because of weakened democratic safeguards, which enable a policy to be used for alternate ends. The European Union, with various member states exhibiting signs of democratic backsliding, offers a natural experiment of sorts of how the same policy carries different risks depending on the strength of democratic safeguards. For example, critics warn how the 'Proposal for a Directive on Transparency of Interest Representation on Behalf of Third Countries' (European Commission, 2023), included in the European Commission's Defence of Democracy package adopted in December 2023, may be used 'to harass NGOs and opposition or target specific groups' (Korkea-aho, 2023). The policy, thereby, would contribute to democratic backsliding, rather than to a strengthening of democracy, with limited possibilities for the Commission to prevent such misuse of the directive.

Another component of time that is worth highlighting relates to the long-lasting harm that a policy can cause. Some policies can quickly be reversed, yet the harm may still be long lasting. In turn, some policies remain even though they cause harm, in some cases knowingly. From a Canadian perspective, the federal government's policies and practices, particularly regarding residential schools for Indigenous peoples, represent an example of a genocidal policy (MacDonald, 2019). Canadian residential schools date back to the 1880s with the last one closing in 1998; these government-sponsored religious schools took children away from their family and community, preventing them from speaking in their mother tongue with the stated purpose of assimilating Indigenous peoples into White Christian society. These schools were the site of brutal physical and psychological abuse. Residential schools generated cross-generational trauma that still reverberates decades later. The federal government apologized to Indigenous people in 2008, though much work remains to foster reconciliation between Indigenous peoples and Canadians. The long-term negative outcomes and harm of a policy have lasting effects in terms of distrust of government and voter disengagement, which are clear signs of erosion in vertical democratic safeguards.

In closing this section there is value in coming back to the issue of political interests and calculus in relation to ineffective policy. The popular perception is that governments and politicians are consumed by the next election, the day-to-day news cycle, and that they are unable or unwilling to govern with a long view. Governments – politicians and the public service – struggle to effectively balance short-term and long-term considerations. In other words, the politics of governing often complicate the actual practice of good government, particularly in a democracy where balancing popular perceptions and interests with sound policy can be difficult when they do not align. Policy makers are bound to adopt ineffective policy if the success or failure of said policy is dependent on its immediate reception among the party faithful. Good and effective policy may require an immediate sacrifice for a gain many years down the road; this requires, however, politicians to have the courage of their convictions. Wicked policy problems such as the climate crisis, wealth inequity, racial discrimination, and preparedness for another pandemic, cannot be solved by the adoption of a single policy in a short amount of time. They require planning and dedicated systematic action over many years. They involve making errors, learning from them, and taking corrective actions. Democratic safeguards have an important role to play in states' ability to address these problems while faced with the political pressures related to nativism, nationalism, and populism. Governing for the greater good is a long-term project. In stating so, this chapter comes full circle to its original argument that good government and ineffective policy are endogenous to policy making and political practices within a democratic environment. Ineffective policy, as such, is both the result of and a factor contributing to democratic backsliding. Ineffective policy, as we have outlined by exploring its relationality to democratic systems, simultaneously weakens democracy and reflects a weakened democratic space. When democratic safeguards are weakened, this, in turn, generates space for (further) ineffective policy to flourish.

Conclusion

This chapter has attempted to draw out the causes of ineffective policy as well as to assess its relationship to democratic failings. We approached the relationship between ineffective policy, on the one hand, and democracy and its (potential) erosion, on the other. This is explored through three vectors of its relationality: the role of interests, ideas, and values in policy making; institutional contexts; and temporality. There is little doubt that democratic failings partially explain ineffective policy and may be exacerbated by a weakening of democratic safeguards. The inability of governments and policy makers to govern for the long term and to overcome everyday managerialism; the multiple ways in which interests affect policy making; how ideology or simply prejudices and preconceived notions prevent policy makers from considering alternatives and better policy; institutional constraints; and policy makers' unwillingness as well as their inability to overcome entrenched practices, among other factors, reflect systemic problems that lead to the adoption and implementation of ineffective policy. At the same time, there is a solid argument to be made that ineffective policy contributes to democratic backsliding and potentially across all – vertical, diagonal, and horizontal – democratic safeguards. While this thought is elaborated elsewhere in the book, it is worth emphasizing here how ineffective policy – bad policy – contributes to a lack of trust in government. When a policy is harmful or discriminatory, populations that have borne the brunt of such a policy are unlikely to trust that governments can work for them, or that policy makers have their best interest at heart. Such sentiment may offer a breeding ground for populism. There is no evidence per se that there is more ineffective policy than in the past, though others such as Fotaki (2010) have asked why policy so often fails. Ineffective policy is neither rare nor anecdotal; because Western democracies are at best strained, or worse, regressing, ineffective policy has become more visible.

This chapter has emphasized that the study of ineffective policy cannot be separated from politics and broader questions about democratic practices. The policy process is inherently political, and policies themselves are more than the simple technical considerations that form them. Viewing the broader field of policy studies in this way provides an opportunity for scholars in the social sciences to engage with questions of effective, good, desirable, ineffective, undesirable, and bad policies more openly. What is at stake is more than just whether a policy has succeeded or failed – the implications are more serious. From failing to address a policy problem, to misaddressing it, to leading to undesirable outcomes, even causing harm, to generating a crisis, the consequences of ineffective policy warrant consideration and the need for better policy is clear. As democratic societies face a barrage of challenges, this book, and this chapter, serve as a call for broader engagement.

References

Baines, D., Brewer, S., and Kay, A. (2020) 'Political, process and programme failures in the Brexit fiasco: exploring the role of policy deception', *Journal of European Public Policy*, 27(5): 742–60.

Bauer, M.W. (2023) 'Public administration under populist rule: standing up against democratic backsliding', *International Journal of Public Administration*, 47(15): 1019–31.

Bermeo, N. (2016) 'On democratic backsliding', *Journal of Democracy*, 27(1): 5–19.

Blankenburg, S. and Palma, J.G. (2009) 'Introduction: the global financial crisis', *Cambridge Journal of Economics*, 33(4): 531–8.

Boese, V.A., Edgell, A.B., Hellmeier, S., Maerz, S.F., and Lindberg, S.I. (2021) 'How democracies prevail: democratic resilience as a two-stage process', *Democratization*, 28(5): 885–907.

Broome, A., Homolar, A., and Kranke, M. (2018) 'Bad science: international organizations and the indirect power of global benchmarking', *European Journal of International Relations*, 24(3): 514–39.

Campbell-Verduyn, M.C. and Hütten, M. (2022) 'Governing techno-futures: OECD anticipation of automation and the multiplication of managerialism', *Global Society*, 36(2): 240–60.

de Lint, W. and Kassa, W. (2015) 'Evaluating US counterterrorism policy: failure, fraud, or fruitful spectacle?', *Critical Criminology*, 23(3): 349–69.

Dunlop, C.A. (2017) 'Policy learning and policy failure: definitions, dimensions and intersections', *Policy and Politics*, 45(1): 3–18.

Eastwood, L.E. (2019) *Negotiating the Environment: Civil Society, Globalisation and the UN*, London: Routledge.

European Commission (2023) 'Proposal for a directive establishing harmonised requirements in the internal market on transparency of interest representation carried out on behalf of third countries', Available from: https://eur-lex.europa.eu/legal-content/EN/TXT/?uri=COM%3A2023%3A637%3AFIN

Fotaki, M. (2010) 'Why do public policies fail so often? Exploring health policy-making as an imaginary and symbolic construction', *Organization*, 17(6): 703–20.

Greer, S.L. (2018) 'The politics of bad policy in the United States', *Perspectives on Politics*, 16(2): 455–59.

Hall, P.A. (1993) 'Policy paradigms, social learning, and the state: the case of economic policymaking in Britain', *Comparative Politics*, 26: 275–96.

Hopkin, J. and Rosamond, B. (2018) 'Post-truth politics, bullshit and bad ideas: "deficit fetishism" in the UK', *New Political Economy*, 23(6): 641–55.

Knutsen, C.H., Marquardt, K.L., Seim, B., Coppedge, M., Medzihorsky, J., Edgell, A.B. et al (2023) 'Conceptual and measurement issues in assessing democratic backsliding', Working Paper Series 2023: 140, Gothenburg: Varieties of Democracy Institute, University of Gothenburg [online], Available from: https://www.v-dem.net/media/publications/wp_140.pdf

Korkea-aho, E. (2023) '"This is not a foreign agents law": the Commission's new directive on transparency of third country lobbying', *Verfassungsblog* [online] 19 December, Available from: https://verfassungsblog.de/this-is-not-a-foreign-agents-law/

Laing, M. and Walter, J. (2020) 'Partisanship, policy entrepreneurs and the market for ideas: what we can learn from policy failure', *Australian Journal of Political Science*, 55(1): 122–34.

Lake, R. (2010) 'MSM blood donation ban: (in)equality, gay rights and discrimination under the Charter', *Appeal: Review of Current Law and Law Reform*, 15: 136–49.

Leijten, I. (2019) 'Human rights v. insufficient climate action: the Urgenda case', *Netherlands Quarterly of Human Rights*, 37(2): 112–18.

Li, L. (2021) 'How to think about media policy silence', *Media, Culture & Society*, 43(2): 359–68.

Little, A. and Meng, A. (2023) 'Measuring democratic backsliding', *PS: Political Science & Politics* [online], Available from: http://dx.doi.org/10.2139/ssrn.4327307

MacDonald, D.B. (2019) *The Sleeping Giant Awakens: Genocide, Indian Residential Schools, and the Challenge of Conciliation*, Toronto: University of Toronto Press.

Maerz, S.F., Edgell, A.B., Wilson, M.C., Hellmeier, S., and Lindberg, S.I. (2023) 'Episodes of regime transformation', *Journal of Peace Research*, 61(6): 967–84.

Matthijs, M. and Blyth, M. (2017) 'When is it rational to learn the wrong lessons? Technocratic authority, social learning, and euro fragility', *Perspectives on Politics*, 16(1): 110–26.

Nair, S. and Howlett, M. (2016) 'Policy myopia as a source of policy failure: adaptation and policy learning under deep uncertainty', *Policy and Politics*, 45(1): 103–18.

Oren, T. and Blyth, M. (2019) 'From big bang to big crash: the early origins of the UK's finance-led growth model and the persistence of bad policy ideas', *New Political Economy*, 24(5): 605–22.

Organisation for Economic Co-operation and Development (2017) *Preventing Policy Capture Integrity in Public Decision Making*, Paris: OECD Publishing.

Orsini, M. (2002) 'The politics of naming, blaming and claiming: HIV, hepatitis C and the emergence of blood activism in Canada', *Canadian Journal of Political Science*, 35(3): 475–98.

Perl, A., Howlett, M., and Ramesh, M. (2018) 'Policy-making and truthiness: can existing policy models cope with politicized evidence and willful ignorance in a "post-fact" world?', *Policy Sciences*, 51(4): 581–600.

Saldin, R.P. (2017) *When Bad Policy Makes Good Politics: Running the Numbers on Health Reform*, New York: Oxford University Press.

Shipan, C.R. and Volden, C. (2021) *Why Bad Policies Spread (And Good Ones Don't)*, Cambridge: Cambridge University Press.

Straka, J.W. and Straka, B.C. (2020) 'Reframe policymaking dysfunction through bipartisan-inclusion leadership', *Policy Sciences*, 53(4): 779–802.

Strobl, D., Bäck, H., Müller, W.C., and M. Angelova (2021) 'Electoral cycles in government policy making: strategic timing of austerity reform measures in Western Europe', *British Journal of Political Science*, 51(1): 331–52.

Whiteford, P. (2021) 'Debt by design: the anatomy of a social policy fiasco – or was it something worse?', *Australian Journal of Public Administration*, 80(2): 340–60.

Wiebrecht, F., Sato, Y., Nord, M., Lundstedt, M., Angiolillo, F., and Lindberg, S.I. (2023) 'State of the world 2022: defiance in the face of autocratization', *Democratization*, 30(5): 769–93.

Wunsch, N. and Blanchard, P. (2023) 'Patterns of democratic backsliding in third-wave democracies: a sequence analysis perspective', *Democratization*, 30(2): 278–301.

PART I

Ineffective policies, contested goals

3

From good to bad? The contested desirability of economic growth

Matthias Kranke

Introduction

For much of the time after the Second World War, the pursuit of economic growth – as measured in terms of gross domestic product (GDP) – officially represented the hallmark of good policy. Governments willingly embraced it (Purdey, 2010; Speich, 2011; Fioramonti, 2016; Barry, 2020), and various international organizations diffused it as a policy norm (Fuchs and Lorek, 2005; Allan, 2019; Andersson, 2019; Meckling and Allan, 2020). The reasoning behind it was – and often still is – that only continuous growth rates allow for the maintenance or enhancement of material living standards. Many policy makers even portray growth as necessary to finance social expenditures and environmental protection. Yet such claims have attracted fundamental criticism given serious threats of irreversible ecological breakdown with all its social ramifications. The underlying argument is that there is an inextricable trade-off between economic growth and ecological sustainability that makes 'green growth' unattainable (Hickel and Kallis, 2020; but see, for example, Stoknes and Rockström, 2018). For these critics, the pursuit of economic growth accordingly represents the hallmark of bad policy.

In this chapter, I engage in the debate on economic growth, starting from the constructivist premise that policies promoting growth are not 'good' or 'bad' in and of themselves. Different actors in fact make diverging inferences from basically the same evidence base, namely the widely recognized fact that so far predominantly relative, rather than absolute, 'decoupling' of economic growth from most environmental pressures has occurred (Haberl et al, 2020). It is therefore important to clarify that while some *deem* growth to be good, others *deem* it to be bad. In the political landscape, the majority view about growth as good builds on expectations that absolute decoupling will be technologically possible in the near future; the minority view about growth as bad derives from more pessimistic expectations about such possibilities. These views – whether for or against economic growth – are social constructions justified by certain ideas shared by a relevant community of actors (see Hay, 2011). Regardless of the actual socio-ecological impacts of growth, its desirability thus remains a bone of contention and is, ultimately, in the eye of the beholder.

The beholder of interest here is the German Federal Ministry for Economic Affairs and Climate Action[1] (*Bundesministerium für Wirtschaft und Klimaschutz* (BMWK)) as an organization that represents the views of the federal German government on matters of economic policy. Given its mandate, we would expect to find a rather firm commitment to economic growth within the BMWK. In contrast to national environmental ministries or, specifically, the relatively growth-critical German Environment Agency (see Lehmann et al, 2022), the BMWK has a clearly defined institutional overall responsibility for the German economy. As the evolution of its official name indicates, the ministry has taken on additional tasks over time: initially, ministers typically carried the simple title of 'Minister for Economic Affairs'; however, all ministers since 1998 have had extensions, specifically 'and Technology', 'and Work', 'and Energy' and now 'and Climate Action'.[2] At the time of writing (February 2024),[3] the ministry is headed by Robert Habeck, a politician from the center-left Green Party (*Bündnis 90/Die Grünen*). Because of the party's credentials for ambitious environmental policies, it appears most likely among the major political parties in Germany to take a growth-critical stance. Indeed, Habeck has publicly stated that good economic policy does not aim only for growth but sees welfare and climate action as inexorably intertwined.[4] By this logic, an exclusive concern with growth could be said to constitute an instance of bad policy, especially against the backdrop of ongoing discussions about economic growth amid rapidly unfolding planetary crises.

Given this context, the chapter asks: how does the BMWK frame economic growth? Undertaking an exploratory analysis, I distill the ministry's views on the goodness, or otherwise, of economic growth under the leadership of Habeck, who assumed office in late 2021. Specifically, I analyze paragraphs from the 2022 and 2023 editions of its annual economic report, the *Jahreswirtschaftsbericht*, that mention the term 'growth'. On the basis of this material, I argue that, even under a Green politician, the BMWK leans strongly towards the idea that economic growth is principally good and can be fully aligned with sustainability efforts.

The chapter is structured into four main sections. First, I briefly summarize the debate between those who call for green growth and those who endorse post-growth ideas, which shows that judging growth to be good or bad is a matter of (evolving) perceptions. Second, I introduce the analytical strategy employed. Third, I present the findings from the empirical analysis. Fourth, I reflect on these findings in light of the volume's overarching theme, suggesting in particular that the complete disregard of current debates on (post-)growth risks leading to ineffective and, ultimately, even bad policies. The conclusion provides a brief summary and outlook.

Good or bad? Constructing growth in economic and environmental policy

Over the years, the widespread assumption that economic growth is good has been regularly challenged. Yet to be clear, much contention to this day has remained within the realms of academia, advocacy, and activism, rather than shaping policy-making processes. Even the widely known *Limits to Growth* report by the Club of Rome (Meadows et al, 1972), which predicted that economic growth would come to an end because of finite resources, did not have a lasting policy impact. While contemporary challenges to growth-friendly policies are arguably less concerned about resource limits than about excessive resource use,[5] mainstream politicians across countries continue to preach the growth gospel over half a century later. Post-growth arguments, which question this gospel, still rarely seep into the routines of policy making.

Seen from a constructivist perspective, it is striking that the debate has taken on such a binary format. In terms of the continuum developed by the editors in the introductory chapter, the mainstream embraces growth-promoting policies as effective, desirable and, hence, 'good', whereas critics cast them as ineffective, undesirable and, hence, 'bad'. Both sides tend to deliver definitive verdicts of (green) growth being either good (for example WEF, 2013; Stoknes and Rockström, 2018) or bad (for example Asara et al, 2015; Hickel and Kallis, 2020). Discussions in the academic literature often mirror and reproduce this division while (also) taking it as a heuristic device for orientation (Pollin, 2018; Jackson and Victor, 2019; Buch-Hansen and Carstensen, 2021; Hasselbalch et al, 2023). There is little in-between, except perhaps the 'a-growth' position most prominently advocated by Jeroen van den Bergh (2011) and the 'precautionary post-growth' agenda (Petschow et al, 2020). Bluntly put, the polarization of the debate between (green) growth advocates and post-growth prophets has obscured or even erased gradations along the continuum from 'good' to 'bad'. In fact, each camp claims to have incontrovertible objective evidence on its side. Remarkably, these arguments revolve around the same object, namely the practical feasibility of decoupling economic growth from various environmental impacts (in terms of both inputs and outside).

We can break this debate down further. Both camps agree that relative decoupling can work and has to some extent already been achieved. Relative decoupling happens when environmental pressures increase at a lower rate than economic growth – for instance, a 3 percent increase in GDP accompanied by 'only' an additional 2 percent in environmental pressures. The real debate is thus about whether absolute decoupling is possible, especially whether it is possible at scale (that is, globally). Those who embrace green growth as a policy objective explicitly or implicitly assume that absolute decoupling will work if enough investment is channeled into new technologies that are then deployed across countries (for example, Pollin, 2018). Post-growth critics respond that such a form of decoupling is historically unprecedented and hence highly unlikely to materialize any time soon, if at all, especially considering that it would have to be sustained over the long run to avert ecological breakdown (Parrique et al, 2019; Hickel and Kallis, 2020; Mastini et al, 2021; for a summary of the debate, see Hasselbalch et al, 2023, pp 1623–4).

Such definitive statements signal a strong commitment, in both camps, to a certain brand of social facts. As a rich vein of scholarship has demonstrated over the years, there is no such thing as purely objective, quasi-natural facts. But 'social facts' do exist. To speak of social facts implies that a certain constellation has come to mean the same thing to a significant number of people. One instructive example is from a constructivist classic by Michael Barnett and Martha Finnemore (2004, p 36), who argue that what constitutes a dysfunctional organizational activity typically varies widely among actors. By implication, if and once enough people agree that a particular activity meets this label, a social fact has formed. Shared social meanings also shape our understanding of seemingly objective facts about the economy, such as capital mobility (Clift and Tomlinson, 2004), money laundering (Hülsse, 2007), or poverty (St. Clair, 2006). Mark Blyth (2003) captures this logic by quipping that 'structures do not come with an instruction sheet'. Other constructivists have similarly underlined that acts of human interpretation can make a difference in otherwise similar settings (Parsons, 2002), and that actors form and change their seemingly obvious interests as they (re)interpret their social environment (Woll, 2008; Hay, 2011).

So what does this fundamental constructivist insight into the production and circulation of social facts entail for the highly polarized debate on (green) growth versus post-growth? The key message here is that it may be productive to take a step back from this debate by seeing the representatives on both sides as (re)negotiating social facts about the desirability of economic growth, rather than attempting to formulate ultimate truths. To paraphrase Barnett and Finnemore (2004, p 36), economic growth is deemed to be good or bad by certain actors in a certain social context. It is not universally good or bad owing to some allegedly intrinsic features that everyone immediately recognizes. In other words, just because higher growth rates have historically been coupled to higher greenhouse gas emissions and more extensive resource use (Haberl et al, 2020) does not mean that everyone will agree with the degrowth position that rich economies have to shrink until they arrive at a steady state. Conversely, just because lackluster or missing growth has often led to higher unemployment rates and lower living standards does not mean that everyone will deem growth to be (unconditionally) desirable.

In the next section, I present an analytical approach that sees the goodness or badness of economic growth along these lines, namely as a social fact.

Analytical approach

For the empirical analysis, I pick a long-standing institution in German national economic policy, namely the Federal Ministry for Economic Affairs and Climate Action, or BMWK. The ministry has evolved over time. As explained in the Introduction, it now bears responsibility for climate questions while being headed – for the first time in German history – by a politician from the Green Party, a center-left political party with a comparatively strong environmental agenda. Moreover, Germany is a rich economy that degrowth proponents would reason has reached levels of material wealth that would allow it to not grow much more easily than poorer countries (Hickel, 2021, pp 1108–10). If historical responsibility for the depletion of global commons is also accounted for, giving up on the objective of aggregate growth should therefore be an imperative for the most affluent countries (O'Neill et al, 2018; Wiedmann et al, 2020). The confluence of these factors may lead us to expect at least some space for growth-critical thinking, potentially manifesting itself in BMWK statements that construct economic growth not as unequivocally good but as insufficient or even somewhat problematic.

My analytical approach revolves around a particular type of report that the ministry publishes annually: its *Jahreswirtschaftsbericht*. Its last ten editions – from 2014 to 2023 – are available from the BMWK's website. Within the scope of this chapter, I concentrate on the 2022 and 2023 reports, both of which were released under Habeck's direction.[6] The two reports have the same broad structure and are of similar length, with the 2022 edition totaling 122 pages and the 2023 edition 159 pages (all inclusive). Using MAXQDA software for qualitative analysis, I followed the same procedure for each report to establish the ministry's position on the growth question. Proceeding from the assumption that a paragraph represents a relatively coherent unit of meaning within a published text, I searched for paragraphs containing the noun *Wachstum* (German for 'growth'). All other paragraphs were ignored. I then applied a simple two-step analysis to the material thus identified.

The first step was deductive and focused on *connotation*, where I assigned one of three predefined codes depending on whether the wording in the relevant paragraph suggested a positive, neutral, or negative meaning of the word. I coded paragraphs as 'growth-positive' if they described growth as necessary, absolute decoupling as technologically feasible, and/or green growth as a possible balance between economic welfare and sustainability (contra Hickel and Kallis, 2020). I coded them as 'growth-negative' if they portrayed growth as problematic, absolute decoupling as unfeasible (yet), and/or green growth as impossible. All other paragraphs from the pool of results were coded as 'growth-neutral' (similar to van den Bergh's a-growth position). The latter category included paragraphs that do not make any substantive claims, such as those that merely reference the name of a law containing the search term (specifically the *Gesetz zur Förderung der Stabilität und des Wachstums der Wirtschaft* (StabG)). In the process of assigning the codes, I discarded all 'paragraphs' that the software had included in the search results, although they turned out upon closer inspection to be section headers, figure titles, and the like.

The second step was inductive and concentrated on *themes*, where I created codes – again at paragraph level – based on the main contents discussed in a given paragraph. Where appropriate, I attributed multiple themes to the same paragraph. This approach aimed to generate somewhat deeper insights into why the ministry sees economic growth in a particular light, especially into how it justifies a stance taken on the subject. This step of the analysis was more sensitive to context and thus complemented the rather schematic initial coding, which had relied on pre-given categories. The next section presents and discusses the results obtained through this exploratory analysis of the two annual reports by the BMWK.

Economic growth and the Ministry

Overall, the documentary evidence is unambiguous. Table 3.1 shows the results from the first step of the analysis: both reports overwhelmingly exhibit positive connotations for the term 'growth' (48 in total) while neutral references are much less common (18 in total) and negative entirely absent (0 in total); the relative distribution is similar across the 2 years of reporting. To further corroborate the finding, I ran a quick separate search for the terms 'degrowth' (English/German) and *Postwachstum* (German). Tellingly, the search yielded no results for either.

The pattern looks even more one-sided if we take into account the themes coded in the second step of the analysis. First of all, some of the neutral references could also be read as having no connotation at all. There are, for example, five paragraphs on investments, as well as several other paragraphs

Table 3.1: References to 'growth' in 2022 and 2023 BMWK annual reports

	2022	2023	Total
Positive	26	22	48
Neutral	10	8	18
Negative	0	0	0

on themes such as wages or digitization, that are kept at a fairly general level. Moreover, four paragraphs referring to the German StabG law and to the European Union Stability and Growth Pact, respectively, could in fact be reinterpreted as positive in the sense of the ministry's acceptance of these legal foundations. Yet I coded as neutral as paragraphs that appeared to be open-ended: while they could fit neatly into the overall positive framing of economic growth, each paragraph on its own could be read differently. For instance, advocates of post-growth measures are not against investments per se, only against certain types of investments (such as into socially or ecologically harmful activities). Overall, then, the count of neutral connotations is likely to be on the high end; correspondingly, the count of positive connotations is rather conservative.

Among those paragraphs coded as positive, many discuss growth in terms of the business cycle (growth as recovery or expansion), innovation, competitiveness, welfare, and sustainability. Together, they sketch a vision of the German economy thriving through what the BMWK repeatedly calls 'sustainable growth'. It is, in many ways, the mainstream rendering of 'green growth', the attempt to square the circle of growth and sustainability via (absolute) decoupling. The 2022 annual report stresses the ambition of decoupling (specifically, the verb *entkoppeln*) economic growth from its typical negative environmental consequences (BMWK, 2022, pp 6, 15, 87). The first such paragraph is worth quoting at length:

> In the socio-ecological market economy, it is also about a differentiated examination of resource use and growth. This is necessary simply because factors of production are principally scarce and resources that get invested in climate protection are not available for extending the supply of consumer products. It is particularly important to account for and address the negative effects of economic activities. We must not support any economic activities that contribute to fossil energy consumption, ecological destruction and social injustice. At the same time, growth needs to be decoupled from resource use and greenhouse gas emissions. Cognizant of the scale of the challenges, the annual economic report with its data gives reason to be optimistic that this is possible. (BMWK, 2022, p 6)

Despite the notable terminological shift from 'social market economy' to 'socio-ecological market economy', it is evident from this quote that the ministry aims to render economic growth green and inclusive. Interestingly, the two reports do not specify what type of decoupling is aspired. They definitely tackle questions of relative decoupling under the banner of (more) efficient resource use or lower resource intensity (BMWK, 2022, p 87; 2023, p 106). But since 'sustainable growth' constitutes the ultimate goal, the underlying assumption seems to be that what is eventually 'possible' is absolute decoupling at scale from all relevant environmental pressures. In this respect, growth as an objective itself is not questioned as long as certain types of economic activities with adverse socio-ecological impacts are avoided.

The BMWK also frequently invokes questions of societal welfare. Across the two annual reports, I coded a total of nine paragraphs as dealing with welfare. Seven of them forge a clear link between economic growth and welfare although some contain pledges to go beyond GDP as the central welfare metric (BMWK, 2022, pp 27–8, 79; 2023, p 107). Both reports dedicate a 'special chapter' to complementary welfare metrics: on 'Sustainable and inclusive growth – making dimensions of welfare measurable' in the 2022 edition (BMWK, 2022, pp 79–101), and on 'Welfare measurement and societal progress' in the 2023 edition (BMWK, 2023, pp 107–33). The following statement aptly summarizes the ministry's position on this matter: 'Aggregate growth, measured in terms of an increasing gross domestic product, is a necessary but not sufficient condition for sustainable welfare, employment, participation and social security' (BMWK, 2022, p 79).

It is important to note in this context that 'beyond GDP' arguments are generally compatible with but not, as such, indicative of post-growth thinking. After all, much mainstream economics is also critical of using GDP as a stand-alone indicator. However, this criticism often culminates in proposals to complement GDP with additional metrics (often called 'dashboards of indicators'), rather than abandon it altogether. The ministry adopts precisely that line of beyond GDP reasoning, as the previous quote illustrates. Further, the BMWK identifies the need to follow the ideal of a socio-ecological market economy that creates and maintains welfare through competitiveness on sustainability issues, among others: 'Germany can master the mentioned mid- and long-term challenges by refining its economic model' (BMWK, 2023, p 10).

The remaining two paragraphs on the welfare theme received neutral codes. While one of them is very generic, the other provides an opening, however timid, for a more critical engagement with the pursuit of economic growth: 'In addition, we want to openly debate what constitutes welfare and quality of life in the long term, where sustainability and growth can complement each other and *where considerations have to be made*' (BMWK, 2022, pp 6–7, emphasis added). The last part hints at potential trade-offs between sustainability goals and economic growth targets without specifying them. The subsequent paragraph, at which I looked for context although it does not use the word 'growth', suggests that the mainstreaming of beyond GDP indicators is the primary strategy for evaluating how sustainability and growth relate to each other. Set against the overarching narrative in favor of sustainable and inclusive growth, this short comment seems to be the exception that proves the rule. In the other paragraphs analyzed across the two annual reports, the ministry makes no such considerations, instead consistently assuming that growth and sustainability can and will go hand in hand.

Pursuing sustainability with and through growth: is it bad policy?

In the remainder of this chapter, I argue that the ministry sidesteps the larger debate by ignoring a wealth of evidence presented by the post-growth community, which includes many well-established academics from various fields of study. At least in the parts of the two reports analyzed, the BMWK almost exclusively sides with green growth proponents, who believe in the possibility of reconciling growth with sustainability through decoupling – as though there were no debate at all. While post-growth ideas remain widely marginalized, academic and activist debates have gathered momentum in recent years. Sometimes, these debates have entered spaces of policy making. We have, for example, witnessed supra- and international bodies questioning the pursuit of growth against the backdrop of deteriorating ecological and social parameters (IPBES, 2019; EEA, 2021a, 2021b). Similarly, growth skeptics in the European Parliament have sought to make their voices heard (Kallis et al, 2024). There is, thus, a more diverse discursive terrain on the intersection between economic growth and socio-ecological crises than the ministry is ready to admit.

And yet the BMWK hastily picks one side over the other, rather than seeking to identify and occupy a middle ground. This middle ground would have to be worked out incrementally. It could plausibly be informed by a mindset of growth indifference for policy making (van den Bergh, 2011); and it could inspire a willingness to build less growth-dependent institutions so that a core argument for why we so badly need economic growth would be countered (Lange et al, 2020, p 214; Büchs, 2021). Such a position would then also duly acknowledge that the desirability of economic growth is increasingly contested because of the long-term divergence between socioeconomic and Earth system indicators (Steffen et al, 2015). It would further link the health of planetary ecosystems, and humans within them, directly to key dimensions of socioeconomic welfare (see Lerner and Berg, 2017; van Woerden et al, 2023), thus developing strategies that do not take growth as their default objective. The hallmark of good economic policy would indeed be to begin to more fully account for the complex interlinkages between growth, ecology, health, and welfare.

As the ministry wholly overlooks the concerns about green growth and, thus, the arguments in favor of post-growth, it risks engaging in a form of 'bad science' (Broome et al, 2018) that can eventually breed ineffective and also bad policies. Such one-sided engagement in fact violates the core principle of rational decision making on which ministries typically pride themselves – that is, the assembling of *all* available information to enable evidence-based decisions that stand the best chance of realizing benefits and avoiding costs or harm (Uzonwanne, 2018, p 5337). Genuinely rational decision makers would care to account for the different arguments made in the (post-)growth debate, carefully weigh the evidence presented, ponder the consequences of their decisions, and regularly revisit them in light of new information. On this count, the BMWK appears to sacrifice a balanced take on what is an increasingly heated debate for the more convenient mainstream stance that economic growth is still good as long as it is (somewhat) green and inclusive.

That said, the ministry's new willingness to work with alternative indicators could, over time, create new space for progressive policies and politics. The crucial question then becomes what kind of metrics make their way into the BMWK and its publications, particularly because beyond GDP indicators may, depending on their design, not depart much from GDP-based valuations (Malay, 2019). As I outlined at the beginning of this chapter, there is a vibrant academic debate about whether economic growth can be made sustainable in the first place. If the ministry is serious about mitigating climate change (and other ecological disasters), its strong focus on rendering growth sustainable may prove ineffective over the long run. However, whether GDP growth remains a desirable policy yardstick even for already affluent economies will still be in the eye of the beholder.

Conclusion

This chapter has adopted a constructivist perspective on the desirability, or otherwise, of economic growth. In other words, there is no 'objectively' bad or good policy. For the BMWK, which I have analyzed in an exploratory fashion, the pursuit of green and inclusive growth is clearly a marker of good policy. Not a single paragraph in its 2022 and 2023 flagship reports discusses economic growth critically or at least recognizes the existence of post-growth thinking and research. It is remarkable that the vivid scholarly and also partly public debate on (post-)growth has left no visible mark on the ministry's official position. One may thus wonder if ignoring such a key debate in the age of climate crisis does not in itself constitute bad policy. Given the highly selective character of this study, however, its evidence base should be deepened and extended to account for discursive patterns over a longer period of time, ideally starting with the first available BMWK report in 2014.

Looking at the bigger picture, we may have to concede that social facts that question or transcend economic growth do not easily enter policy makers' minds and institutions of political power. Notably, the chapter has explored a case in which some openness to growth-critical thinking would seem reasonably likely, or at least more likely than in most other situations, even for an economic ministry: the BMWK hails from an affluent country with a high cumulative contribution to contemporary global socio-ecological problems while, at the time of writing, being under the helm of a politician from an environmentally minded political party that tends to recognize this historical responsibility. The German case could be meaningfully seen as representative of a larger class of cases of political institutions in high-income economies in Europe and beyond (under varying leaderships). Would any of them not so readily subscribe to a (green) growth agenda and seriously process deviating evidence? If not, do growth-critical views at least blossom within political institutions in countries in the Global South with little historical responsibility for planetary crises but high exposure to them?

Addressing these questions is a worthy task for future research that aims to investigate the normative underbelly of the pursuit of economic growth, green or otherwise. Self-reflexive scholars should exercise particular care in identifying and assessing the stakes enveloped in debates about (green) growth versus post-growth, as well as helping to ensure that each side gets a fair hearing in the corridors of political power. Speaking truth to power would at the very least demand that researchers with access to high-profile institutions, such as ministries, point political leaders and professional bureaucrats to competing evidence. The beholder should see it all.

Acknowledgments

I am grateful for the support and feedback that Malcolm Campbell-Verduyn, Heather McKeen-Edwards, and Ian Roberge extended to me in their capacity as volume editors. This work was supported by the Eva Mayr-Stihl Foundation through a one-year Young Academy for Sustainability Research Fellowship at the Freiburg Institute for Advanced Studies (FRIAS), University of Freiburg, Germany (from October 2023 to September 2024).

Notes

[1] This is the official translation to be found on the ministry's website.

[2] Relevant information on the ministry name can be obtained from the 'gallery of ministers' at https://www.bmwk.de/Navigation/DE/Ministerium/Ministergalerie/ministergalerie.html.

[3] The final draft of the chapter was completed on 7 February 2024, which represents the cut-off point for the analysis.

[4] As in the video provided as part of the gallery.

[5] I thank Matthew Paterson for making this point in a conversation unrelated to this chapter.

[6] The 2024 edition had not been released by the time the final draft of the chapter was completed. All annual economy reports since 2014 have had a main title combining the German term *Jahreswirtschaftsbericht* with the respective year, followed by a unique subtitle. The 2022 report is subtitled *For a Socio-Ecological Market Economy – Designing Transformation Innovatively*; the 2023 report is subtitled *Renewing Welfare*. The English subtitles are my translations from the German original, as are all passages or terms quoted from these two reports from this point in the chapter onwards.

References

Allan, B.B. (2019) 'Paradigm and nexus: neoclassical economics and the growth imperative in the World Bank, 1948–2000', *Review of International Political Economy*, 26(1): 183–206.

Andersson, J. (2019) 'The future of the Western world: the OECD and the Interfutures project', *Journal of Global History*, 14(1): 126–44.

Asara, V., Otero, I., Demaria, F., and Corbera, E. (2015) 'Socially sustainable degrowth as a social–ecological transformation: repoliticizing sustainability', *Sustainability Science*, 10(3): 375–84.

Barnett, M. and Finnemore, M. (2004) *Rules for the World: International Organizations in Global Politics*, Ithaca, NY: Cornell University Press.

Barry, J. (2020) 'A genealogy of economic growth as ideology and Cold War core state imperative', *New Political Economy*, 25(1): 18–29.

Blyth, M. (2003) 'Structures do not come with an instruction sheet: interests, ideas, and progress in political science', *Perspectives on Politics*, 1(4): 695–706.

BMWK (2022) *Jahreswirtschaftsbericht 2022: Für eine Sozial-ökologische Marktwirtschaft – Transformation innovativ gestalten*, Berlin: Bundesministerium für Wirtschaft und Klimaschutz [online], Available from: https://www. bmwk.de/Redaktion/DE/Publikationen/Wirtschaft/jahreswirtschaftsberi cht-2022.pdf?__blob=publicationFile&v=1

BMWK (2023) *Jahreswirtschaftsbericht 2023: Wohlstand erneuern*, Berlin: Bundesministerium für Wirtschaft und Klimaschutz [online], Available from: https://www.bmwk.de/Redaktion/DE/Publikationen/ Wirtschaft/jahreswirtschaftsbericht-2023.pdf?__blob=publicationFile&v=3

Broome, A., Homolar A., and Kranke, M. (2018) 'Bad science: international organizations and the indirect power of global benchmarking', *European Journal of International Relations*, 24(3): 514–39.

Buch-Hansen, H. and Carstensen, M.B. (2021) 'Paradigms and the political economy of ecopolitical projects: green growth and degrowth compared', *Competition & Change*, 25(3–4): 308–27.

Büchs, M. (2021) 'Sustainable welfare: independence between growth and welfare has to go both ways', *Global Social Policy*, 21(2): 323–7.

Clift, B. and Tomlinson, J. (2004) 'Fiscal policy and capital mobility: the construction of economic policy rectitude in Britain and France', *New Political Economy*, 9(4): 515–37.

EEA (2021a) 'Growth without economic growth', Briefing no 28/2020, 11 January, Copenhagen: European Environment Agency [online], Available from: https://www.eea.europa.eu/publications/growth-without-econo mic-growth

EEA (2021b) *Reflecting on Green Growth: Creating a Resilient Economy within Environmental Limits*, EEA Report no 11/2021, Copenhagen: European Environment Agency [online], Available from: https://www.eea.europa. eu/publications/reflecting-on-green-growth

Fioramonti, L. (2016) 'A post-GDP world? Rethinking international politics in the 21st century', *Global Policy*, 7(1): 15–24.

Fuchs, D.A. and Lorek, S. (2005) 'Sustainable consumption governance: a history of promises and failures', *Journal of Consumer Policy*, 28(3): 261–88.

Haberl, H., Wiedenhofer, D., Virág, D., Kalt, G., Plank, B., Brockway, P. et al (2020) 'A systematic review of the evidence on decoupling of GDP, resource use and GHG emissions, part II: synthesizing the insights', *Environmental Research Letters*, 15(6): 065003.

Hasselbalch, J.A., Kranke, M., and Chertkovskaya, E. (2023) 'Organizing for transformation: post-growth in International Political Economy', *Review of International Political Economy*, 30(5): 1621–38.

Hay, C. (2011) 'Ideas and the construction of interests', in D. Béland and R.H. Cox (eds) *Ideas and Politics in Social Science Research*, Oxford: Oxford University Press, pp 65–82.

Hickel, J. (2021) 'What does degrowth mean? A few points of clarification', *Globalizations*, 18(7): 1105–11.

Hickel, J. and Kallis, G. (2020) 'Is green growth possible?', *New Political Economy*, 25(4): 469–86.

Hülsse, R. (2007) 'Creating demand for global governance: the making of a global money-laundering problem', *Global Society*, 21(2): 155–78.

IPBES (2019) *Summary for Policymakers of the Global Assessment Report on Biodiversity and Ecosystem Services of the Intergovernmental Science-Policy Platform on Biodiversity and Ecosystem Services*, Bonn: IPBES Secretariat [online], Available from: https://zenodo.org/record/3553579#.Y8frBRWZNdg

Jackson, T. and Victor, P.A. (2019) 'Unraveling the claims for (and against) green growth', *Science*, 366(6468): 950–1.

Kallis, G., Mastini, R., and Zografos, C. (2024) 'Perceptions of degrowth in the European Parliament', *Nature Sustainability*, 7(1): 64–72.

Lange, S., Schmelzer, M., and Sharp, H. (2020) 'Raus aus dem Elfenbeinturm! Mit der "Third Mission" zur Wachstumsunabhängigkeit', in L. Hochmann (ed) *Economists4future: Verantwortung übernehmen für eine bessere Welt*, Hamburg: Murmann Verlag, pp 207–18.

Lehmann, C., Delbard, O., and Lange, S. (2022) 'Green growth, a-growth or degrowth? Investigating the attitudes of environmental protection specialists at the German Environment Agency', *Journal of Cleaner Production*, 336: 130306.

Lerner, H. and Berg, C. (2017) 'A comparison of three holistic approaches to health: One health, EcoHealth, and Planetary Health', *Frontiers in Veterinary Science*, 4: 163.

Malay, O.E. (2019) 'Do beyond GDP indicators initiated by powerful stakeholders have a transformative potential?', *Ecological Economics*, 162: 100–7.

Mastini, R., Kallis, G., and Hickel, J. (2021) 'A Green New Deal without growth?', *Ecological Economics*, 179: 106832.

Meadows, D.H., Meadows, D.L., Randers, J., and Behrens, W.W. (1972) *The Limits to Growth*, report for the Club of Rome's project on the Predicament of Mankind, New York, NY: Universe Books.

Meckling, J. and Allan, B.B. (2020) 'The evolution of ideas in global climate policy', *Nature Climate Change*, 10(5): 434–8.

O'Neill, D.W., Fanning, A.L., Lamb, W.F., and Steinberger, J.K. (2018) 'A good life for all within planetary boundaries', *Nature Sustainability*, 1(2): 88–95.

Parrique, T., Barth, J., Briens, F., Kerschner, C., Kraus-Polk, A., Kuokkanen, A., and Spangenberg, J.H. (2019) *Decoupling Debunked: Evidence and Arguments Against Green Growth as a Sole Strategy for Sustainability*, Brussels: European Environmental Bureau [online], Available from: https:// eeb.org/library/decoupling-debunked/

Parsons, C. (2002) 'Showing ideas as causes: the origins of the European Union', *International Organization*, 56(1): 47–84.

Petschow, U., Lange, S., Hofmann, D., Pissarskoi, E., aus dem Moore, N., Korfhage, T., and Schoofs, A. (2020) *Social Well-Being within Planetary Boundaries: the Precautionary Post-Growth Approach*, partial report for the 'Approaches to Resource Conservation in the Context of Post-Growth Concepts' project, Dessau-Roßlau: Umweltbundesamt [online], Available from: https://www.umweltbundesamt.de/sites/default/files/medien/ 5750/publikationen/2020_12_14_texte_234-2002_precautionary_post-growth.pdf

Pollin, R. (2018) 'De-growth vs a Green New Deal', *New Left Review*, 112: 5–25.

Purdey, S.J. (2010) *Economic Growth, the Environment and International Relations: The Growth Paradigm*, Abingdon: Routledge.

Speich, D. (2011) 'The use of global abstractions: national income accounting in the period of imperial decline', *Journal of Global History*, 6(1): 7–28.

St. Clair, A.L. (2006) 'The World Bank as a transnational expertised institution', *Global Governance*, 12(1): 77–95.

Steffen, W., Broadgate, W., Deutsch, L., Gaffney, O., and Ludwig, C. (2015) 'The trajectory of the Anthropocene: The Great Acceleration', *The Anthropocene Review*, 2(1): 81–98.

Stoknes, P.E. and Rockström, J. (2018) 'Redefining green growth within planetary boundaries', *Energy Research & Social Science*, 44: 41–9.

Uzonwanne, F.C. (2018) 'Rational model of decision-making', in A. Farazmand (ed) *Global Encyclopedia of Public Administration, Public Policy, and Governance*, Cham: Springer International Publishing, pp 5334–9.

van den Bergh, J.C.J.M. (2011) 'Environment versus growth: a criticism of "degrowth" and a plea for "a-growth"', *Ecological Economics*, 70(5): 881–90.

van Woerden, W.F., van de Pas, R., and Curtain, J. (2023) 'Post-growth economics: a must for planetary health justice', *Globalization and Health*, 19: 55.

WEF (2013) *The Green Investment Report: The Ways and Means to Unlock Private Finance for Green Growth*, report of the Green Growth Action Alliance, Geneva: World Economic Forum [online], Available from: http://www3.weforum.org/docs/WEF_GreenInvestment_Report_2013.pdf

Wiedmann, T., Lenzen, M., Keyßer, L.T., and Steinberger, J.K. (2020) 'Scientists' warning on affluence', *Nature Communications*, 11(1): 3107.

Woll, C. (2008) *Firm Interests: How Governments Shape Business Lobbying on Global Trade*, Ithaca, NY: Cornell University Press.

4

What a bad policy idea! Exploring views on wind farms in Italy

Alberto Asquer

This chapter aims to develop a framework for the analysis of arguments about what constitutes 'bad policies' during the policy-making stage. The framework provides a way to categorize bad policies, spanning from ideal policies to disastrous policies, based on their perceived effectiveness and desirability from the perspectives of both target groups and other stakeholder groups. This framework is applied to the analysis of the discourse about wind farms in Italy, using a Q Methodology study. Distinct perspectives emerge, ranging from endorsement of wind farms as a pathway to sustainable energy to concerns about their impact on local aesthetics, tourism, and biodiversity. A more nuanced understanding of the reasons for characterizing a policy option as a bad one is important to help policy makers and stakeholders participate in the policy discourse.

The role of bad policies in public policy decision making

The process of making public policy decisions has been extensively researched. The stages approach dissects it into components like issue framing, agenda setting, search for policy options, appraisal of policy options, and decision (Lindblom, 1959; Kingdon, 1984). The process entails that policy options are weighted against their potential benefits and drawbacks, and that inferior policy options are filtered out before the preferred one is selected. In a pluralist context, selecting policy options involves multiple stakeholders. They engage in negotiations to evaluate the merits of various policy options within institutionalized and discursive venues, ultimately influencing the selection of candidate policies.

Relatively little attention has been placed on how policy options are filtered out and selected within the public policy-making process. Policy making is based on calculative or utilitarian assumptions that individuals choose among alternative options by selecting the option with the highest net merit, while taking into account expected benefits, costs, and risks (Boadway, 2006; Brent, 2006). Alternative approaches extend the utilitarian model by highlighting that individuals may apply the calculative logic to intangible effects, like 'credit' and 'blame' (Leong and Howlett, 2017). Yet, these approaches neglect that policy options are also appraised on the basis of their reasons, that is, the justifications that are given for the merits of a policy option. When facing decisions, individuals often seek to construct order, resolve conflict, and justify their choices to themselves and others by offering reasons (Shafir et al, 1993).

The role of reasons in the selection of policy options seems important to explain which policy option is selected as the policy choice. Reasons may build on different grounds. Reasons for a policy option may consist of an appraisal of the expected effects of the policy, that can be conducted by means of a cost-benefit analysis or other techniques (Turnpenny et al, 2009). Policy options that are expected to be ineffective or inefficient or unwelcomed by any social, economic, or environmental standards are plausibly rejected. Reasons for a policy option may also consist of an appraisal of the policy by normative criteria. This involves weighing the meaning of a policy and the policy-making process against the principles of equity, social justice, human rights, and cultural acceptance (McKay et al, 2012; Hitzig, 2020). Policy options that do not conform to the accepted principles are undesirable and likely ostracized as 'disastrous' policies, and they would be contrasted with 'ideal' policy options that deliver effective and desirable effects. Following the theme of this volume, policies that are ineffective and undesirable – that is, bad policies – are likely pushed out of consideration in the policy agenda, at least in the types of democratic and human-centered systems that are examined in the volume.

This chapter aims to investigate the role of bad policies in the making of public policies. The investigation builds on the premise that identifying the presence of bad policy options in the policy-making process is important to explain how policy decisions are eventually made. In public policy making, several policy options may contend to be elected as the preferred course of action. Understanding how some options are discarded because they are labeled as 'bad' can help polish theories of public policy making, explain the outcome of the policy-making process, and contribute to improving the quality of public policy decisions.

The role of bad policies in the making of public policies is examined here by means of a study on the reasons for and against wind farms in Italy. Wind farms, also often referred to as wind power plants, are clusters of wind turbines strategically placed in areas with consistent and strong wind patterns. Wind farms harness the kinetic energy of the wind, converting it into mechanical energy through the rotation of their blades, which subsequently drives a generator to produce electricity. The process of making, shipping, and installing the turbines does emit greenhouse gasses (GHGs), but wind farms result in the generation of renewable energy without the emission of GHGs, with the overall effect that wind farms are considered 'climate positive' over a life cycle (Uddin and Kumar, 2014; Alsaleh and Sattler, 2019; Wang et al, 2019).

Governments worldwide are increasingly promoting the installation of wind farms for several compelling reasons. Firstly, the global imperative to combat climate change calls for a transition to cleaner energy sources. Wind farms, being a zero emission energy source, directly contribute to the reduction of carbon footprints. Secondly, wind energy diversifies the energy mix, reducing dependency on finite and often geopolitically sensitive fossil fuel reserves. This diversification enhances energy security and can stabilize energy prices. Lastly, the development and maintenance of wind farms create employment opportunities, stimulating economic growth in both urban and rural areas.

Given these multiple benefits, it is unsurprising that many governments are using various policy tools to expedite the adoption of wind energy solutions. Policy tools that are intended to stimulate the development of wind farms include financial incentives, like tax credits for investment in wind energy projects, direct support via grants and subsidies to reduce the initial capital cost, loan guarantees, and feed-in tariffs that guarantee a fixed price for electricity generated from wind farms, ensuring a stable revenue stream for producers. Additional policy tools consist of regulatory measures, such as requiring utilities to source a certain share of their electricity from renewable sources (the so-called Renewable Portfolio Standards or RPS), streamlining permission and approval processes to reduce the bureaucratic hurdles and expedite the start of wind projects, and ensuring that wind farms have priority or guaranteed access to the power grid. Further measures include funding on research and development to improve wind turbine technologies, launching campaigns to educate the public about the benefits of wind energy, offering public land at subsidized rates or facilitating the leasing process to ease the search for suitable locations for wind farms, investing in infrastructure such as roads and grid connections, adopting green certificates (or renewable energy certificates) to attest that electricity was generated from wind as a renewable energy source, offering long-term guaranteed purchase agreements by government or utilities to wind farms to ensure a market for the electricity that they produce, and implementing carbon taxes or other mechanisms that make fossil fuels more expensive relative to wind and other renewable energy sources, with the effect of making wind energy more competitive. These policies, when implemented effectively, can significantly boost the development and adoption of wind farms, helping countries transition to a more sustainable energy mix.

Yet, the discourse on wind farm policies is populated by contrasting claims about the merits of wind farms, which include arguments holding that they are a bad policy option to green energy transition. Arguments against the installation of wind turbine farms often revolve around environmental, aesthetic, and practical concerns. They include the claim that wind turbines can pose a threat to wildlife, particularly birds and bats, as the spinning blades can lead to fatal collisions; that wind turbines produce a low frequency sound that can be disturbing to nearby residents, leading to complaints about noise pollution; that wind farms are often considered an eyesore, as they can significantly alter the natural landscape and visual aesthetics of a region; that the presence of wind farms can reduce property values in nearby areas, especially due to their visual impact and noise; that wind is an intermittent and unpredictable energy source, which can make wind energy less reliable compared to other energy sources; that the initial setup cost for wind turbines can be high and the return on investment may be disappointing, especially in areas with less wind; that suitable locations for wind farms can be far from the places where electricity is most needed, and they may trigger disputes on land use and ownership; and that investment in wind farms should be accompanied by an expansion of existing power grids. The 'badness' of wind farm policy options, therefore, needs to be carefully assessed to understand its role in the making of energy policies and green energy transition strategies.

The chapter is structured as follows. The next section will discuss the concept of bad policies, especially in the context of public policy making. The section following this will present a framework to analyze bad policies within a discourse on policy options. Next, a Q Methodology study of the views on wind farms in Italy will be illustrated. The final section will provide the conclusions.

Bad policies: ineffective and undesirable

In various social, political, and economic contexts, the term 'bad policies' frequently emerges in discussions. Bad policies are often associated with issues of short-termism, neglect, misdirected interventions, and harmful effects, among other criticisms. Bad policies are those that may fail to adequately address the core policy issue, exhibit excessive or insufficient intervention, and demonstrate a lack of preparedness. Furthermore, bad policies may perpetuate discrimination, exacerbate inequalities, instill overregulation, and lack transparency. Communication failures with the public or media and misplaced priorities further compound the challenges associated with bad policies. These multifaceted criticisms underscore the complexity and multifarious nature of what constitutes a bad policy (Hogwood and Gunn, 1984).

In the context of this volume, bad policies are delineated as those that are both ineffective and undesirable. Ineffectiveness pertains to the failure in achieving a set objective, while undesirability implies that the policy is unwelcome based on normative standards. This dual criterion provides a

Figure 4.1: A typology of policies depending on effectiveness and desirability

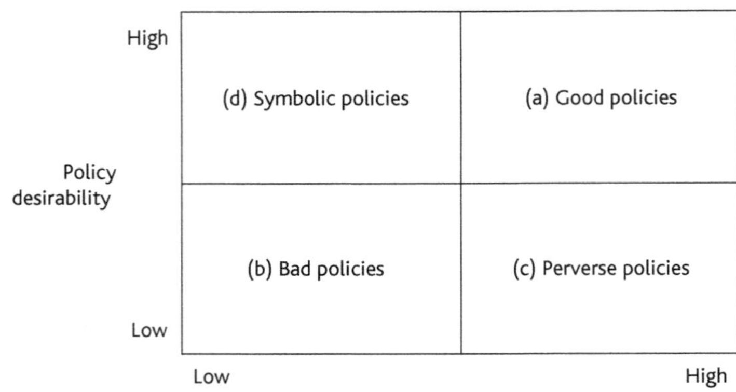

starting point for zooming into what bad policies are. The very concept of bad policies is clarified by exploring the intersections of the effectiveness and desirability dimensions. Figure 4.1 shows a typology of policies depending on two axes. The horizontal axis represents the policy's effectiveness, while the vertical axis indicates its desirability. Figure 4.1 yields four distinct categories: (a) good policies that are both effective and desirable, (b) bad policies that are ineffective and undesirable, (c) 'perverse policies' that, while effective, are undesirable, and (d) 'symbolic policies' that are desirable but ineffective. The rest of the discussion will focus on bad policies only, although it may be relevant to perverse and symbolic policies as well.

Within the context of public policy making, it is crucial to clearly differentiate between the appraisal of policy options (*ex ante*) and the evaluation of policies after the implementation (*ex post*). The appraisal of policies that have been implemented calls for the application of theories, tools, and techniques of policy evaluation. Policy evaluations help assess, on the basis of evidence, whether policies have been bad, meaning that the implemented policy is shown to be ineffective and unwelcome. Conversely, the *ex ante* appraisal of policy options builds on expectations about whether the policy is going to be effective and desirable.

Policies that are indicated as 'bad' in the public policy-making process can play an important role. Labels of 'bad policy' serve as red flags, indicating courses of action that are anticipated to be ineffective and undesirable. By identifying and discarding these options early in the process, policy makers can potentially streamline policy making, ensuring that the final policy choice is well-informed and effective. The preemptive identification and elimination of bad policy options are instrumental in refining the policy-making process, especially in anticipatory governance approaches (Ramos, 2014; Maffei et al, 2020). Questions arise, though, concerning how it is that a policy option is labeled as 'bad', who labels policy options as 'bad', and how the stigma of 'badness' attached to a policy eventually affects the selection of the policy choice.

In pluralistic contexts, any stakeholder can potentially label a policy option as 'bad'. A claim that a policy option is bad enters the policy discourse, where the 'policy is bad' claim competes against other claims about the relative merits of the policy option with respect to others. Stakeholders conceivably assess the persuasiveness of the claim that a 'policy is bad' by canons of reasonableness and plausibility (Nickerson, 2020). The capacity of a claim that a 'policy is bad' to affect the outcome of a public policy-making process, however, is also dependent on the identity, role, and credibility of the stakeholders who argue about the badness of the policy (Majone, 1989; Mols, 2012; Eising et al, 2020). Influential stakeholders may be able to throw their resources against the diffusion and acceptance of policy options that they regard as bad ones. Relatively weaker or marginalized stakeholders, instead, may denigrate a policy as bad in an effort to advance their preferred options by rhetorical means.

Bad policies in arguments about public policies

Several studies highlighted the importance of arguments and discourse in the making of public policies. Majone (1989) observed that policy analysis is not merely a technical exercise but fundamentally an argumentative one. Setting empirical data and factual evidence aside, policy appraisals and decisions largely rest on the persuading power of arguments. Among institutionalist approaches, Schmidt (2010) contributed to the development of discursive institutionalism, that focuses on the role that arguments and discourse play in coordinating stakeholders and communicating with the public and the media. In a broader perspective, critical discourse analysis (Weiss and Wodak, 2007) or critical discourse studies (van Dick, 2015) address how language, power, and ideology affect the policy discourse, influencing the framing and understanding of policy issues and options. Policy analysis, therefore, should be attentive to arguments that are made about the effectiveness and desirability of policies.

In a pluralist context, arguments about policy options can be made about how good or bad policies are for the intended target and how good or bad their effects are for other groups, including those that are to bear the consequences of a policy in the distant future. Figure 4.2 shows how policy options can be appraised depending on two dimensions. The horizontal axis shows how a policy is assessed from the perspective of the target group. The vertical axis indicates how a policy is assessed from the perspective of other groups. Figure 4.2 results in nine types of policies. On the one polar corner, (a) an ideal policy is one that delivers effective

Figure 4.2: A typology of policies depending on degree of goodness for the target group and for other groups

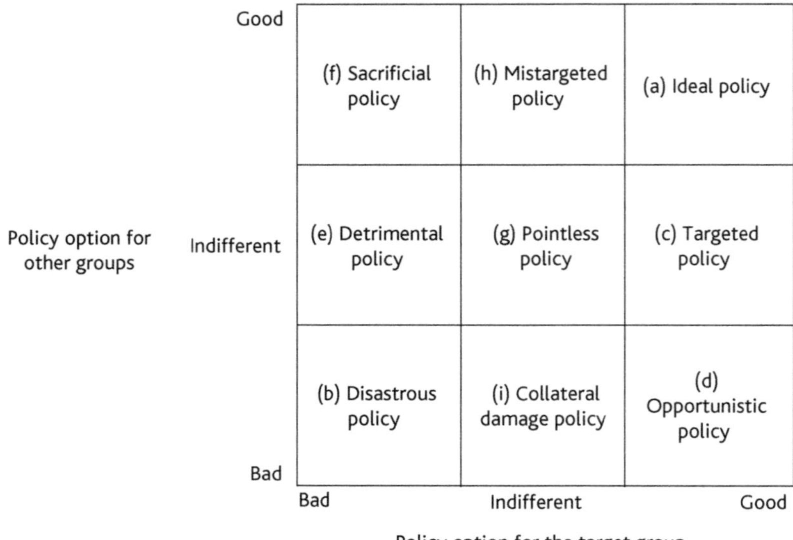

and desirable effects for both the target group and other groups. On the opposite polar corner, (b) a disastrous policy is one that results in ineffective and undesirable effects for both the target group and other groups. Policies that are considered 'good ones' for the target group may be indifferent for other groups – and these policies may be labeled as (c) targeted ones – or may deliver bad consequences for other groups – and these policies may be labeled (d) opportunistic. Policies that are regarded as 'bad ones' for the target group may be indifferent for other groups, and they may be labeled as (e) detrimental ones, or may be rather good for other groups, and they may be labeled as (f) sacrificial ones – as the target group would be worse off to the benefit of other groups. Finally, policy options that are indifferent for the target group and which are immaterial to other groups can be labeled as (g) pointless policies; those that are indifferent for the target group but deliver good effects to other groups are (h) mistargeted policies; those that are indifferent for the target group but entail bad effects on other groups can be called (i) collateral damage policies.

The taxonomy of policy options depending on their degree of 'goodness' for the target group and for other groups can be related to the structure and interplay of argument that populate policy discourses. Needless to say, an ideal policy is likely to gain support from both the target group and other stakeholders, while a disastrous policy is likely to trigger resistance from everyone. Advocates of a policy option that bears immaterial or negative effects to other groups but the target one would need to craft rhetorical strategies to persuade about the merits of the policy. For example, arguments for an opportunistic policy need to anticipate resistance from the side of other groups, who would be negatively affected by the opportunistic policy option. In converse, target groups that resist policies that have a negative impact on them need to be attentive about whether other groups can be allies (as when facing disastrous bad policies), or neutral observers (as when facing a detrimental bad policy), or profiteers (as when facing a sacrificial bad policy). Policy discourses are also influenced by the length of time stakeholders expect it will take to see the effects of policy options. Some groups may hold a more short-termist perspective than others, with consequential effects on their appraisal of the degree of 'goodness' of policy options. For example, stakeholders who care about the long-term prospects for future generations or the environment would appraise a policy option as bad, indifferent, or good with respect to its likely implications decades into the future.

The taxonomy in Figure 4.2 can be also related to previous works on rhetoric and public deliberation. Hirshman's (1991) *Rhetoric of Reaction* offered, for example, a distinction between futility, perversity, and jeopardy arguments that populate reactionary rhetoric. The futility thesis, that aims to undermine a proposed course of action because it would be inconsequential, can be related to pointless and mistargeted policies. The perversity thesis, that flags the worsening effects of a proposed course of action, can be related to disaster, detrimental, and collateral damage policies. The jeopardy thesis, which warns that the proposed course of action would undermine other arrangements in the political regime, can be related to opportunistic and sacrificial policies, where attaining good for one part of stakeholders entails bad consequences for another one, with the resulting effect of compromising political stability.

The analysis of bad policies in arguments about policy options can be enriched further in at least two ways. First, in the policy-making context where appraisals of policy options consist of arguments that build on empirical as much as normative ground, stakeholders may strategically argue about policy options for advancing their own agendas. A stakeholder, for example, may rhetorically craft arguments that a given policy option results in worsening effects for them, for the sake of obtaining an improved bargaining position, possibly on other policy issues. In this respect, claims that a given policy option is bad may be pretentious and instrumental to attain some other gains.

Second, the argument about the merits of a policy option may be enriched by considering sources of uncertainties. Figure 4.3 shows further nuances to policy arguments when two dimensions are added. The horizontal axis shows the degree of uncertainty that the intended effects of the policy

Figure 4.3: A typology of arguments about policies depending on uncertainty about their effects and about the stability of the context

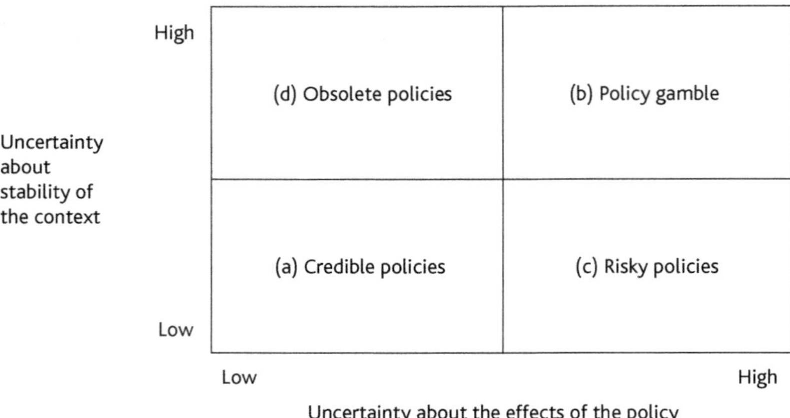

on the target group materialize. The vertical axis indicates the degree of uncertainty regarding the stability of the context conditions. Figure 4.3 results in four possible scenarios. If uncertainty about the policy effects and about the stability of the context are low, then an argument can be made that (a) the policy is credible. If, on the other hand, there is high uncertainty that the intended effects of the policy materialize and that the context remains stable, then (b) the policy is a gamble. If the effects of the policy are uncertain while the context is stable, then (c) the policy is risky. Finally, if the effects of the policy are relatively certain but the context may change, an argument can be made that (d) the policy is obsolete because of its inadequacy to address the policy issues under changed context conditions. Adding uncertainty, therefore, opens up additional rhetorical strategies around the pitfalls of bad policies.

The framework that has been illustrated in this section provides a way to map out the variety of arguments about what constitutes bad policy options. Building on this volume's argument that bad policies are characterized as being ineffective and undesirable, the attractiveness of policy options depends on their effects on the target group and on other groups in society. Further nuances arise, moreover, depending on uncertainties about the effects of a policy and about the stability of the context. The rest of this chapter shows an application of the framework to the reasons for and against wind farms in Italy. By analyzing a variety of claims on the merits and drawbacks of wind farms, the study will shed some light onto the reasons for labeling wind farms as a bad policy and, relatedly, it will illustrate how the framework can be used to inform argumentative strategies in public policy discourse.

Wind farms in Italy as a bad policy option: a Q methodology study

Italy has been progressively embracing wind energy as part of its commitment to renewable energy sources. The country's journey with wind energy began in earnest in the early 2000s, driven by European directives and national targets to reduce carbon emissions and increase the share of renewables in the energy mix. The Italian government introduced various incentives and support mechanisms, such as feed-in tariffs and green certificates, to promote the development of wind farms. By the 2010s, Italy had made significant strides in increasing its wind energy capacity, with numerous onshore wind farms spread across regions like Sicily, Puglia, and Calabria. The total installed capacity in the country exceeds 11 GW. In recent years, there has also been interest in exploring offshore wind potential, given Italy's extensive coastline. The Italian government and energy stakeholders continue to invest in research, infrastructure, and policy frameworks to further harness the potential of wind energy and contribute to a sustainable energy future.

As part of Italy, the island of Sardinia has a rich history of wind energy utilization. The island's topography and geographical location make it an ideal spot for harnessing wind energy. The first wind farms were established in Sardinia in the 1990s with a combined power capacity of around 15 MW. The 2000s marked a period of rapid expansion for wind energy, when the number of wind farms increased substantially. By the end of the decade, the total installed capacity reached approximately 90 MW. During the 2010s, advancements in technology and increased investments led to an exponential growth of the island's wind energy capacity. Eventually, the total capacity of wind farms in Sardinia came to exceed 1 GW. Notably, the wind farm in Buddusò, located in the northern part of the island, is one of the largest in the country with a capacity of about 138 MW.

Total wind energy capacity in Sardinia is relatively high by international standards (for instance, in the United Kingdom, the offshore Walney Extension wind farm has a capacity of 659 MW; in the United States, the Alta Wind Energy Centre has a capacity of about 1.5 GW; and in China the onshore Gansu wind farm operates at about 8 GW). However, and despite the promising potential for enlargement, the wind energy sector in Sardinia has faced challenges. The island's unique landscape and the presence of protected areas have posed constraints on the development of new wind farms. Additionally, concerns related to visual impact and noise pollution have been raised by local communities. The Sardinian government also opposed offshore wind farm development, in contrast with European Union and central government orientation to stimulate the wind energy capacity.

The contemporary public discourse in Sardinia is populated by several views that cast the policy of installing further wind farms as a bad one.

Specific arguments about the ineffective or undesirable features of wind farms include that wind farms disrupt the natural beauty of the pristine landscapes of the island; that the presence of wind farms can deter tourists, especially if they are built near popular attractions and coastal areas; that wind farms may detract the integrity and significance of the numerous archeological sites and areas of historical importance; and that wind farms would result in the enrichment of investors while bringing negligible effects to the regional economy and employment. These arguments are counteracted, however, by other views that support wind energy in Sardinia as a sustainable way to meet the energy needs of the island and reduce dependency on fossil fuels. The debate over wind farms in Sardinia reflects, in this sense, a broader global conversation about the balance between renewable energy development and preserving the natural environment, as well as the cultural heritage.

As a way to empirically ground the investigation of arguments about wind farms as bad policy, a Q Methodology study was carried out. Q Methodology is a statistical approach designed to discern patterns of individual subjective viewpoints within a group (Stephenson, 1953; Brown, 1980). Unlike other quantitative research methods, Q Methodology does not aim to test hypothesized causal links but rather to pinpoint clusters of shared ideas, represented as statements, among participants. Furthermore, while Q Methodology incorporates statistical correlations to deduce connections between ideas (expressed as statements), it distinguishes itself from other qualitative research methods that predominantly depend on the researcher's interpretation. Nevertheless, interpreting the results remains crucial, particularly as the ideas must be contextualized within the specific political discourses of the policy domain.

The Q study began by identifying a set of statements, termed the Q sample, which encapsulated the diverse opinions concerning the matter in question, known as the 'concourse' (Dryzek and Berejikian, 1993; Steelman and Maguire, 1999; Dryzek and Holmes, 2002). This study's Q sample was derived from the review of local media and social outlets (Facebook, which features as the second main source of information in Italy after TV news; Censis, 2022), which resulted in a collection of 85 statements. Statements conveyed a variety of views on wind farms held by a diverse range of individuals, from representatives of the energy industry to local businesses to residents. The statements were then consolidated into a more manageable number of 27. It is acknowledged that the Q sample may not capture the full spectrum of perspectives on wind farms. However, the size of the Q sample is influenced by the practical task required from respondents during data gathering.

In the Q study next phase, respondents, referred to as the P sample, were asked to indicate their level of concurrence with the statements from the Q sample. The Q study collected 40 respondents, who were recruited via a Facebook social media discussion group on wind farms in Sardinia of about 800 members. Respondents were asked to organize the Q sample's statements on a 'grid' designed as a normal distribution. This grid, resembling a pyramid, consisted of 'slots' set on a scale from the statement a respondent least agrees with (scored −4) to the one they most concur with (scored +4). The sorting process was facilitated using the FlashQ software (Braehler and Hackert, 2013). The grid's purpose was to have respondents prioritize the statements based on their relative agreement level, rather than just indicating their level of agreement, which is a common approach in questionnaire surveys. Subsequently, the collected responses, termed Q sorts, underwent a by-person factor analysis (Stephenson, 1953) to identify clusters of similar statement preferences. The factors derived from the analysis can be interpreted as sets of assertions linked to specific perspectives on wind farms.

The factor analysis resulted in the extraction of four factors that explain 69 percent of cumulative variance. Table 4.1 shows the correlation scores between the factors. Table 4.2 displays the factor characteristics. Figures 4.4 to 4.7 visualize the factors by positioning the sentences of the Q sort grids. The results of the Q Methodology analysis shed some light onto the variety of arguments that populate the discourse on wind farms in Sardinia. Factor 1 shows that several arguments are made that broadly support the installation of wind farms. Statements that respondents agree with include that wind farms are a sustainable alternative to fossil fuel energy sources and that wind farms are a necessary solution to address climate change, indicating a connection between wind farms and the contemporary climate change and energy

Table 4.1: Correlation scores between factors

	Factor 1	Factor 2	Factor 3	Factor 4
Factor 1	1.0	−0.17	−0.12	0.52
Factor 2	−0.17	1.0	−0.02	0.06
Factor 3	0.12	−0.02	1.0	−0.15
Factor 4	0.52	0.06	−0.15	1.0

Table 4.2: Factor characteristics

	Factor 1	Factor 2	Factor 3	Factor 4
No. of defining variables	20	4	2	7
Avg. rel. coef.	0.8	0.8	0.8	0.8
Composite reliability	0.99	0.94	0.89	0.97
SE of factor Z-scores	0.11	0.24	0.33	0.18

Figure 4.4: Factor 1 of the Q Methodology study on wind farms in Sardinia

-4	-3	-2	-1	0	1	2	3	4
I am against the installation of wind farms.	Wind farms cause noise pollution.	I am concerned about the noise produced by wind farms.	Offshore wind farms have a negative impact on fishing.	Wind farms can cause electromagnetic interference problems.	Wind farms are a preferable option compared to thermal power plants.	Wind farms can be effectively integrated into the surrounding environment.	Wind farms are a sustainable alternative to fossil energy sources.	I am in favor of the installation of wind farms.
	Wind farms are inefficient compared to other renewable energy sources.	Wind farms are a temporary and unsustainable solution to the energy crisis.	Wind farms have a negative impact on human health.	Wind farms scan interfere with radio and television signals.	Wind farms can creaate jobs in the commuiity.	Wind farms can help reduce greenhouse gas emissions.	Wind farms are a necessary solution to address climate change.	
		Wind farms are a threat to biodiversity.	I am concerned about the environmental effects of wind farms.	Wind farms have a negative impact on tourism.	I am concerned about the future disposal of wind turbine blades.	Wind farms are a clean and renewable energy source.		
		Wind farms can be a danger to air navigation.	Wind farms have a negative impact on wildlife.	Wind farms have a negative impact on the aesthetics of the landscape.	Wind farms are too expensive to build and maintain.	Wind farms can bring economic benefits to the community.		
				Wind farms can cause soil erosion / problems.				

Figure 4.5: Factor 2 of the Q Methodology study on wind farms in Sardinia

-4	-3	-2	-1	0	1	2	3	4
Wind farms can be effectively integrated into the surrounding environment.	Wind farms are inefficient compared to other renewable energy sources.	Wind farms can cause electromagnetic interference problems.	Wind farms cause noise pollution.	Wind farms can bring economic benefits to the community.	Wind farms can cause soil erosion problems.	Wind farms can help reduce greenhouse gas emissions.	Offshore wind farms have a negative impact on fishing.	Wind farms have a negative impact on tourism.
	Wind farms can be a danger to air navigation.	I am in favor of the installation of wind farms.	Wind farms are too expensive to build and maintain.	Wind farms have a negative impact on wildlife.	Wind farms are a sustainable alternative to fossil energy sources.	I am concerned about the future disposal of wind turbine blades.	Wind farms have a negative impact on the aesthetics of the landscape.	
		I am concerned about the noise produced by wind farms.	Wind farms scan interfere with radio and television signals.	I am concerned about the environmental effects of wind farms.	Wind farms are a clean and renewable energy source.	I am against the installation of wind farms.		
		Wind farms are a necessary solution to address climate change.	Wind farms can creaate jobs in the commuiity.	Wind farms have a negative impact on human health.	Wind farms are a threat to biodiversity.	Wind farms are a temporary and unsustainable solution to the energy crisis.		
				Wind farms are a preferable option compared to thermal power plants.				

Figure 4.6: Factor 3 of the Q Methodology study on wind farms in Sardinia

-4	-3	-2	-1	0	1	2	3	4
Offshore wind farms have a negative impact on fishing.	I am in favor of the installation of wind farms.	Wind farms can be a danger to air navigation.	Wind farms are a sustainable alternative to fossil energy sources.	Wind farms have a negative impact on the aesthetics of the landscape.	Wind farms have a negative impact on wildlife.	I am concerned about the environmental effects of wind farms.	Wind farms can creaate jobs in the commuiity.	Wind farms cause noise pollution.
	Wind farms can be effectively integrated into the surrounding environment.	Wind farms can cause electromagnetic interference problems.	Wind farms are a clean and renewable energy source.	Wind farms have a negative impact on tourism.	I am concerned about the future disposal of wind turbine blades.	Wind farms are inefficient compared to other renewable energy sources.	Wind farms can bring economic benefits to the community.	
		Wind farms are a preferable option compared to thermal power plants.	Wind farms are a temporary and unsustainable solution to the energy crisis.	Wind farms scan interfere with radio and television signals.	Wind farms can help reduce greenhouse gas emissions.	Wind farms have a negative impact on human health.		
		I am against the installation of wind farms.	Wind farms can cause soil erosion problems.	Wind farms are a threat to biodiversity.	Wind farms are too expensive to build and maintain.	I am concerned about the noise produced by wind farms.		
				Wind farms are a necessary solution to address climate change.				

Figure 4.7: Factor 4 of the Q Methodology study on wind farms in Sardinia

-4	-3	-2	-1	0	1	2	3	4
Wind farms have a negative impact on human health.	Wind farms are a threat to biodiversity.	Wind farms have a negative impact on tourism.	Wind farms cause noise pollution.	Wind farms can creaate jobs in the commuiity.	Wind farms can be effectively integrated into the surrounding environment.	Wind farms can help reduce greenhouse gas emissions.	Wind farms are a temporary and unsustainable solution to the energy crisis.	I am in favor of the installation of wind farms.
	Wind farms can be a danger to air navigation.	Wind farms are inefficient compared to other renewable energy sources.	Wind farms can cause electromagnetic interference problems.	Wind farms are too expensive to build and maintain.	Wind farms are a preferable option compared to thermal power plants.	Wind farms are a clean and renewable energy source.	Wind farms have a negative impact on the aesthetics of the landscape.	
		I am concerned about the environmental effects of wind farms.	Wind farms are a sustainable alternative to fossil energy sources.	I am concerned about the noise produced by wind farms.	Wind farms can bring economic benefits to the community.	Wind farms are a necessary solution to address climate change.		
		I am against the installation of wind farms.	Wind farms scan interfere with radio and television signals.	Offshore wind farms have a negative impact on fishing.	Wind farms can cause soil erosion problems.	Wind farms have a negative impact on wildlife.		
				I am concerned about the future disposal of wind turbine blades.				

transition discourses. Also other statements broadly support wind farms, which can be effectively integrated into the surrounding environment, can help reduce greenhouse emissions, provide a clear and renewable energy source, and can bring economic benefits to the community. Arguments that flag potential issues with wind farms highlight practical concerns, like the future disposal of wind turbine blades and the cost of their construction and maintenance.

Factor 2 highlights that wind farms raise concerns about their negative impact on tourism, on fishing, and on the aesthetics of the landscape. Other sentences that respondents especially agree with include those about the future disposal of wind turbine blades, soil erosion problems, and biodiversity, but the respondents associated with this view also acknowledge that wind farms can reduce greenhouse emissions and that they are a sustainable alternative to fossil energy sources. Part of the views of Factor 2 also address the futility of wind farms, which are considered a temporary and unsustainable solution to the energy crisis. Factor 2 flags some reasons why wind farms may be regarded as a bad policy. Negative views towards wind farms relate to multiple reasons from the negative impact that wind farms have on other groups (for instance, on operators of tourism and fishing industries), to the ineffectiveness of wind farms to tackle energy crisis, to the undesirable consequences of wind farms on biodiversity and natural environment preservation.

Factor 3 indicates that some respondents hold ambivalent views towards wind farms. Sentences that respondents agree on include positive claims that wind farms can create jobs in the community and that they can bring economic benefits to the community. On the other hand, they also agree that wind farms cause noise pollution that is a source of concern to them, that wind farms have negative effects on the environment and on human health, and that they may be inefficient compared to other renewable energy sources. With respect to Factors 1 and 2, Factor 3 seems to hold rather vague beliefs towards wind farms, and probably to lack any strong policy standing towards them; in fact, Factor 3 indicates that they disagree with both being in favor and being against the installation of wind farms.

Factor 4, lastly, expresses a supportive view of wind farms, albeit in a pragmatic understanding of wind farms as a 'necessary evil'. Respondents are in favor of the installation of wind farms, which are a necessary solution to address climate change, are a clean and renewable energy source, and can help reduce greenhouse emissions. On the other hand, they believe that wind farms are a temporary and unsustainable solution to the energy crisis, particularly as it has a negative impact on the aesthetics of the landscape, and has a negative impact on wildlife. Factor 4 is similar to Factor 1 in acknowledging the advantages of wind farms, but it also admits some of their negative sides.

The Q Methodology study helps identify the views that characterize wind farms as a bad policy option. The views that are associated with Factors 2 and 3 flag that the policy to install wind farms is both ineffective (that is, wind farms are inefficient with respect to other energy sources, and they provide a temporary and unsustainable solution to the energy crisis) and undesirable (that is, wind farms have a negative impact on tourism, on fishing, and on the aesthetics of the environment). In this respect, the views associated with Factors 2 and 3 would arguably oppose wind farms because of inefficiency and undesirability reasons.

Views associated with Factors 2 and 3 also regard wind farms as an opportunistic policy, where the energy industry gains from wind farm investment while other stakeholders – like the tourism and the fishing industry – would be worse off. These views would also resist casting wind farms as beneficial to local communities because of their effects on the local economy and employment; rather, they regard wind farms as a sacrificial policy, where local residents would suffer the loss of aesthetics, biodiversity, and wildlife while the renewable industry would thrive. In this respect, the framework proposed in this chapter (Figure 4.2) helps elucidate that some views frame wind farms as highly contentious policy options. Different stakeholder interests are pitted one against the other, in a rhetorical posture that papers over room for agreement on a middle ground course of action.

Views associated with Factors 2 and 3 also indicate that wind farms face uncertainties concerning both their effects and the context. On the one hand, some views hold that there are risks arising from the disposal of wind turbine blades, the erosion of the soil, and human health. On the other hand, they also hold that wind farms are inefficient with respect to other renewable energy sources and a temporary and unsustainable solution only to the energy crisis. These views indicate that wind farms can be also characterized as a policy gamble, as defined in this chapter (Figure 4.3), which would act as a rhetorical strategy to discredit wind farms policy options because of the uncertainties arising from their use and from changing alternatives to handle the energy transition.

This Q Methodology study reveals a multifaceted landscape of the discourse on wind farms in Italy, particularly in Sardinia. By mapping out four different views ranging from the most supportive to the most critical towards wind farms (associated to four factors resulting from the by-person factor analysis), the study underscores the variety of public sentiment towards wind farms. Some views, in particular, characterize wind farms as a bad policy option, which can be framed as an opportunistic or a sacrificial policy that is detrimental to some stakeholders (namely, the tourism and the fishing industry and the local residents) while being beneficial to others (namely, the renewable industry and investors). The option to install wind farms is also framed as a policy gamble because of facing uncertainties concerning both their effects and the context. In sum, the framework proposed in this chapter helps appreciate the nuances of the view of wind farms as a bad policy. This results in a more detailed understanding of the challenges to advance wind farms because of the intersection of environmental, economic, and social concerns, which may be relevant more generally to appreciate the challenges faced in transitioning to renewable energy sources globally.

Conclusion

The process of making public policy involves considering various policy options, each of which is evaluated based on its merits, especially in terms of effectiveness and desirability. A policy option that is characterized as a bad policy may be ostracized in the policy discourse and discarded. It is important, therefore, to analyze what the features of bad policy options are. This chapter presented an analytical framework for the analysis of arguments about what constitutes bad policies during the policy-making stage. The framework provides a way to map out views about a policy option along the dimensions of the degree of goodness (or badness) of the effects of the policy on target and other groups, and depending on the degree of uncertainty about the effects of the policy and the stability of the context. The application of the framework results in a more nuanced understanding of the arguments that are put forward about why a policy is characterized as a bad one.

The chapter illustrated the application of the framework to the study of the reasons for and against wind farms in Italy. The analysis resulted in the identification of four views (factors), namely one that expresses support to wind farms, one that highlights the negative effects of wind farms, one that holds ambivalent views towards wind farms, and one that accepts wind farms as a 'necessary evil' to the energy transition issue. The framework helps appreciate nuances of the views that regard wind farms as a bad policy option, including those that consider wind farms as an opportunistic or a sacrificial policy, or one that may be considered as a policy gamble because of the uncertainties concerning both their effects and the context. Understanding these nuances is important with respect to the development of wind farms in the country, which – at the time of writing – still exhibits contradictory tendencies between continuous growth of installed wind energy capacity and persistent issues arising from resistance of local communities and regulatory hurdles.

In conclusion, a more nuanced understanding of the reasons for characterizing a policy as a bad one is important to help policy makers and stakeholders participate in the policy discourse. Reasons for the 'badness' of a policy option may take different forms. Stakeholders who want to label a policy as a bad one may deploy rhetorical strategies that cast the policy option as bearing negative or indifferent effects to the target or other groups, or as facing uncertainties concerning either their effects or the context or both. Stakeholders who want to counteract the argument about the 'badness' of a policy, instead, may need to develop alternative policy proposals that offset the concerns of those who resist the adoption of bad policies. Policy makers must be attentive to the variety of voices, concerns, and arguments presented, ensuring that decisions are not just technically sound but are also resonant with the values, needs, and aspirations of the communities they impact. The framework that has been presented in this chapter, possibly coupled with Q Methodology or other techniques to map out the variety of views on a contentious policy option, may help achieve this goal.

References

Alsaleh, A. and Sattler, M. (2019) 'Comprehensive life cycle assessment of large wind turbines in the US', *Clean Technologies and Environmental Policy*, 21: 887–903.

Boadway, R. (2006) 'Principles of cost–benefit analysis', *Public Policy Review*, 2(1): 1–44.

Braehler, G. and Hackert, C. (2013) 'FlashQ 1.0, Q Sorting via the internet' [online], Available from: http://www.hackert.biz/flashq/home/

Brent, R.J. (2006) *Applied Cost-Benefit Analysis*, Cheltenham: Edward Elgar Publishing.

Brown, S.R. (1980) *Political Subjectivity: Applications of Q Methodology in Political Science*, New Haven and London: Yale University Press.

Censis (2022) *18th Report on Communication* [online], Available from: https://www.censis.it/comunicazione/18%C2%B0-rapporto-censis-sulla-comunicazione

Dryzek, J.S. and Berejikian, J. (1993) 'Reconstructive democratic theory', *American Political Science Review*, 87(1): 48–60.

Dryzek, J.S. and Holmes, L. (2002) *Post-Communist Democratization: Political Discourses Across Thirteen Countries*, Cambridge: Cambridge University Press.

Eising, R., Rasch, D., Rozbicka, P., Fink-Hafner, D., Hafner-Fink, M., and Novak, M. (2020) 'Who says what to whom? Alignments and arguments in EU policy-making', in R. Eising, D. Rasch, and P. Rozbicka (eds) *National Interest Organizations in the EU Multilevel System*, London: Routledge, pp 19–42.

Hirschman, A.O. (1991) *The Rhetoric of Reaction*, Cambridge, MA: Harvard University Press.

Hitzig, Z. (2020) 'The normative gap: mechanism design and ideal theories of justice', *Economics & Philosophy*, 36(3): 407–34.

Hogwood, B.W. and Gunn, L.A. (1984) *Policy Analysis for the Real World*, New York: Oxford University Press.

Kingdon, J.W. and Stano, E. (1984) *Agendas, Alternatives, and Public Policies*, Boston: Little, Brown and Company.

Leong, C. and Howlett, M. (2017) 'On credit and blame: disentangling the motivations of public policy decision-making behaviour', *Policy Sciences*, 50: 599–18.

Lindblom, C.E. (1959) 'The science of "muddling through"', *Public Administration Review*, 19(2): 79–88.

Maffei, S., Leoni, F., and Villari, B. (2020) 'Data-driven anticipatory governance: emerging scenarios in data for policy practices', *Policy Design and Practice*, 3(2): 123–34.

Majone, G. (1989) *Evidence, Argument, and Persuasion in the Policy Process*, New Haven, CT: Yale University Press.

McKay, S., Murray, M., and Macintyre, S. (2012) 'Justice as fairness in planning policy-making', *International Planning Studies*, 17(2): 147–62.

Mols, F. (2012) 'What makes a frame persuasive? Lessons from social identity theory', *Evidence & Policy*, 8(3): 329–45.

Nickerson, R.S. (2020) *Argumentation: The Art of Persuasion*, Cambridge: Cambridge University Press.

Ramos, J.M. (2014) 'Anticipatory governance: traditions and trajectories for strategic design', *Journal of Futures Studies*, 19(1): 35–52.

Schmidt, V.A. (2010) 'Taking ideas and discourse seriously: explaining change through discursive institutionalism as the fourth "new institutionalism"', *European Political Science Review*, 2(1): 1–25.

Shafir, E., Simonson, I., and Tversky, A. (1993) 'Reason-based choice', *Cognition*, 49(1–2): 11–36.

Steelman, T.A. and Maguire, L.A. (1999) 'Understanding participant perspectives: Q-methodology in national forest management', *Journal of Policy Analysis and Management*, 18(3): 361–88.

Stephenson, W. (1953) The Study of Behavior: Q-Technique and its Methodology, Chicago: University of Chicago Press.

Turnpenny, J., Radaelli, C.M., Jordan, A., and Jacob, K. (2009) 'The policy and politics of policy appraisal: emerging trends and new directions', *Journal of European Public Policy*, 16(4): 640–53.

Uddin, M.S. and Kumar, S. (2014) 'Energy, emissions and environmental impact analysis of wind turbine using life cycle assessment technique', *Journal of Cleaner Production*, 69: 153–64.

Van Dijk, T.A. (2015) 'Critical discourse analysis', in D. Tannen, H.E. Hamilton, and D. Schiffrin (eds) *The Handbook of Discourse Analysis*, Hoboken, NJ: Wiley, pp 466–85.

Wang, S., Wang, S., and Liu, J. (2019) 'Life-cycle green-house gas emissions of onshore and offshore wind turbines', *Journal of Cleaner Production*, 210: 804–10.

Weiss, G. and Wodak, R. (eds) (2007) *Critical Discourse Analysis*, New York: Palgrave Macmillan.

5

Satoshi meets the state: bad policy in Uncle Sam's initial encounters with Bitcoin and distributed ledger technology

Malcolm Campbell-Verduyn

Bad and good technological innovations in finance

American financial innovation, or 'finnovation', has had a rough recent history. As the American economist and former Chair of the Federal Reserve, Paul Volcker (2009) once noted, the mundane automatic teller machine (ATM) is considered to be the most worthwhile finnovation by leading financial regulators and economics commentators. This is despite the vast turn-of-the-century technological changes that saw massive expansions of the commercial Internet and web-based commerce. Even earlier technological advances adopted in finance had limited success, contributing in part to severe market volatilities in crises of the 1980s and 1990s that Susan Strange (2015) identified as an era of 'casino capitalism' (see also Campbell-Verduyn et al, 2019). As *Financial Times* columnist and 'undercover economist', Tim Harford (2023) suggests, the ATM facilitated a shift in financial resources towards packaging risky mortgages into tradable securities.[1] These asset-backed securities were exchanged worldwide in the run-up to the 2007–08 global financial crisis, along with other finnovations like credit default swaps (CDS), a tradable derivative that both promised efficiencies in spreading risks and enhancing access to credit (see Chapter 10). Together, these and other finnovations concentrated risks into several systemically important and 'too-big-to-fail' financial institutions whose insolvencies might have led to the collapse of the global financial system were it not for a series of government 'bailouts' in 2008 (Woll, 2014). This crisis was associated with a loss of national income equivalent to that of a world war (Aldrich, 2012). Post-crisis inquiry commissions linked the worst period of financial volatility since the Great Depression, to hands-off policies towards finnovation (Financial Services Authority, 2009; United Nations, 2009).

One consistent exception to the 'hands-off' policy approach to finnovation has been money. Since the advent of national monies in the 19th century and the Federal Reserve system in the US in the early 20th century, governments have staunchly sought to maintain monopolies over monetary policy (Helleiner, 1999; Polillo, 2013). Finnovation was rarely, if ever, encouraged in the monetary realm. Beyond more efficient payments systems, finnovation was not geared towards *money itself*. Indeed, any finnovation that even tangentially touched on the dominant international currency, the US dollar, was strictly and severely discouraged. A prominent case at the outset of the 2007–08 crisis illustrated this exception to the wider trend of encouraging finnovation when executives of a Florida-based digital payments mechanism called e-gold were indicted. Founded in 1996, e-gold had grown within a decade to process US$2 billion in payments. This finnovation was shut down in 2007 and its directors were charged with conspiracy to engage in money laundering and operating an unlicensed money transmitting business in 2008 (Zetter, 2008).

In the same year that the e-gold executives were charged and which the global financial system was suffering its most turbulent period since the 1920s, a technical white paper was circulated on a cryptography mailing list by a person or persons writing under the pseudonym Satoshi Nakamoto (2008). This still unidentified person(s) directly invoked the ongoing financial crisis in calling for a new form of digital money called Bitcoin that would be produced, exchanged, and circulated in decentralized Internet-based networks. This was a call for an alternative where computer code-based monetary policy architecture was positioned as a direct challenge to the dollar and other monies that are produced and maintained by central banks. Under the Bitcoin standard, monetary policy would not be conducted by central bankers, but by computer code, created and maintained by a global network of people (Champagne, 2014; Vigna and Casey, 2016; Ammous, 2018). Given the longstanding monetary exception to the general approach to promoting finnovation, most commentators initially expected a crackdown on Bitcoin (Hughes and Middlebrook, 2014). After all, Bitcoin proponents are actively associated with the likes of e-gold, often referring to terms such as 'cryptocurrency' and likening the token to 'digital gold' (Popper, 2015).

This chapter traces the initial encounter between the US and Satoshi Nakamoto's creation. During 2009–22, the federal government pursued two policy objectives that conflicted with one another. First, was a continued stress on the national security implications of digital money, particularly its potential on finance terrorism. Second, there was an emphasis on promoting technological experimentation with blockchain, the technology behind the first cryptocurrency, while avoiding a complete crackdown on Bitcoin. In the words of the head of the Commodity Futures Trading Commission (CFTC), the policy approach was to 'avoid undue restrictions', 'do no harm', and to rely on a 'bottom-up' policy that followed the decentralized 'nature of the technology' itself to let markets regulate themselves (Giancarlo, 2016). The long-standing exception to promoting finnovation in the realm of money was overturned in pursuit of a largely hands-off approach to Bitcoin and its underlying blockchain, or 'distributed ledger technology'.

Initial American policy towards Bitcoin bucked both historical and international trends. It stood out when compared to other digital currencies that were clamped down on in this very same period, such as Liberty Reverse, shut down in 2013, and Facebook's plans for Libra in 2019 (Mullan, 2016; Gerard, 2020). The US approach to Bitcoin also stood out internationally as countries pursued far more hands-on approaches, including outright bans on their use as in China (Kai and Zhang, 2017), or detailed regional regulations as in the European Union (Donnelly et al, 2024).

How then can the US response to the initial advent of Bitcoin in 2009 be understood? This chapter argues that the first encounters between the US and Satoshi Nakamoto-inspired finnovations were characterized by persistent bad policy. The federal government's two-pronged approach sought to reconcile the need to contain the potential national security harms associated with Bitcoin, while encouraging wider applications of its underlying blockchain technology on the other hand. These dual policy objectives succeeded in containing some of the worst *potential* excesses of Bitcoin-related experimentation. Yet they failed to address the rapid growth of *actual* consumer harms as scams and frauds proliferated along with environmental harms as a large part of the energy intensive Bitcoin and cryptocurrency production industry located in the US. Efforts at reversing the initial policy as its harms became increasingly recognized in the late 2010s were constrained as the growth of this finnovation sector in the US had formed a powerful new lobbying force.

These arguments are laid out in three steps. First, the surprising and unsurprising elements of the US' two-pronged approach to Bitcoin are exposed alongside tensions in the pursuit of these two policy goals. Second, the limits to overcoming this initial bad policy are identified as growing recognition of harms were in part stymied by an industry that had grown in size and influence. Third, wider conclusions from this case are drawn out suggesting that legacies of initial policy goals are difficult but must not be seen as impossible to overcome. Learning from the past and generating more active policy approaches to novel technology entails that bad policy may not be inevitable in complex, fast changing decentralized policy environments like the US.

Curtailing potential national security risks, promoting cool computer code

The circulation of the Bitcoin white paper in 2008 immediately spurred efforts to create a computer protocol for producing, exchanging, and publishing digital tokens on a shared digital ledger of transactions. While produced in esoteric online communities in 2009, Bitcoin rose in public prominence during multiple boom and bust cycles that saw its dollar exchange value rise over US$1,000 for the first time in 2013 and then over US$10,000 in 2017. The US federal government's reception of this novel digital token was both unsurprising and surprising in emphasizing its potential national security risks while doing very little about the actual consumer harms in indirectly promoting experimentation with what became perceived as a cool new set of computer code (Aziz, 2015).

On the one hand, the US government response to Bitcoin was unsurprising. Regulators widely and consistently invoked the litany of pathologies associated with digital monies, including the cases of e-gold and Liberty Reserve whose executives and founders were charged with illicit financing. Money laundering and terrorism financing were continually deemed to be major *possible* problems for national security (Campbell-Verduyn, 2018). Yet *actual* cases of Bitcoin and its growing competitors' use in terrorist activities were few and far between. For instance, a 2014 announcement by Islamic State of Iraq and the Levant (ISIS) that it would accept donations in Bitcoin was quickly reversed when the group realized the potential for donations to be tracked through the permanent ledger of transactions recorded on the underlying blockchain technology. The frenzied media speculation of cryptocurrency involvement in the 2015 Paris attacks turned out to have been unfounded (Perez, 2015). While these security risks were acknowledged, the 'long-term promise' provided by the technology for finnovation was also stressed by leading policy makers, such as the then-head of the Federal Reserve, Ben Bernanke: 'while these types of innovations may pose risks related to law enforcement and supervisory matters, there are also areas in which they may hold long-term promise, particularly if the innovations promote a faster, more secure, and more efficient payment system' (cited in Aziz, 2015).

On the other hand, and more surprising given the historical exception of finnovation in monetary affairs, experimentation with what was framed as cool computer code underlying Bitcoin and its competing digital tokens was actively encouraged. For instance, the Senate hearings on virtual currencies in 2013 'were described by one reporter as "lovefests"' in which national security agencies praised the traceability of digital transactions permitted by Bitcoin's underlying blockchain technology (Hughes and Middlebrook, 2014, p 833). The federal non-policy largely deferred decisions on how to regulate these technologies to the state level, resulting in a decentralized approach to applications of blockchains, also known as 'distributed ledger technology'. States were effectively encouraged to compete in welcoming cryptocurrency-related finnovations. What emerged were both races-to-the-top, in which states competed to develop and apply regulations more strictly than the other, as well as races-to-the-bottom, in which states competed by relaxing existing regulations. In the former instance, New York state in 2015 developed a BitLicense that was widely regarded as overly stringent. This led start-ups in the industry to move jurisdictions both within and beyond the US with laxer regulations, particularly to states that were eager to attract the production of Bitcoin and other cryptocurrencies, such as Georgia and Texas, as discussed further in this chapter.

The active encouragement of Bitcoin-related finnovation did little to counter the growing scams, ransomware, and frauds afflicting an increasingly large array of citizens and organizations (Swartz, 2022). Granted, the likes of the Consumer Financial Protection Bureau (2014) did issue warnings about the 'Wild West' nature of cryptocurrencies and the potential for scams and hacking. Yet no new federal legislation explicitly targeted Bitcoin and the decentralized nature of cryptocurrency-specific operation. Instead, policy was largely restricted to countering the worst excessive uses of Bitcoin for other illicit means. Most prominently, the online marketplace Silk Road whose initial version only accepted Bitcoin for exchange of drugs and illicit services, was targeted by the Federal Bureau of Investigations (FBI) in 2013 and its founder Ross Ulrich convicted for life in prison. Yet, beyond this international headline grabbing case, most of the US's initial stress was on the potential for Satoshi Nakamoto's creations to pose potential national security problems that rarely materialized.

What the two-pronged initial policy approach by the US to Satoshi Nakamoto's creations did was open space for Bitcoin and its underlying technology to be linked with both illicit activity and innovation. Blockchain technology was held up and hyped up as the 'next big thing' and one that entrepreneurs, technologists, and financiers alike *ought* to engage with. With the major exception for national security risks of terrorism financing, the hands-off policy approach that had long guided finnovation more generally was effectively extended to Bitcoin and blockchain experimentation which boomed as a result.

What this initial policy approach recognized were two interrelated idiosyncrasies that distinguished Bitcoin and its blockchain-based competitors from other digital monies. First, and despite claims that they represent new forms of digital money, neither Bitcoin nor any of its competitors anywhere nearly resembled the traditional functions of money (Campbell-Verduyn, 2018). The term cryptocurrency became a complete misnomer as the technology's challenge was less about *monetary* policy and more about whose *jurisdiction's* laws apply. Second and relatedly, recognition of Bitcoin-related experimentation as a normal yet novel form of finnovation also conceded that the technology was 'too complicated to regulate' centrally. As discussed later in this chapter, debates over whether Bitcoin was a security or commodity led to regulatory disputes. Moreover, that no single person, in a single office based in a single country was in charge of the digital token, led the Financial Stability Oversight Council, a group of Treasury, Federal Reserve, and other financial regulators, to call for international cooperation.[2] Finally, despite efforts to identify Satoshi Nakamoto, the author(s) of the white paper remained mysterious. Most nodes in the early Bitcoin network, moreover, were based outside the US. Nevertheless, the initial US policy approach set the stage for an expansion of experimentation with the technology within the country.

The initial encounter between Uncle Sam and Satoshi Nakamoto's creations, in sum, focused largely on *potential* harms to national security while overlooking and indeed even encouraging experimentation that induced *real* individual and systemic harm. As individual scams proliferated and individual cases gained significant media coverage, the systemic perils of blockchain-based finnovations became recognized (Jopson, 2016). In 2017, leading financial trader Thomas Peterffy took out a full-page ad in the *Wall Street Journal* to warn that the formalization of experiments with derivatives related to Bitcoin could spark a crisis not unlike that of the 2007–08 period (Robert, 2017). Meanwhile, the energy intensive production, or 'mining', of Bitcoin was encouraged to relocate to the US from countries such as China where steps towards a total ban on Bitcoin were being taken. According to the US Energy Information Administration (2024), cryptocurrency production 'expanded rapidly in 2019' with an estimated consumption totaling between 0.6 percent and 2.3 percent of the country's electricity consumption by 2022. These trends were confirmed in several detailed studies tracking the global production of mining, which revealed that the US overtook China as the leading producer of Bitcoin in 2021. Additionally, it also revealed that states having significant but environmentally damaging electricity sources, such as Georgia and Texas, attracted a significant portion of the mining industry (Cambridge Bitcoin Electricity Consumption Index, n.d.; Statista, 2023).[3]

Increasing attention to the growing individual and systemic harms of this dual policy sparked attempts at shifts towards active federal policies in the late 2010s. The next section, however, argues that these efforts were highly constrained by the initial encounters between the US and Satoshi, as well as entailing continuations of bad policies set out in the 2009–18 period.

Closer encounters of the continually bad kind

By 2018, growing attention to problems in the US's initial policy towards Satoshi Nakamoto-inspired creations instigated attempts to change course. This re-calibration, however, was ultimately limited in several ways that led to continually bad policy. This section reviews in turn how the 'bad policy start' constrained attempts at reversal and how, while not inevitable, efforts to overcome bad policy need to address their potential constraining initial effects.

A first constraint on attempts to overcome initial bad policy in the US's encounter with Satoshi Nakamoto's creations was the scaling up of earlier definitional battles into who regulates 'the space', as the cryptocurrency industry labeled itself. The Federal Reserve's recognition that neither Bitcoin nor any of its competitors formed actual currencies led chair Jerome Powell (2018) to declare that:

> We don't have jurisdiction over cryptocurrency. We have jurisdiction over banks, and so we know their activities with cryptocurrency companies and cryptocurrency, we can address that ... but again we don't have this regulatory authority to deal with it, so that's the key thing, is to be looking at the places where there is that regulatory authority ... I think it should be well-regulated, but I don't see us as the right group to do that.

What ensued was an inter-regulator turf war between two other financial regulators in the US's fractured regulatory system. The CFTC, the regulator overseeing commodities, argued for cryptocurrencies to be classified as commodities and to fall under its purview. The Securities and Exchange Commission (SEC), meanwhile, maintained that cryptocurrencies were securities and effectively fell under its jurisdictions. Initial positions laid out in 2014–15[4] led to a more heated phase after 2018 as each agency sought to assert jurisdiction through enforcement actions. The SEC, for instance, instigated a series of fines for unregistered securities offerings, targeting companies like blockchain developer Block.one, which faced a US$24 million penalty in 2019.[5] The Commission similarly sued US-based remittance firm Ripple in 2020 to prevent offerings of its XRP token, which the SEC argued constituted unregistered securities.[6] Meanwhile, the CFTC took on cryptocurrency exchanges Bitfinex (2021) and Binance (2023) for similarly unregistered operations. A 'Digital Commodities Consumer Protection Act' was also introduced in Congress in 2022 to place cryptocurrencies under CFTC mandate.[7] SEC head Gary Gensler went on a public relations blitz in 2021–22 to argue for the SEC's jurisdiction.[8]

A second constraint on attempts to overcome Uncle Sam's initial bad policy was the growth in the size and influence of the industry surrounding Satoshi's creations. Bitcoin embassies, professional associations, and foundations had all formed lobbyists for promoting lenient policy towards this type of what was argued to be normal finnovation. A Congressional Blockchain Caucus emerged in 2015 with House of Representatives members receiving three times more industry donations than non-caucus members supporting a 'light touch regulatory approach' to the technology

(Buckley and O'Neil, 2023). By the early 2020s, the digital currency industry generally and blockchain-based cryptocurrency projects had become a major lobbying force in the US Congress. Donations to both major political parties were made by the likes of FTX cryptocurrency CEO Sam Bankman-Fried, known as SBF, who came into the top-10 of overall donations in 2022 with an estimated US$38 million in donations (Buckley and O'Neil, 2023).[9] The industry aggressively lobbied elected representatives, as well as making very vocal public statements about the perceived unfairness of SEC and CFTC fines and other enforcement actions. It was argued that the existing rules were being enforced inconsistently, in an ad hoc and random manner. Wealthy investors like Mark Cuban complained how it was 'impossible to know' whether tokens could or could not constitute securities (Lindrea, 2023) and called for clearer rules to be formulated by Congress. Such calls were echoed in traditional media where the likes of the *Financial Times* argued that 'Trying to shoehorn new asset classes into old definitions is not the wisest course' (Masters, 2023). Even consumer advocates organizations, such as Dennis Kelleher, the head of the non-governmental organization Better Markets, emphasized the lack of clear rules albeit in critiquing the political power of the cryptocurrency industry:

> The problem is not just a lawless industry, but a lawless industry that's making a lot of money and using hundreds of millions of dollars in campaign contributions and lobbying to buy elected officials and other allies, like academics, trade groups, and the media. They're engaged in a massive lobbying campaign to get their special interest put above the public interest. (Cited in Parramore, 2023)

Industry lobbying led to regulatory arbitrage in which the likes of the CFTC were regarded as having 'spent most of its time cheerleading the industry and trying to expand its jurisdiction rather than worrying about investor, customer, and markets protection' (Kelleher, 2022).

Reversing bad policy then had become extremely difficult due in large part to growth in size and influence of an industry, as well as disputes between regulators. In lieu of new industry-specific formal legislation, seemingly 'random enforcement' actions by regulators locked in turf battles and worsened industry's perception of US policy. Little was done beyond the most egregious cases to curtail harms of frauds. It is estimated that these frauds amounted to around US$1 billion between January 2021 and March 2022 (Federal Trade Commission, 2022), with US$2.3 billion lost in scams in 2022 alone (Table 5.1).

While regulators bickered and the industry lobbied politicians, the FBI's Internet Crime Complaint Center reported 'unprecedented increases in the

Table 5.1: Cryptocurrency scams per state (2022)

State	Victim count (crypto-currency, 2022)	Victim loss, $ (crypto-currency, 2022)	State	Victim count (crypto-currency, 2022)	Victim loss, $ (crypto-currency, 2022)
Alabama	222	17,147,815	Montana	68	6,678,328
Alaska	89	1,807,138	Nebraska	100	4,316,079
Arizona	732	81,325,502	Nevada	512	33,891,782
Arkansas	152	4,205,810	New Hampshire	108	15,829,513
California	4,879	572,581,744	New Jersey	895	81,591,234
Colorado	584	48,415,674	New Mexico	138	6,025,235
Connecticut	276	23,860,521	New York	1,710	153,005,623
Delaware	87	10,531,602	North Carolina	631	38,547,655
District of Columbia	161	6,817,900	North Dakota	35	1,773,126
Florida	2,535	213,744,150	Ohio	615	30,951,848
Georgia	680	93,586,136	Oklahoma	206	9,423,438
Hawaii	137	10,368,849	Oregon	388	37,031,209
Idaho	122	7,848,800	Pennsylvania	813	54,836,895
Illinois	875	56,212,989	Rhode Island	67	4,319,150
Indiana	270	11,763,654	South Carolina	319	15,682,757
Iowa	144	8,510,336	South Dakota	39	38,922,814
Kansas	150	16,775,086	Tennessee	397	24,260,005
Kentucky	222	15,191,583	Texas	2,174	180,983,946
Louisiana	205	10,810,591	Utah	322	28,676,949
Maine	79	4,122,836	Vermont	30	800,505
Maryland	785	61,736,724	Virginia	693	45,632,489
Massachusetts	598	46,926,018	Washington	787	69,561,954
Michigan	574	38,172,901	West Virginia	82	2,424,223
Minnesota	379	28,138,345	Wisconsin	321	19,673,198
Mississippi	120	1,786,094	Wyoming	47	1,652,095
Missouri	343	18,153,432	**The US**	**26,897**	**2,317,034,280**

Source: Surfshark (2023) drawing on FBI (2022)

number of victims and the dollar losses to these investors as cryptocurrency investment fraud rose from US$907 million in 2021 to US$2.57 billion in 2022, an increase of 183 per cent' (FBI, 2022, p 12). This growth was highly racialized, with Black Americans targeted in the industry's advertising and forming comparatively larger holders of cryptocurrency than White Americans (Ariel-Schwab, 2022). Even largely hypothetical harms to national security began to materialize, albeit not entirely in manners predicted initially by policy makers. Reports began to detail increasing cryptocurrency donations to *domestic* terrorist organizations, such as white supremacist groups (Gartenstein-Ross et al, 2022), such as several of the groups who are involved in the 6 January 2021 take-over of the US Capitol (Stone, 2021). National security concerns also arose in revelations of Chinese involvement in cryptocurrency production sites located near strategic power plants (Dance and Forsythe, 2023).

In sum, what emerged from attempts to overcome the harms from the initial two-pronged policy were further individual and systemic harms as the US's policy and closer encounters with Satoshi's creations appeared to be failing on its own terms.

Conclusion

Uncle Sam's initial reception to Satoshi Nakamoto-inspired creations, Bitcoin and other cryptocurrencies based on blockchain technology, pursued two policy goals that were not entirely aligned and were ineffective in preventing harm to citizens and the environment. Unsurprisingly, given the history of American approaches to finnovation, national security risks were stressed in the potential for Bitcoin and its competitors to support illicit financing. Surprisingly, authorities expanded the long-standing encouragement of finnovation within American fintech policy to include the monetary realm. In promoting experimentation with the blockchain technology underlying Bitcoin, US policy discounted individual harms to consumers targeted by rampant cryptocurrency-related frauds and scams, as well as systemic harms to the environment from the production of Bitcoin. The policy promotion of 'cool' technological innovation encouraged the growth in the US of a high energy consuming industry whose growing political power was reflected in campaign donations to political parties. US policy makers attempting a U-turn after 2018 faced an increasingly powerful industry that actively encouraged regulatory turf wars while decrying ad-hoc enforcement of industry-unspecific rules. Neither such crypto-specific rules, nor a complete ban on (elements) of this set of finnovations resulted. The far harder and unified approach taken to the Bitcoin-inspired digital currency suggested by Facebook/Meta in its 2019 plans for Libra, which were first severely curtailed and then abandoned by 2022, was not extended to cryptocurrencies whose global networks made them 'too complicated to regulate'. Regulation was instead effectively left to industry leaders like FTX whose infamous CEO Sam Bankman-Fried was quoted (in Piper, 2023) as saying 'Fuck regulators … they make everything worse … they don't protect customers at all'. While commentators declared that 'the US is one of the most crypto-friendly countries in the world' (Ozelli, 2022), a 2024 essay entitled *The Cruelty of Crypto*, argued that American policy 'exposes the vulnerable to fraud and scams, and loads risk onto the poor' (O'Dwyer, 2024).

The case of cryptocurrency policy in the US provides three major take-aways for the conceptualization of bad policy, as well as for how to both avoid and counter it: first, bad policy is more likely when goals pursued are in tension with each other and policy makers are at pains to reconcile them; second, that temporalities matter to the conceptualization of bad policy; third, that more active policy making can both prevent and reverse the legacies stemming from initial bad policy approaches. The 'power of inaction' (Woll, 2014), however, must be overcome in avoiding the continuation of harms from finnovation fetishism.

A first overarching lesson from the initial encounter of Satoshi and the US is that bad policy becomes likely when two potentially contradictory goals are pursued in decentralized environments in which regulators compete rather than work with one another to reconcile such goals. The US loosened its longstanding strict approach to finnovations that touched on national security objectives, such as preventing terrorism financing. While blockchain technology continues to receive an emphasis in policy discussions concerning Bitcoin, the promotion of blockchain technology across financial agencies and across states conflicted with national security objectives. Granted, cases of Bitcoin funding terrorism were initially few and far between. Emphasis on this potential was overshadowed by the potential 'revolutionary' contributions blockchain technology could make to finance and the economy more generally. This first lesson about reconciling twin policy goals is important as the US and other countries lay out frameworks for artificial intelligence and other technologies said to be part of the 'Fourth Industrial Revolution' (Swab, 2017).

Second, it is important to consider temporalities both conceptually and practically. Ineffective policies become ineffective as evidence of harm mounts over time. For almost a decade, American authorities recognized but did very little beyond addressing the most egregious cases in countering the illicit uses of cryptocurrencies. The average American citizens, and particularly Black Americans, were encouraged to engage in highly volatile markets characterized by rampant scams and frauds. As other countries took on stricter, more hands-on approaches by, for instance, banning cryptocurrencies, American policy let an industry flourish under the banner of encouraging technological 'innovations' and financial 'inclusion'.

Mounting evidence of harm to local populations and to the environment from reports of the growing energy consumption required to produce Bitcoin did eventually spur authorities to react. However, such delayed action was constrained by lobbying and turf battles as improved policy paths continued either not to be taken (for example, legislating the cryptocurrency industry) or to consist of random enforcement actions.

A third related take away is that although ineffective policies are revealed over time, they still can be anticipated and prevented. Looking back at history and acting on precedent before undertaking policy reversals is difficult but not impossible to do. The US was long attuned to the perils of 'wild cat banking' wherein expansions of credit beyond official channels resulted in harms in the 19th century (Polillo, 2013) as well as the 20th century (Strange, 2015). The un-learning of historical lessons as the US turned to actively encouraging finnovations in the 1970s onwards can be overcome with more active learning from history and the kind of actions being increasingly pursued at the time of writing.

The year 2023 witnessed larger high-profile penalties issued from the CFTC, including a US\$4.3 billion money laundering plea deal with the world's largest exchange, Binance, that was explicitly intended to serve as a 'warning shot' to the industry (Chipolina et al, 2023). The November 2023 conviction of Sam Bankman-Fried on more than a half dozen counts of conspiracy, money laundering, and fraud also signaled a potential policy shift that is less accommodating to major political campaign donors. Finally, legislative attempts such as the Lummis-Gillibrand Digital Asset Bill for A Responsible Financial Innovation Act reintroduced to the US Senate in the summer of 2023 indicated a potential for the supply of rules to finally meet growing demands for laws tailored to Bitcoin-inspired and blockchain-based finnovations. At the state level, California's Department of Financial Protection and Innovation was also tasked in the fall of 2023 to develop a BitLicense akin to the one developed in New York state. The sum of these and other developments at the time of writing indicate that the persistence of bad policy is not inevitable and that active learning and effort is required by all stakeholders, including the academics, media industry, and regulators, all of whom need to be transparent about where their funding and sources of knowledge and expertise come from (for example, CoinTelegraph Innovation Circle, 2023).

Notes

[1] 'Consider the ATM: it did not make bank tellers redundant. Instead, it freed them to cross-sell subprime mortgages.' (Harford, 2023).

[2] 'Since the set of market participants which makes use of a distributed ledger system may well span regulatory jurisdictions or national boundaries, a considerable degree of coordination among regulators may be required to effectively identify and address risks associated with distributed ledger systems' (quoted in Jopson, 2016).

[3] The Bitcoin Mining Council (2023), a mining industry association, claims that around half of electricity used for mining stems from renewable energy sources.

[4] CFTC (24 September, 2015), Available from: http://www.cftc.gov/idc/groups/public/@lrenforcementactions/documents/legalpleading/enfteraexchangeorder92415.pdf

[5] Specifically for undertaking an unregistered initial coin offering (ICO) that was argued to be akin to initial public offerings or IPOs for traditional corporate securities.

[6] A US District Court ruled in July 2023 that the security designation only applied to institutional investors.

[7] See: https://www.congress.gov/bill/117th-congress/senate-bill/4760/text.

[8] See: https://www.sec.gov/news/speech/gensler-aspen-security-forum-2021-08-03.

[9] This is a conservative estimate, at least compared to that of Ferguson et al (2022) whose US$89 million figure includes:

> the many streams of political money from SBF, his senior associates, and all other employees of FTX, together with the executives of Alameda Research, the crypto hedge fund that SBF had co-founded and remained involved with. We include individual donations and political action committee (PAC) contributions, but also the often gigantic 527 transfers reported to the Internal Revenue Service (IRS). We counted his brother, but not his parents.

References

Aldrich, P. (2012) 'Loss of income caused by banks as bad as a "World War," says BoE's Andrew Haldane', *The Telegraph* [online] 3 December, Available from: https://www.telegraph.co.uk/finance/financialcrisis/9719300/Loss-of-income-caused-by-banks-as-bad-as-a-world-war-says-BoEs-Andrew-Haldane.html

Ammous, S. (2018) *The Bitcoin Standard: The Decentralized Alternative to Central Banking*, Hoboken, NJ: John Wiley & Sons.

Ariel-Schwab (2022) 'Black investor survey' [online], Available from: https://www.schwabmoneywise.com/tools-resources/ariel-schwab-survey-2022

Aziz, J. (2015) 'The US government is surprisingly cool with Bitcoin', *The Week* [online] 9 January, Available from: https://theweek.com/articles/456114/government-surprisingly-cool-bitcoin

Bitcoin Mining Council (2023) 'Bitcoin Mining Council survey confirms year on year improvements in sustainable power and technological efficiency' [online], Available from: https://bitcoinminingcouncil.com/bitcoin-mining-council-survey-confirms-year-on-year-improvements-in-sustainable-power-and-technological-efficiency-in-h1-2023/

Buckley, O. and O'Neil, C. (2023) 'Cryptocurrency', *Open Secrets* [online] July, Available from: https://www.opensecrets.org/news/issues/crypto

Cambridge Bitcoin Electricity Consumption Index (n.d.) 'Bitcoin mining map' [online], Available from: https://ccaf.io/cbnsi/cbeci/mining_map

Campbell-Verduyn, M. (2018) 'Bitcoin, crypto-coins, and global anti-money laundering governance', *Crime, Law and Social Change*, 69: 283–305.

Campbell-Verduyn, M., Goguen, M., and Porter, T. (2019) 'Finding fault lines in long chains of financial information', *Review of International Political Economy*, 26(5): 911–37.

Champagne, P. (2014) *The Book of Satoshi: The Collected Writings of Bitcoin Creator Satoshi Nakamoto*, Austin, TX: E53 Publishing.

Chipolina, S., Asgari, N., and Stafford, P. (2023) 'Binance's $4.3bn fine was set high as a warning, says US regulator', *Financial Times* [online] 5 December, Available from: https://www.ft.com/content/81bdaf30-3f61-4ff4-b579-805a4af8f8e1

CoinTelegraph Innovation Circle (2023) '11 things the United States can learn from other nations' crypto regulations' [online] 11 June, Available from: https://cointelegraph.com/innovation-circle/11-things-the-united-states-can-learn-from-other-nations-crypto-regulations

Consumer Financial Protection Bureau (2014) 'CFPB warns consumers about Bitcoin' [online] 11 August, Available from: https://www.consumer finance.gov/about-us/newsroom/cfpb-warns-consumers-about-bitcoin/

Dance, G. and Forsythe, M. (2023) 'Across US, Chinese Bitcoin mines draw national security scrutiny', *New York Times* [online] 18 October, Available from: https://www.nytimes.com/2023/10/13/us/bitcoin-mines-china-united-states.html

Donnelly, S., Ríos Camacho, E., and Heidebrecht, S. (2024) 'Digital sovereignty as control: the regulation of digital finance in the European union', *Journal of European Public Policy*, 31(8): 2226–49.

Energy Information Administration (2024) 'Tracking electricity consumption from US cryptocurrency mining operations' [online] 1 February, Available from: https://www.eia.gov/todayinenergy/detail.php?id=61364

Federal Bureau of Investigation (FBI) (2022) *2022 Internet Crime Complaint Center Annual Report* [online], Available from: https://www.ic3.gov/Media/PDF/AnnualReport/2022_IC3Report.pdf

Federal Trade Commission (2022) 'Reports show scammers cashing in on crypto craze' [online] 3 June, Available from: https://www.ftc.gov/news-events/data-visualizations/data-spotlight/2022/06/reports-show-scamm ers-cashing-crypto-craze

Ferguson, T., Jorgensen, P., and Chen, J. (2022) 'Bankman-Fried, political money, and the crash of FTX', Institute for New Economic Thinking [online] 15 December, Available from: https://www.ineteconomics.org/perspectives/blog/bankman-fried-political-money-and-the-crash-of-ftx

Financial Services Authority (2009) *The Turner Review*, London: FSA.

Gartenstein-Ross, D., Koduvayur, V., and Hodgson, S. (2022) *Crypto-Fascists: Cryptocurrency Usage by Domestic Extremists*, Foundation for the Defense of Democracies [online] 15 March, Available from: https://www.fdd.org/wp-content/uploads/2022/03/fdd-monograph-crypto-fascists.pdf

Gerard, D. (2020) *Libra Shrugged: How Facebook Tried to Take Over The Money*, Independently published.

Giancarlo, C. (2016) 'With blockchain, regulators should first do no harm', *Financial Times* [online] 12 April, Available from: https://www.ft.com/content/8090cc80-fff6-11e5-99cb-83242733f755

Harford, T. (2023) 'What neo-Luddites get right – and wrong – about Big Tech', *Financial Times* [online] 26 May, Available from: https://www.ft.com/content/f312c9ff-633d-480e-8887-4b5ad3f0ae5e

Helleiner, E. (1999) 'Historicizing territorial currencies: monetary space and the nation-state in North America', *Political Geography*, 18(3): 309–39.

Hughes, S.J. and Middlebrook, S.T. (2014) 'Regulating cryptocurrencies in the United States: current issues and future directions', *William Mitchell Law Review*, 40(2): 813–48.

Jopson, B. (2016) 'Regulators say bitcoin poses "financial stability risks"', *Financial Times* [online] 22 June, Available from: https://www.ft.com/content/e0880cf6-3800-11e6-9a05-82a9b15a8ee7

Kai, J. and Zhang, F. (2017) 'Between liberalization and prohibition: prudent enthusiasm and the governance of Bitcoin/Blockchain technology', in M. Campbell-Verduyn (ed) *Bitcoin and Beyond: Cryptocurrencies, Blockchains and Global Governance*, New York: Routledge, pp 88–108.

Kelleher, D. (2023) *Crypto, FTX, Sam Bankman-Fried, SEC, CFTC, Banking Regulators and the Revolving Door*, Better Markets [online] 8 March, Available from: https://bettermarkets.org/wp-content/uploads/2022/11/Better_Markets_FTX_FactSheet.pdf?trk=public_post_comment-text

Lindrea, B. (2023) '"Near impossible to know" what is and isn't a security: Mark Cuban on SEC', *CoinTelegraph* [online] 12 June, Available from: https://cointelegraph.com/news/impossible-to-know-what-is-a-security-mark-cuban-on-sec

Masters, B. (2023) 'When tackling crypto, the SEC should be wary of overreach', *Financial Times* [online] 27 August, Available from: https://www.ft.com/content/77ec670e-7bb1-4d26-8370-7d0c567d9070

Mullan, P.C. (2016) 'Liberty reserve', in P.C. Mullan (ed) *A History of Digital Currency in the United States: New Technology in an Unregulated Market*, London: Palgrave Macmillan, pp 171–96.

Nakamoto, S. (2008) 'Bitcoin: a peer-to-peer electronic cash system' [online], Available from: https://bitcoin.org/bitcoin.pdf

O'Dwyer, R. (2024) 'The cruelty of crypto', *Aeon* [online] 6 February, Available from: https://aeon.co/essays/the-cruelty-of-crypto-in-its-promise-to-revive-the-american-dream

Ozelli, S. (2022) 'Why the US is one of the most crypto-friendly countries in the world', *CoinTelegraph* [online] 8 October, Available from: https://cointelegraph.com/news/why-the-us-is-one-of-the-most-crypto-friendly-countries-in-the-world

Parramore, L. (2023) '"Crypto is a fraud on the public": financial watchdog explains ties between crypto and the banking crisis', Institute for New Economic Thinking [online] 11 May, Available from: https://www.ineteconomics.org/perspectives/blog/crypto-is-a-fraud-on-the-public-financial-watchdog-explains-ties-between-crypto-and-the-banking-crisis

Perez, Y. (2015) 'Bitcoin, Paris and terrorism: what the media got wrong', Coindesk [online] 20 November, Available from: https://www.coindesk.com/markets/2015/11/20/bitcoin-paris-and-terrorism-what-the-media-got-wrong/

Piper, K. (2023) 'Sam Bankman-Fried tries to explain himself', *Vox* [online] 16 November, Available from: https://www.vox.com/future-perfect/23462333/sam-bankman-fried-ftx-cryptocurrency-effective-altruism-crypto-bahamas-philanthropy

Polillo, S. (2013) *Conservatives Versus Wildcats: A Sociology of Financial Conflict*, Redwood City, CA: Stanford University Press.

Popper, N. (2015) *Digital Gold: Bitcoin and the Inside Story of the Misfits and Millionaires Trying to Reinvent Money*, New York: Harper.

Powell, J. (2018) 'Fed chair Jerome Powell testifies before the house – July 18', Video [online], Available from: https://www.youtube.com/watch?v=A4tWrEKbTBc&t=26s

Roberts, J.J. (2017) 'Bitcoin futures could trigger a Lehman-style collapse, billionaire warns', *Fortune* [online] 4 December, Available from: https://fortune.com/crypto/2017/12/04/bitcoin-futures/

Statista (2023) 'Distribution of Bitcoin mining hashrate from September 2019 to January 2022, by country' [online], Available from: https://www.statista.com/statistics/1200477/bitcoin-mining-by-country/

Stone, P. (2021) 'US far-right extremists making millions via social media and cryptocurrency', *The Guardian* [online] 10 March, Available from: https://www.theguardian.com/world/2021/mar/10/us-far-right-extremists-millions-social-cryptocurrency

Strange, S. (2015) *Casino Capitalism*, Manchester: Manchester University Press.

Surfshark (2023) 'Average losses of crypto scams in the US' [online] 6 June, Available from: https://surfshark.com/research/chart/us-cryptocurrency-scams

Swab, K. (2017) *The Fourth Industrial Revolution*, London: Penguin.

Swartz, L, (2022) 'Theorizing the 2017 blockchain ICO bubble as a network scam', *New Media & Society*, 24(7): 1695–713.

United Nations (2009) *UN Commission of Experts on Reforms of the International Monetary and Financial Systems, Recommendations*, New York: United Nations.

Vigna, P. and Casey, M. (2016) *The Age of Cryptocurrency: How Bitcoin and the Blockchain are Challenging the Global Economic Order*, London: Macmillan.

Volcker, P. (2009) 'Think more broadly', *Wall Street Journal*, 14 December.

Woll, C. (2014) *The Power of Inaction: Bank Bailouts in Comparison*, New York: Cornell University Press.

Zetter, K. (2008) 'E-gold founder pleads guilty to money laundering', *Wired*, 25 July.

6

Toronto's failed smart city: intellectual property, data, and bad governance

Natasha Tusikov

Introduction

Google publicly announced its bid to build a smart city in Toronto on 17 October 2017 at a press conference attended by the Prime Minister of Canada, the Premier of Ontario, and the Mayor of Toronto. Alongside were Executive Chair Eric Schmidt of Alphabet, Google's parent company, and Sidewalk Labs' Chief Executive Officer (CEO) Daniel L. Doctoroff. At the press conference, Schmidt said, years before, Google founders Larry Page and Sergey Brin had mused about how Google could build a smart city 'if someone would just give us a city and put us in charge' (Barth, 2020). In Toronto, Google appeared to get that wish.[1]

It was the little-known Sidewalk Labs that was the public face of the smart city project. Sidewalk Labs, a Google company created in 2015, is best understood as operating as Google's 'Division of Urban Policy' (Haggart, 2019). The project was to develop Quayside, a valuable 12-acre plot adjacent to downtown Toronto, part of a much larger parcel of more than 800 acres of formerly industrial land on Lake Ontario owned by various public and private parties. Sidewalk Labs' vision for its smart city would 'blend human-centered urban design with cutting-edge digital technology, cleantech, and advanced building materials. It will be a global testbed where people can use data about how the neighborhood works to make it work better' (Sidewalk Labs, 2017, p 15). Left unexplained in this vision were core smart-city issues, specifically control over data flows and intellectual property (IP) rights related to the technologies and services that were to be developed and used in Quayside (Tusikov, 2019). As a result, Sidewalk Labs faced criticism from residents, the local tech industry, and policy experts over its ambitious plans to capture, control, and monetize smart city data, plans that would disproportionately benefit one (American) company (Balsillie, 2018).

In the end, these concerns were moot. On 7 May 2020, Sidewalk Labs announced that it was officially pulling out of the world's most high-profile

83

and controversial smart city project (Doctoroff, 2020). The COVID-19 pandemic was the final twist in the 3-year unfolding of what a Swedish urban studies colleague called an 'urban development thriller'. The death of the Quayside project raises the question, why study a failure? Although the Quayside smart city did not materialize, studying Sidewalk Labs' plans offers a useful opportunity to reflect upon oversights and errors by policy makers and regulators in order to counter such problems in future smart city projects. Sidewalk Labs' plans published in its 1,500-page *Master Innovation and Development Plan* in June 2019,[2] revealed key details about how the company conceptualized and valued data as well as IP, and the governance relationships it foresaw having with Toronto city officials.

The key public body was Waterfront Toronto, a quasi-independent governmental agency created by the Canadian federal government, the province of Ontario, and the city of Toronto to manage the redevelopment of Toronto's waterfront. Controversially, Waterfront Toronto planned to collaborate on governance frameworks with the successful technology vendor, that is a part of Google, including on rules to govern IP relating to the project (Waterfront Toronto, 2017). A key governance problem was that the proposed multi-billion-dollar Quayside project brought together a government land-development agency, Waterfront Toronto, with no track record in smart city policy areas like data governance and IP rights, and a Google-affiliated tech company with no track record in urban development at this scale (see, for example, Flynn and Valverde, 2019). Complicating the matters further, government officials and regulators involved generally lacked expertise on digital policy issues, specifically on how to manage smart city-related data and IP (Auditor General of Ontario, 2018).

This chapter reflects upon the Quayside case to consider the concept of ineffective policy in the context of smart cities and governance of digital issues. As set out in this book's Introduction, ineffective policy refers to policies that decision makers deliberately adopted and maintained even though these measures demonstrably cause harm, are ineffective, or generate undesirable outcomes. In the Quayside case, the chapter argues ineffective policy refers to a two-fold situation: (1) Waterfront Toronto's decision to collaboratively develop smart city-related policies on IP and data governance with the tech vendor, Sidewalk Labs, and (2) the adoption of specific IP and data governance policies that unfairly and harmfully privileged Sidewalk Labs' commercial interests over the public interest. In part, this ineffective policy stemmed from public officials' poor understanding of IP and data governance.

In order to explain the central roles of IP and data governance in smart cities, this chapter draws from critical data studies and the International Political Economy literature. Additionally, the chapter examines the primary documents related to the project, specifically Sidewalk Labs' June 2019 four-volume, 1,500-page project plan. The chapter then concludes by offering practical suggestions to policy makers about lessons learned.

Designing smart cities

Sidewalk Labs' strategic downplaying of its plans to control data and IP related to smart city technologies was not the only problematic elements of the Quayside project. At the time of its Toronto bid, Sidewalk Labs had no experience in urban planning, despite promising self-driving garbage bins, underground package-delivering robots, 'climate-positive' building designs, and advanced construction methods that would improve housing affordability (Sidewalk Labs, 2019a). Compounding its expertise gap was Sidewalk Labs' weak public consultations, which were a requirement of the bid process. Critics argued that the company's engagement was troubled by 'delayed information releases and staged consultations on already or nearly consummated agreements' (Goodman and Powles, 2019, p 497). More a public relations exercise than consultation, Sidewalk Labs proposed a free summer camp for children under 12 and a travel program that would take students aged between 19 and 24 to three international cities over 6 months to learn about urban development. Such consultations were insufficient to evaluate a multi-billion-dollar project, leading some commentators to characterize Sidewalk Labs' efforts as 'empty, Potemkin, pretend consultations' (Haggart, 2020, p 46).

Alongside its omissions on data and IP, as well as its public consultation woes, Sidewalk Labs offered ambitious, controversial proposals, expanding the project area. It expanded from the approved 12 to 150 acres and created a vast bureaucracy of five new 'management entities', with Sidewalk Labs at the heart of the action. These agencies, formed by combining existing departments or by creating new agencies, would manage transportation, water and energy, open spaces, housing, and data, under a revamped 'super-public administrator' that would either reform or replace Waterfront Toronto. Dramatic changes to Toronto's regulatory agencies were not only controversial because they came from a technology vendor rather than from elected officials, but also because they would have required creating new or amending existing legislation, including traffic laws, municipal bylaws, and zoning rules.

Given these multiple, serious challenges, those unfamiliar with the Quayside project may wonder why Toronto seriously considered Sidewalk Labs' smart city plans. A key reason is that Sidewalk Labs' promises of technological innovation and economic benefits were welcome announcements to politicians across the political spectrum, as were its plans to locate the Canadian Google headquarters on the Toronto waterfront, further building Canada's Silicon Valley North. Sidewalk Labs, moreover, wanted Quayside to serve as an incubator for smart city IP that could be sold to customers around the world,[3] placing Toronto on the urban tech innovation map globally. Additionally, Canadian politicians were also captivated by Sidewalk Labs' technological solutionism arguments, which claimed that complex social problems of unaffordable housing and traffic congestion could be effectively addressed by data-driven technologies (see Haggart and Tusikov, 2023).

Centrality of data in smart cities

Drawing from the critical data studies literature, this chapter defines data as a socially constructed form of knowledge (see Gitelman, 2013). People make decisions about what information to collect and how, what technologies to use to analyze data, and whether to share data freely or treat data as proprietary. In other words, data does not exist independently from human actions, and once collected, data must be interpreted for them to have meaning and value (Kitchin, 2014). Deciding to commodify data is a political decision, as is rendering it for public or commercial use.

Capturing and disseminating data enables smart cities to function, often through proprietary data-collecting sensors. These sensors are attached to real objects embedded in the urban environment to form networks of communications technologies that enable real-time data collection, streaming, and analysis to deliver services, as well as integrate information and physical infrastructure (Edwards, 2016, p 31; see also Kitchin, 2014; Meijer and Bolivar, 2016). The sensors enable 'ubiquitous trackability', a core smart city feature, as the provision of services relies upon the real-time continuous tracking of people and objects within the urban environment (Edwards, 2016, p 39).

Smart cities collect both non-personal and personal data. Non-personal data, such as data from sensors that measure pollution and detect wastewater leaks, does not relate to identifiable persons. Technologies may also collect personal data, such as through facial recognition software, automated license plate readers, or services tied to individuals' smartphones. Personal data, according to the European Union's General Data Protection Regulation, is 'a name, an identification number, location data, an online identifier' or 'one or more factors specific to the physical, physiological, genetic, mental, economic, cultural or social identity of that natural person' (Art 4(1)) (European Parliament, 2016).

Sidewalk Labs' proposals for the Quayside smart city were data intensive: the company proposed to create systems to coordinate mobility services with sensors collecting data on the presence of pedestrians and cyclists, as well as the volume and speed of vehicles and bicycles. Traffic sensors would detect vehicles waiting to use intersections in order to prioritize transit, bicycles, and pedestrians (Sidewalk Labs, 2019b).

Geolocational data would provide users with real-time updates on weather, traffic, and vehicle arrival times to streamline trips. Even private spaces would not have been off limits from data collection, albeit with the permission of residents. To manage and improve the diversion of recyclables from waste, tenants could subscribe to a 'pay-as-you-throw' program billing for their waste and then the weight of their waste would be tracked over time (Sidewalk Labs, 2019a). Energy usage would also be tracked with dynamic pricing to encourage tenants to decrease energy waste and lower energy use to peak hours.

Although its city plans relied upon collecting and transmitting data (Sidewalk Labs MIDP), Sidewalk Labs was tight-lipped on how data would be collected, stored, used, and governed through much of its 2-year public consultation (Tusikov, 2020). In Toronto, civil society groups and privacy activists raised concerns about how data would be governed and by whom, as well as the effects from monetizing smart city data (see Tusikov, 2020). Critics feared that Sidewalk Labs, more specifically, Google, would primarily benefit from the capture of smart city data to the detriment of other partners, including local industry, government, and civil society (Tusikov, 2019). Such concerns were not unwarranted. Smart city vendors could sell access to data on energy or water usage, while also monetizing personal data flows by selling access to advertisers, alongside selling their smart city products and licensing their technologies.

In response to concerns about the collection and commodification of residents' personal data, Sidewalk Labs offered an ambitious plan that would have significantly reshaped how personal data would be defined in law and governed in Canada. There were three main elements to this plan: a new definition of data, establishing a data trust to govern data, and a set of color-coded symbols on signs in public settings. These symbols would constitute a new way to obtain people's consent for data collection (Sidewalk Labs, 2018).[4] While a full discussion of Sidewalk Labs' data proposals is beyond the scope of this chapter, the company's most ambitious proposal was that smart city-related data would be governed by a data trust (Sidewalk Labs, 2019c). The structure and legal authority of the trust was not clear when Sidewalk Labs proposed the idea, but data trusts are legal instruments that have stewards to manage data on behalf of the beneficiary or beneficiaries (McDonald, 2019). According to Sidewalk Labs, its data trust was intended to assuage public concerns over privacy and ensure the data collection and use practices would facilitate both 'innovation and investment' (Sidewalk Labs, 2018, p 13). Rather than restrict or prohibit the collection of personal data, however, Sidewalk Labs attempted to insert itself into governance practices by proposing a new legal definition for data and a new legal structure to manage data, but both plans fell through when Sidewalk Labs canceled the Quayside project.

Capture of data flows

Decisions regarding what data is collected, how it is used and by whom, and the rules governing it – understood as data governance – are important to understand, as are the resulting effects. Data governance is an expression of structural power, as theorized by an International Political Economist Susan Strange (1994), which determines the rules of the game for economic and social activity. Those who have the authority and capacity to govern data, whether public or private actors, can therefore wield considerable power in determining how data is used, whether it is freely shared or monetized, and how economic and social benefits are distributed (Haggart and Spicer, 2022). Proprietary control over data can also allow for the exercise of network effects, in which the generation of data is used to refine existing products and processes (Srnicek, 2017). A vendor, for example, that uses sensors to track traffic patterns throughout a city could amass knowledge about transit usage and congestion valuable to both businesses and government officials, which the vendor can then monetize into additional products.

Cities are rich sources of data and by inserting themselves into the bureaucracy through operating key services, technology companies can set rules and standards over infrastructure that benefit their commercial interests. Companies prefer to treat the data they collect as proprietary property from which they will extract value even when the data originates in the public realm, such as from transit systems. Power accrues to those actors that can exert control through the accumulation, interpretation, and commodification of both personal and non-personal data (Haggart and Tusikov, 2023), like Google's Waze app that offers real-time traffic updates and directions. In the Quayside project, the fear was that, by shaping the creation and funding models of these proposed public bodies, Quayside could end up favoring Google's commercial interests through the involvement of Sidewalk Labs. By proposing new legal definitions and structures to govern data, technology companies can set rules and standards over infrastructure that benefit their commercial interests (Haggart and Tusikov, 2023).

Large actors may be able to translate their capacity to amass, interpret, and control insights from data into monopolies over data, thereby capturing the dominant share of economic value produced by data. The societal risks from data monopolies, like other monopolies, include stifled innovation, higher prices, greater barriers to entry, and economic benefits disproportionately captured by the 'data-opoly' actors. Concerns about data monopolies speak to broader issues of anti-competitive behavior that results when private actors assume a dominant role in the creation of and proprietary control over digital technologies and datasets (Haggart and Tusikov, 2023). Sidewalk Labs, which is a part of Google, could capture a disproportionate share of value from Quayside because of its control over data flows and the IP rights related to smart city technologies created in the project area.

Centrality of IP in smart cities

This chapter adopts a critical perspective on IP that underlines its economic and political importance (see Drahos and Braithwaite, 2002; Sell, 2003) to explain the importance of IP in smart cities. In the modern globalized economy, ownership of IP rights is central to economic dominance because economic benefits from IP primarily flow to those who own these rights, which disproportionately tends to be large multinational rights holders in the United States and Europe (Schwartz, 2021). Owning IP rights enables those actors to capture a disproportionate share of the value as all others must pay the IP owner for use of the knowledge covered by the rights, such as software licensing fees.

Smart city-related technologies can be protected not only through patents, but also through trademarks, trade secrets, and copyrights. Patents safeguard novel inventions, particularly new and useful processes like pharmaceutical formulas. Although software programs were traditionally ineligible for patent protection, as the source code and scripts are covered under copyright law, functionable aspects of software may now be patentable, such as new computer-configured methods for processing information. Trademarks, meanwhile, protect words, drawings, symbols, logos, pictures, or a combination of these, like Nike's swoosh. Trade secret law, on the other hand, protects competitive business information, often the result of innovation, with the value of this information being derived from its secrecy, such as Google's proprietary search algorithms. Copyright law safeguards creative and artistic works like music, films, and books, along with software, such as software programs operating the sensors and technologies operating within smart cities.

IP functions as an instrument of control and provides its holders with the power to determine who is allowed to use the knowledge protected by the IP rights in question. This right can involve denying or allowing use, as well as requiring payment for the use of IP, such as through patent licensing fees. Central to Sidewalk Labs' plans was the control of technologies developed in the Quayside project to commercialize technologies for markets outside of Toronto. As former Blackberry co-CEO and prominent Quayside critic Jim Balsillie noted, 'You can only commercialize IP or data when you own or control them' (Balsillie, 2018).

Capture of IP flows

For some critics and the local technology industry, the key issue was who would control the IP relating to the creation of smart city technologies.

Specifically, the concern was that Sidewalk Labs, not the Canadian technology industry, would disproportionately benefit from control over IP (McBride, 2018). This fear was realized in August 2018 when *The Globe and Mail* newspaper in Toronto obtained a confidential design procurement document in which Sidewalk Labs set conditions for companies that would work in the Quayside project (O'Kane and Bozikovic, 2018). In the document, Sidewalk Labs asked potential consultants to sign over IP to Sidewalk Labs and 'in cases where that's not possible, to give Sidewalk an exclusive, royalty-free, worldwide license to use it' (O'Kane and Bozikovic, 2018). In addition to these ambitious demands, Sidewalk Labs proposed to share only 10 percent of revenue with the government from some of the technologies developed, tested, or piloted in the project area for a 10-year period (O'Kane, 2019). In other words, Sidewalk Labs envisioned capturing the lion's share of value from IP rights stemming from technologies created for the project area.

An expert advisory panel that Waterfront Toronto set up to independently assess Sidewalk Labs' plans, the Digital Strategy Advisory Panel, concluded that the 10 percent revenue sharing proposal of net profits was too little and the 10-year term was too short as 'city building takes time and innovations that involve city development play out over decades, not years' (Digital Strategy Advisory Panel, 2019, p 19). Sidewalk Labs' proposal only covered technology, leaving out any valuable insights the company would gain in executing its plans that could be exported to other smart cities (Digital Strategy Advisory Panel, 2019, p 1). The company could, for example, capture economically valuable data about residents' transit habits from monitoring traffic patterns and transit usage that it could transfer to other products.

After almost 2 years of industry and expert pressure, as well as demands from Waterfront Toronto, Sidewalk Labs amended its proposals to share more of the anticipated economic benefits. The new provisions included an expanded 'patent pledge' that would grant Canadian innovators access to Sidewalk patents registered globally, instead of those only in Canada (O'Kane, 2019). The company also conceded on sharing benefits with Waterfront Toronto. Sidewalk Labs' concession on patents meant that Canadian companies could build upon Sidewalk innovations without fear of infringement claims (O'Kane, 2019). Sidewalk Labs also agreed to increase the revenue sharing with Waterfront Toronto from its original 10 percent, although at the time it did not specify either the amount or timeframe (O'Kane, 2019).

While Sidewalk Labs' changes were welcomed by IP experts (O'Kane, 2019), they amounted to a rear-guard action made necessary because of the lack of attention that Waterfront Toronto accorded to IP rights. Waterfront Toronto, pressured by activists and experts, had to play catch-up against a partner, which is Google, that understood precisely why setting the terms of an IP agreement is a form of structural power, since its entire business model is based on the control of intangible knowledge (see Haggart and Tusikov, 2023). Without an agreement stating otherwise, the benefits that accrue to those who hold IP – licensing revenues and control over how the IP is deployed – rest with the owner and can be easily moved out of the country. Toronto's tech community and Canadian IP experts understood exactly that Sidewalk Labs' plans would place both Quayside and the local tech community into a subservient position, restricting knowledge spillovers into the local community while reducing Waterfront Toronto's ability to profit from the marketing of any Quayside tech (see, for example, Balsillie, 2018).

Effective and ineffective policies in smart cities

Sidewalk Labs' entry into the smart city market in Toronto ended in May 2020 when CEO Daniel L. Doctoroff claimed that it had become 'too difficult to make the 12-acre project financially viable without sacrificing core parts of the plan' (Doctoroff, 2020). Sidewalk Labs had proposed expanding the project to 150 acres of Toronto's eastern waterfront, but Waterfront Toronto, which does not control the 150 acres, limited the project to the original 12 acres (Diamond, 2019). Following the project's cancellation, Google dissolved the company and absorbed its technologies (Lyons, 2021). Despite its cancellation, the failed Quayside smart city has several lessons to offer policy makers on operating and governing digital technologies.

The Quayside project, particularly its relatively public battles over the control of IP rights and data flows from smart city technologies, highlights how policy makers can identify and counter ineffective policy in smart cities. These lessons also extend to other digital projects. In the Quayside case, ineffective policy can be traced back to Waterfront Toronto's decision to jointly develop policies with Sidewalk Labs, which unsurprisingly led to the proposal of IP and data policies that would benefit the commercial interests of Sidewalk Labs. This ineffective policy was compounded by ideology, specifically when officials conceptualized smart cities as solely or primarily a technical endeavor in which the integration of digital into physical infrastructure inevitably leads to innovation, as well as economic and social growth. Similarly, ineffective policy arises when key actors, including policy makers, tacitly or actively accept the key, albeit highly problematic, principles underlying the data-driven economy. These principles assert that amassing and interpreting data from individuals, objects, and environments, both personal and non-personal, are essential for economic growth and innovation (Haggart and Tusikov, 2023). The Quayside project demonstrated that smart cities are not merely technical projects. Rather, they are socio-technical endeavors where power flows to actors that create and operate the technologies embedded within these cities (see Haggart and Tusikov, 2023). Additionally, economic development is contingent, disproportionately benefiting those who control the IP and data relating to smart city technologies.

On the other hand, effective policy clearly outlines the roles of government and industry actors, ensuring a clear separation between rule-setting entities, ideally carried out by democratically accountable government entities, and those who are subject to the rules. Government actors must perform the necessary role of oversight and regulation of digital technologies with a focus on serving the public interests. In some cases, this direct governmental intervention in regulating the digital economy contradicts the longstanding preference of democratic states for industry self-regulation. Moreover, effective policy also requires that policy makers recognize the importance of governing data flows and IP rights. Those who control such knowledge can capture the economic benefits, including requiring others to pay licensing fees to access data or use proprietary technologies (see Schwartz, 2021). To build this critical understanding, policy makers who are likely more accustomed to focusing on procurement issues, must become thoroughly knowledgeable in IP laws and establish effective working relationships with privacy regulators and data protection authorities. Access to 'independent policy-relevant research' is crucial for policy makers to cultivate digital expertise (Haggart and Spicer, 2022, p 15). Furthermore, independent research matters because industry groups typically work to promote their commercial interests, while civil society groups may not have the capacity to advise the government as effectively or as comprehensively as may be needed (Haggart and Spicer, 2022).

Effective policy rejects the automatic default in the data-driven economy that prioritizes relentless collection of data to achieve industry and government goals. In contrast, effective policy situates problems within their contexts instead of assuming that technology will solve intractable social problems, such as congested traffic and unaffordable housing in the case of smart cities. In essence, it begins by accurately defining the specific problem and evaluating which technology may be appropriate to address the problem. This demands policy makers to resist the urge to oversimplify problems by relying on digital data collection and instead, maintain a healthy respect for subject-matter expertise.

Conclusion

Google's failed smart city project in Toronto – the ill-fated Quayside project – was supposed to be Sidewalk Labs' entry into the smart city industry. This failed project highlights a key lesson in the construction and operation of smart cities: the actor(s) who control data flows and IP rights stemming from smart city technologies can wield significant power. If the project had proceeded, Google would have been the primary actor, enabling it to capture much of the value from data and IP rights relating to the technologies developed in the smart city, disadvantaging the local tech industry. Google, a data company, recognized immediately the importance of controlling data and IP rights. It seized the opportunity, offered by Waterfront Toronto, to jointly develop rules on data and IP governance (Waterfront Toronto, 2017) that would have disproportionately benefited its commercial interests (see Tusikov, 2020).

Failure can serve as a useful teacher. The Quayside project offers a fruitful opportunity to reflect upon what factors contribute to effective or ineffective policies in the governance of digital technologies. Some of the lessons of effective policy are enduring, such as the necessity of separate roles for industry and government actors, coupled with transparent accountability mechanisms. Other lessons are relatively new. For instance, policy makers at all levels of government must acquire expertise in digital issues, such as modes of data governance like data trusts and how IP rights, like licenses for patents, may affect the construction and operation of networked digital infrastructure. A critical comprehension of these matters is essential in establishing effective governance of smart cities that is focused on serving the public interest, as well as addressing digital issues on a broader level.

This failed smart city project also offers broader insights into the governance of digital technologies. Smart cities serve as the intersection between the digital and physical realms, 'their incorporation of networks, data and infrastructure ... the physical embodiment of the "last mile" of internet governance' (Reia and Cruz, 2021, p 219). Understanding smart cities, therefore, equates to comprehending the broader digital economy. Smart cities serve an ideal case for exploring how companies and governments are increasingly assigning economic, political, and social significance to the control of digital data and IP, foundational elements of the digitizing global political economy (see Haggart and Tusikov, 2023). Just as municipal policy makers who are working on physical public infrastructure projects must adapt to a world where previously overlooked issues surrounding data and IP have become prominent concerns, policy makers at other levels must also familiarize themselves with digital matters to effectively govern areas such as trade, national security, or agricultural issues.

As policy makers need to become proficient in digital issues, society's perception of who qualifies as an expert is changing. Google's Sidewalk Labs, a technology company with little urban development experience, won a valuable land development contract to propose a smart city project because of its association with Google's surveillance (data collection) and data processing capacities. Waterfront Toronto seemingly assumed that Sidewalk Labs' technical expertise was equivalent to urban development expertise, a widely held belief, termed 'dataism', in which technical proficiency in surveillance and in collecting and processing digital data translates into expertise in any public policy area (van Dijck, 2014). The belief in tech companies as experts outside of their narrow, technical domains is rooted in a belief in the power of data itself, particularly digital data, to allow us to understand and interpret the world. Facility with data has become synonymous with all-purpose expertise, displacing old-fashioned subject-matter proficiency (Haggart and Tusikov, 2023, p 120).

It is crucial to learn from the Quayside project's ineffective policies (see, for example, Flynn and Valverde, 2019; Haggart and Spicer, 2022). But it is also equally crucial to strengthen and normalize practices of effective policies, particularly in relation to the governance of digital technologies and, more broadly, the digital economy.

Notes

[1] The chapter draws from ideas developed in Haggart, B. and Tusikov, N. (2023) *The New Knowledge: Information, Data, and the Remaking of Global Power*, Lanham, MD: Rowman and Littlefield.

[2] For all Sidewalk Labs' plans, see https://www.sidewalklabs.com/toronto.

[3] As Sidewalk Labs CEO Daniel L. Doctoroff noted in testimony before the Canadian House of Commons Standing Committee on Access to Information, Privacy and Ethics, 'we'll hopefully develop a small group of products that would be operational here, which we think have the potential to be taken beyond Toronto into other markets around the world' (Doctoroff, 2019).

[4] Sidewalk Labs' new definition of data (termed 'urban data') eliminated the legal distinction between personal and non-personal data, which is a foundation within the privacy law in Canada and other western countries (see Tusikov, 2020). Waterfront Toronto rejected the term, stating that the project would comply with existing regulatory frameworks (Diamond, 2019). For further details on these elements – new definition, new governance model, and new consent system – see Tusikov (2020).

References

Auditor General of Ontario (2018) 'Section 3.15: Waterfront Toronto', in *2018 Annual Report*, Ontario: Auditor General of Ontario [online], Available from: http://www.auditor.on.ca/en/content/annualreports/arbyyear/ar2018.html

Balsillie, J. (2018) 'Sidewalk Toronto has only one beneficiary, and it is not Toronto', *The Globe and Mail* [online] 5 October, Available from: https://www.theglobeandmail.com/opinion/article-sidewalk-toronto-is-not-a-smart-city/

Barth, B. (2020) 'Death of a smart city', *OneZero* [online] 12 August, Available from: https://onezero.medium.com/how-a-band-of-activists-and-one-tech-billionaire-beat-alphabets-smart-city-de19afb5d69e

Diamond, S. (2019) 'Open letter from Waterfront Toronto board chair', Waterfront Toronto [blog], 31 October, Available from: https://www.waterfrontoronto.ca/news/open-letter-waterfront-toronto-board-chair-stephen-diamond-regarding-quayside

Digital Strategy Advisory Panel (2019) 'Preliminary Commentary and Questions on Sidewalk Labs' Draft Master Innovation and Development Plan (MIDP)', Waterfront Toronto's DSAP, pp 1–41.

Doctoroff, D.L. (2019) 'Testimony', House of Commons Standing Committee on Access to Information, Privacy and Ethics, 42nd Parliament, 1st session, 2 April, Ottawa [online], Available from: https://www.our commons.ca/DocumentViewer/en/42-1/ethi/meeting-141/evidence

Doctoroff, D.L. (2020) 'Why we're no longer pursuing the Quayside project – and what's next for Sidewalk Labs', *Medium* [online] 7 May, Available from: https://medium.com/sidewalk-talk/why-were-no-lon ger-pursuing-the-quayside-project-and-what-s-next-for-sidewalk-labs-9a61de3fee3a

Drahos, P. and Braithwaite, J. (2002) *Information Feudalism: Who Owns the Knowledge Economy?* Oxford: Oxford University Press.

Edwards, L. (2016) 'Privacy, security and data protection in smart cities: a critical EU law perspective', *European Data Protection Law Review*, 2(1): 28–58.

European Parliament (2016) Regulation (EU) 2016/679 of the European Parliament and of the Council of 27 April 2016 on the protection of natural persons with regard to the processing of personal data and on the free movement of such data, and repealing Directive 95/46/EC (General Data Protection Regulation), O.J., L. 119/1.

Flynn, A. and Valverde, M. (2019) 'Where the sidewalk ends: the governance of Waterfront Toronto's Sidewalk Labs deal', *Windsor Yearbook of Access to Justice*, 36: 263–83.

Gitelman, L. (2013) *Raw Data Is an Oxymoron*, Cambridge, MA: MIT Press.

Goodman, E.P. and Powles, J. (2019) 'Urbanism under Google: lessons from Sidewalk Toronto', *Fordham Law Review*, 88(2): 457–98.

Haggart, B. (2019) 'No longer liveblogging Sidewalk Labs' Master Innovation and Development Plan, Bonus entry 9: can Sidewalk Labs find any independent experts to support it?', Blayne Haggart's Orangespace [blog] 10 September, Available from: https://blaynehaggart.com/2019/09/10/no-longer-liveblogging-sidewalk-labs-master-innovation-and-developm ent-plan-bonus-entry-9-can-sidewalk-labs-find-any-independent-expe rts-to-support-it/

Haggart, B. (2020) 'The selling of Toronto's Smart City', in *Smart Cities in Canada: Digital Dreams, Corporate Designs*, Toronto: Lorimer, pp 38–51.

Haggart, B. and Spicer, Z. (2022) 'Infrastructure, smart cities and the knowledge economy: lessons for policymakers from the Toronto Quayside Project', *Canadian Public Administration*, 65(2): 1–19.

Haggart, B. and Tusikov, N. (2023) *The New Knowledge: Information, Data, and the Remaking of Global Power*, Lanham, MD: Rowman and Littlefield.

Kitchin, R. (2014) 'The real time city? Big data and smart urbanism', *GeoJournal*, 79: 1–14.

Lyons, K. (2021) 'Sidewalk Labs will be folded into Google as CEO steps down for health reasons', *The Verge* [online] 16 December, Available from: https://www.theverge.com/2021/12/16/22840028/sidewalk-labs-google-doctoroff-health-toronto-quayside

McBride, K. (2018) 'Monetizing smart cities: framing the debate', Centre for International Governance Innovation [blog] 28 March, Available from: https://www.cigionline.org/articles/monetizing-smart-city-data/

McDonald, S.M. (2019) 'Reclaiming data trusts', Centre for International Governance Innovation [online] 5 March, Available from: https://www.cigionline.org/articles/reclaiming -data-trusts/

Meijer, A. and Bolívar, M.P.R. (2016) 'Governing the smart city: a review of the literature on smart urban governance', *International Review of Administrative Sciences*, 82(2): 392–408.

O'Kane, J. (2019) 'New Sidewalk deal strikes better balance on IP and innovation but questions still unanswered, experts say', *The Globe and Mail* [online] 1 November, Available from: https://www.theglobeandmail.com/business/article-experts-and-others-weigh-in-on-new-sidewalk-deal/

O'Kane, J. and Bozikovic, A. (2018) 'Sidewalk Labs taking steps to control intellectual property on Toronto's "smart city" document shows', *The Globe and Mail* [online] 31 August, Available from: https://www.theglobeandm ail.com/business/article-sidewalk-labs-taking-steps-to-control-intellect ual-property-on-toronto/

Reia, J. and Cruz, L.F. (2021) 'Seeing through the smart city narrative', in B. Haggart, N. Tusikov, and J. A. Scholte (eds) *Power and Authority in Internet Governance*, Abingdon: Routledge, pp 219–42.

Schwartz, H.M. (2021) 'Global secular stagnation and the rise of intellectual property monopoly', *Review of International Political Economy*, 29(5): 1448–76.

Sell, S.K. (2003) *Private Power, Public Law: The Globalization of Intellectual Property Rights*, Cambridge: Cambridge University Press.

Sidewalk Labs (2017) 'Project vision' [online], Available from: https://qua ysideto.ca/wp-content/uploads/2019/04/SWL-Vision-Sections-of-RFP-Submission-October-27-2017.pdf

Sidewalk Labs (2018) *Digital Governance Proposals for DSAP Consultation*, Toronto: Sidewalk Labs [online], Available from: https://quaysideto.ca/wp-content/uploads/2019/07/Digital-Governance-Proposals-for-DSAP-Consultation.pdf

Sidewalk Labs (2019a) *Toronto Tomorrow (Master Innovation and Development Plan)*, Volume 1: The Plans [online], Available from: https://www.sidew alklabs.com/toronto

Sidewalk Labs (2019b) 'Mobility', in: *Master Innovation and Development Plan*, Volume 2 [online], Available from: https://www.sidewalklabs.com/toronto

Sidewalk Labs (2019c) 'Digital innovation', in: *Master Innovation and Development Plan*, Volume 2 [online], Available from: https://www.sidew alklabs.com/toronto

Srnicek, N. (2017) *Platform Capitalism*, Cambridge: Polity.

Strange, S. (1994) *States and Markets* (2nd edn), New York: Continuum.

Tusikov, N. (2019) 'Sidewalk Toronto's master plan raises urgent concerns about data and privacy', *The Conversation* [online] 30 July, Available from: https://theconversation.com/sidewalk-torontos-master-plan-rai ses-urgent-concerns-about-data-and-privacy-121025

Tusikov, N. (2020) 'Privatized policymaking in Toronto's proposed smart city', in M. Valverde and A. Flynn, (eds), *Smart Cities in Canada: Digital Dreams, Corporate Designs*, Toronto: James Lorimer Ltd. Publishers, pp 68–82.

van Dijck, J. (2014) 'Datafication, dataism and dataveillance: big data between scientific paradigm and ideology', *Surveillance and Society*, 12(2): 197–208.

Waterfront Toronto (2017) 'Request for Proposals: Innovation and Funding Partner for the Quayside Development Opportunity' [online], Available from: https://www.waterfrontoronto.ca/news/statement-quayside-innovat ion-and-funding-partner-request-proposals

7

Letting the solution define the problem: Canada's COVID Alert app as a case of failed policy

Blayne Haggart

Introduction

On 17 June 2022, the Canadian federal government quietly issued a statement decommissioning its COVID Alert app (Health Canada, 2022). The contact notification app had been launched to great fanfare just under 2 years earlier, on 31 July 2020, in the depths of the first wave of the COVID-19 pandemic. Designed and promoted as a way to use digital technologies to automate the intensive manual contact tracing process and thus mitigate the pandemic's spread while also respecting Canadians' privacy, neither this app nor the many similar apps deployed by governments worldwide lived up to expectations.

Reflecting other countries' experiences, the COVID Alert app was a failure for many reasons: relatively low uptake by Canadians limited its effectiveness; an insufficiently context-sensitive Bluetooth-based system, in which a 'contact' is determined by how close two smartphones running the app are to each other; insufficient integration with the country's wider pandemic-response systems, among others (Haggart and Tusikov, 2023, p 141). Due to these reasons, the COVID Alert app failed to contribute in any meaningful way to countering the pandemic. Nevertheless, this alone is not enough to condemn either the app or the people behind it. Experimentation, especially during the depths of a pandemic at a time when vaccines were more hope than reality, is something to be encouraged. Trying something new always involves the risks of failure; in other words, not every policy innovation is a success. There are also lessons in failure. As a wise teacher once noted, 'the greatest teacher, failure is' (Johnson, 2017).

A failed policy is, by definition, an ineffective policy. This book defines ineffective policies as 'policies that are developed, adopted and/or sustained despite being shown to be ineffective/ineffectual and generating undesirable and/or unanticipated negative outcomes'. As the chapters in this book attest, ineffectiveness has many possible origins and manifests itself in various ways. In this case, the ineffectiveness of the COVID Alert app and other

COVID-19 apps can be traced to its origins. Specifically, the solution – implementing a digital COVID-19 app to track and notify those infected with the virus – was allowed to reshape, or redefine, the actual policy problem: how to best mitigate the spread of COVID-19.

In this case, what made the COVID Alert app and other smartphone-based COVID-19 apps generally ineffective – even bad – policy, was the result of two related, increasingly prevalent, pathologies masquerading as common sense in policy-making processes. First, it was their embrace of 'technological solutionism' (Morozov, 2014) – the misguided belief that any social problem can best (or adequately) be addressed through the application of digital technologies – instead of evaluating the app as one among several possible health policy options. Second, and related, the COVID Alert app reflected an ideology that media studies scholar José van Dijck refers to as 'dataism', which is the presumption that social reality can be fully captured by the collection of digital data (van Dijck, 2014).

These two related ideologies blinded politicians and policy makers to the fatal flaws in an app-based approach to contact tracing. As this chapter argues, they shifted the focus away from addressing the primary goal – fighting the pandemic – and towards adapting their response to fit the affordances of the technology itself. The result was a short-circuited policy-making process, creating a situation where policy makers failed to assess fully the significant drawbacks of their preferred solution. Policy makers instead focused more on the tech itself and the needs of the tech giants providing the digital infrastructure – Apple and Google – than on the nominal health policy objective. In the end, failure was inevitable.[1]

Policy makers have much to learn from the COVID Alert app. As van Dijck and others note (for example, Haggart and Tusikov, 2023), dataism and technological solutionism are the ideologies of our time, their reach is extending into every corner of public policy, from health (Sharon, 2018) to social welfare (Mann, 2020) to finance (Gerard, 2020). While dataism and technological solutionism are powerful ideologies, they can be countered relatively simply, by ensuring that digital tech-driven policy proposals are evaluated according to the same issue-specific criteria applied to other potential solutions. In the case of the COVID Alert app, the automation of the contact tracing process using smartphones produced by companies whose business interests are closely linked to maximizing surveillance, led to a counterproductive focus on protecting individual privacy at the cost of its utility as a contact tracing or contact notification tool.

This chapter explores how dataism and technological solutionism shaped the development of COVID-19 apps in general and the Canadian COVID Alert app in particular. The chapter proceeds in two sections. The first section defines and discusses the ideologies of technological solutionism and dataism. The second section explores the phenomenon of COVID-19 apps, with special attention paid to the introduction, implementation, and retirement of the Canadian COVID Alert app. The chapter then concludes with specific policy recommendations.

Dataism and technological solutionism: the ideology of our times

The experts to whom we turn in moments of crisis reveal a great deal about a society. In early 2020, as the reality of the COVID-19 pandemic became inescapable, several authorities came to the fore: political leaders, the World Health Organization (WHO), local public health authorities, as well as the tech companies. Almost immediately, companies began proposing, to very receptive governments, ways in which digital technologies could be used to fight the pandemic. Facebook CEO Mark Zuckerberg argued that data is 'a new superpower' to counter COVID-19, that there were opportunities to use 'aggregate data [from social media platforms] to benefit public health' (Haggart and Tusikov, 2023, p 130). Governments, academics, and companies adopted the idea that digital technologies – particularly smartphones – could be used to track the spread of this novel virus almost immediately. Apple and Google, which dominated the smartphone operating system market, played (and were allowed to play) a significant role in designing these apps (Sharon, 2020; Taylor et al, 2021).

Dataism and the new knowledge

Identifying the source of authority of government officials and health specialists is relatively straightforward. In the midst of a pandemic, health officials are deemed to have relevant subject matter expertise, while government officials control the means to address large-scale, systemic challenges like the global spread of an unknown virus. But what about tech companies? Why was there an assumption that they had a fundamental role in fighting the pandemic? The answer is, to most people, obvious – because they are seen as experts in collecting, manipulating, and interpreting data. This is the measure of the emergence of a new ideology of knowledge, what media studies scholar José van Dijck (2014) calls 'dataism'. Dataism is the belief that all social life – all reality, in fact – can be unproblematically represented as data, and that if you have enough computing power and enough data, you can interpret the world through correlations alone, no theories necessary (Anderson, 2008, p 200). This represents a new form of knowledge, based on the 'belief that large datasets offer a higher form of intelligence and knowledge that can generate insights that were previously impossible, with the aura of truth, objectivity, and accuracy' (boyd and Crawford, 2012, p 663).

To be blunt, this view is nonsense. Critical data scholars (for example, Gitelman, 2013; Loukissas, 2019), along with philosophers of knowledge (for instance, Berger and Luckmann, 1966), have long highlighted that data is never neutral. It is a form of knowledge that is always and necessarily partial, shaped by decisions about what phenomena to turn into data, how to measure these phenomena, and how to store and use this data (Haggart and Tusikov, 2023). Correlations can never speak for themselves; when we assume that they can, we merely end up sublimating our pre-existing assumptions, biases and interests into our creation, interpretation, and use of the data. This is the reason why, time and again, algorithms are found to 'act' in racist and misogynist ways (Eubanks, 2018; Noble, 2018). The idea of a neutral algorithm, or large language model, is a myth. Data is a thoroughly human creation. Like any other human artifact, anything that uses data will always reflect the biases and interests of the people who designed it. You can never escape people.

The significance of data does not lie in its potential to provide a purer, more objective form of knowledge, but rather in our belief that it does (Haggart, 2023). This belief, in turn, sanctifies new categories of experts – the technologist, the data scientist, the techbro, the (usually male) tech executive – who, because of their supposed facility with the technical knowledge of data manipulation, are believed to possess knowledge that transcends specific areas of expertise. Therefore, a search engine and advertising company is treated seriously when it attempts to enter domains as disparate as healthcare and urban development, not as the hired help, but as the project leaders, because a facility with data manipulation – a technical skill – is seen as equivalent, as superior, to subject-matter expertise.

Technological solution: hammer, meet nail

Expertise itself is never neutral. At the very least, it reflects one's training: a lawyer sees the world differently from a social scientist. Different forms of expertise naturally predispose the expert toward some solutions and away from others. For example, a lawyer may favor black-letter regulation, while a political scientist may be more sensitive to the role of informal norms in regulating behavior.

Technologists, and those who ascribe to an ideology of dataism, see the world as consisting of raw data, ready to be scooped up and manipulated. In turn, this leads those who subscribe to dataism down the path of what prescient tech critic Evgeny Morozov calls 'technological solutionism' (Morozov, 2014). Simply put, technological solutionism is the tendency to assume that digital-based approaches to public policy problems are inherently superior compared to the others, non-digital-tech approaches. It assumes that there is, or should be, a digital component to any public-policy issue.

The problem with this approach to policy making is not that digital tech never has a role to play in public policy. Rather, by beginning with the solution – digital technology – one ends up redefining the problem in terms of the capacities and limitations of the tool. Rather than choosing the best tool for the job, technological solutionism effectively shapes the job to fit the tool. While doing so, they often end up failing to address the essence of the problem at hand, as what went down with the COVID-19 apps. Instead of focusing on the problem, they focus on the parts of the problem that can be quantified, or turned into digital data, which may not be the most important parts of the problem.

Taken together, dataism and technological solutionism present a pernicious habit of mind that can lead policy makers to pursue policies that consider the problem in terms of the tool, rather than in and of itself. Such an approach places too much faith in data and data experts, producing outcomes that fail to account for the whole problem, or how the act of 'datafication' – the rendering of social life exclusively in terms of the digital data that can be collected about it (Mayer-Schönenberger and Cukier, 2013) – itself represents a partial interpretation of complex underlying phenomena. While these attitudes are prevalent throughout the policy making world, they were particularly on clear display in the rush to adopt COVID-19 contact notification and tracing apps.

The rise and fall of Canada's COVID Alert app

The idea that a smartphone-based app could potentially contribute to a country's pandemic response, at first glance, is not obviously ridiculous.[2] Faced with a nebulous challenge of the unknown scope and indeterminate duration of the pandemic, it made sense to consider all possible options. However, good policy, even (or especially) in times of emergency, requires an appropriate evaluative framework. At its base, such a framework must consider whether the action will have the desired effect on the problem at hand, as well as how a proposed action compares with other viable options. In the case of COVID-19 apps, including Canada's COVID Alert app, this basic framework was short-circuited. Key questions regarding the effectiveness in managing the pandemic were either downplayed or effectively ignored, while other, less-relevant concerns ended up driving app (and thus policy) design.

COVID-19 apps differ in their goals and in some aspects of how they function, but they all follow a similar method. The apps use Bluetooth functionality in a user's smartphone to define a contact. In the case of Canada's COVID Alert app, a contact was defined as two Bluetooth signals from users' phones that were within 2 m (6 ft) of each other for at least 15 minutes. Apps differed in what they did with this contact information. In the case of Canada, privacy concerns led the app's designers – a mix of actors from both the public and private sector – to create a *contact notification*, rather than a *contact tracing* app. Briefly described, a person who had tested positive for COVID-19 would upload to their phone a code that they received from their local health authority. If a phone with a 'positive' code 'contacted' another phone as defined previously, it would automatically 'notify' the other person's phone that they had come into contact (as defined by the programmers) with a person who tested positive for COVID-19 (or, more precisely, with their phone).

Initial claims for these apps were quite utopian. An early article in *Science*, by several Oxford University academics, argued that if used by enough people, a contact tracing app could 'be sufficient to stop the epidemic' (Ferretti et al, 2020). While contact notification apps, designed so in large part because of fears of the government and corporate surveillance that would be necessary for public health officials to trace the disease, would depend on individual actions rather than centralized public-health responses, hopes were similarly high.

Problems with these claims, rooted in dataist and solutionist ideologies, were obvious at the time. An article published just 2 weeks after the COVID Alert app's launch, noted that the high cost of smartphones meant that the app (and therefore contact notification) would not be available to lower income individuals and households. These groups were least able to restrict their movements, which, before the vaccines, was the only guaranteed way to keep from catching and spreading a virus whose full effects were still unknown (Haggart, 2020). In Brazil, the government's Monitora COVID-19 app, created 'in a partnership between public and private institutions', was 'underused in impoverished areas due to a lack of economic access to the technology and wireless network' (Lemos et al, 2022, p 84).

Such apps, far from automating the contact notification process, displaced this labor, handing responsibility for responding to the pandemic to individuals, who had to: download the app; run the app in the appropriate way; contact their local health agency to receive a code if they tested positive; seek out legitimate information about what to do in the case of a positive test; and follow through on this advice. Individuals who may or may not know where to turn for many of these steps, and who would still have to deal with life pressures like other people in the home and (for many) the need to keep working outside the home.

Beyond these socioeconomic aspects, others pointed out that Bluetooth itself was a poor measure of meaningful contact (epistemologically speaking), since it could not tell whether two phones were being held by people standing face-to-face in a crowded room, or whether there was a wall between them. While we are used to thinking of digitization as making things more efficient, here, its creation of many false positives demonstrates how digital efficiency is often an illusion. There were also mixed messages that such an app would send: at a time when restricting social movement in the absence of vaccines was (correctly) seen as limiting the disease's spread, the app seemed to suggest it would be fine to carry on as normal so long as the app was active.

Technological solutionism in action: privacy and centralized versus decentralized data storage

COVID-19 apps were flawed policy instruments from the outset. The misguided debate over privacy and these apps helps to further illustrate this point. Concerns about privacy played a central role in app design in most Western countries. When Canada unveiled its app on 31 July 2020, its government web page emphasized the protection of individuals' privacy, providing links to Canada's privacy regulator, the Privacy Commissioner of Canada, who attested to the app's privacy measures. To their credit, they managed to design an app that prioritizes individual privacy, evident in every aspect of the design, starting with the decision to create a contact notification, rather than a contact tracing app. Ironically, though, it quickly became clear that they had made the app so airtight, so protective of individual privacy, that they had left themselves no way to evaluate the app's effectiveness in mitigating the pandemic.

In other words, they ended up designing the app to protect individuals' privacy, not to stop the pandemic. The tool dictated the focus. In this case, the decision to rely on Apple and Google's operating systems placed these two companies in a position to largely dictate how data would be used, and they favored a decentralized approach. This decentralized approach makes sense for these two companies. In an era characterized by increasing suspicion of tech surveillance, and recognizing their own ambitions to enter the multi-billion-dollar healthcare market, advocating for decentralized data storage was a way to buttress their privacy bona fides. They were effectively creating a latent surveillance capacity that they could later turn on, should they so desire (Sharon, 2020; Taylor et al, 2021). This singular focus on privacy also reflects the ideological predisposition of many digital rights activists whose main (often justified) focus is surveillance overreach by companies and governments.

The COVID-19 apps, in general, privileged a corporate view of privacy over what we could call the epidemiological view of privacy. The benefits of privacy are highly contextual (Nissenbaum, 2004); more privacy is not always better. In a pandemic, too-strong individual privacy rights can literally be a killer, making it difficult for health authorities to stop the spread of a virulent disease. For instance, contact tracing as a practice requires access to data of how a disease is traveling through a population. In other words, it requires high levels of surveillance. From the perspective of healthcare, such surveillance is not only unobjectionable; it is imperative. However, from the perspective of the technology companies, as well as the technology activists and experts intervening in this debate, such surveillance was an anathema.

To be clear, digital rights activists are certainly correct to be suspicious of data grabs by these companies. Although relatively little was made of the fact that, even though these companies committed to not centralizing this data collection, in setting up the apps to work on their systems, they effectively created the capacity to undertake such surveillance sometime in the future (Sharon, 2020). However, it is not obvious why privacy should be the primary criterion for judging a pandemic policy response *during a pandemic*, or, more precisely, why the need for epidemiologically contextual privacy did not drive the debate. In particular, if this type of surveillance is so problematic, why was it considered at all? Concerns around surveillance should have prompted questions about whether relying on commercial platforms to deliver such sensitive services was appropriate. These concerns should have been assessed in a context where other options, such as significantly increasing manual contact tracing, were also considered. Instead, the starting point was the tech, not the problem. Rather than focusing on the best way to mitigate the pandemic and considering how to build the trust that is the lifeblood of any society, let alone during a pandemic, the main focus was maximizing users' privacy against governments and companies.

Along the same lines, why was the obvious alternative – manual contact tracing undertaken via a wartime-like deployment – never seriously considered? While the Oxford University *Science* article argued that it would be 'infeasible' to control 'the epidemic by manual contact tracing' (Ferretti et al, 2020), the immediate wake of the pandemic created a potential volunteer army of idled workers and students, who could have been sent into their communities as contact tracers. The billions of deficit dollars spent by governments around the world in response to the pandemic served as a reminder that the state, facing existential threats, will do what it believes needs to be done to survive. Expansive manual contact tracing could easily have been one of those things. Instead, true to a solutionist mindset, policy makers' minds immediately went to the shiny digital response.

Dataism, trust, and contact tracing

Dataism is the belief that society can be reduced to data points. When expressed through algorithms, it implies a bias toward automation. Automation is the process of reducing a process to those steps the designer believes are essential to that process. In practice, though, these steps are usually those that are most amenable to datafication. Importantly, automation redefines the thing that is being automated, this also applies to the dynamic between app-based contact tracing and manual contact tracing. In this case, the datafication (and appification) of the manual contact tracing process transformed it into something else entirely, while also eliminating many, if not most, of the features that make manual contact tracing valuable.

Contact tracing is not just about identifying infected individuals. As philosophy of technology scholar Tamar Sharon notes:

> much of the work of human contact tracers has to do with ensuring that people have the material conditions required to sustain an (at the time) 14-day quarantine, including food in their homes, the ability to care for children who may need to be removed, how to isolate in small spaces and when to seek medical attention. (Sharon, 2020, p 551)

In this case, access to food and childcare and proper isolation practices are effectively downloaded onto the infected (or presumed infected) individuals.

The underlying philosophies of the two processes, moreover, are diametrically opposed. Canada's contact notification app was designed to minimize the need for trust. As early critic of the app Sean McDonald wryly noted, the government's app privacy-focused messaging was effectively 'The app probably won't help us hurt you', rather than stressing its role as a pandemic-mitigation measure (McDonald, 2020).

In contrast, manual contact tracing is designed to build trust. The purpose of manual contact tracing with respect to infectious diseases is to identify infected individuals and the people with whom they have been in contact. This can be a delicate process. Transmissible diseases are often accompanied by feelings of shame, embarrassment, or fear. Identifying potential disease vectors thus requires public health workers to 'build a relationship of trust' with the people they are interviewing (Sharon, 2020, p 551). This trust is necessary 'so that people feel safe revealing personal details', including personal contacts, and allow the health workers to provide them with the 'targeted information' that is necessary when it comes to dealing with the infection, such as quarantine guidelines (Sharon, 2020, p 551). Trust between public health workers and infected individuals allows public health officials to engage in the surveillance that is necessary to map and fight the pandemic.

Contact tracing is indeed a form of data collection. Like all forms of data collection, it involves surveillance of individuals and groups, in this case by health professionals, who usually are employed by the state. Implicit in this approach is the idea that the more data amassed, the better equipped a society will be to fight a pandemic. Manual contact tracing, as Sharon (2020) notes, requires that (trained) contact tracers work to gain the trust of the people they work with, often to supply very private information, such as sexual encounters. That manual contact tracing is about building trust makes the (non-) decision to forego a dramatic expansion in manual contact tracing even more disappointing, a lost opportunity to increase social cohesion at a time when social bonds were being placed under significant strain.

Conclusion

The record of COVID-19 apps as a tool to fight the pandemic is, to be kind, mixed. Probably the most favorable report came from researchers studying the United Kingdom's National Health Service COVID-19 app. In England and Wales, between 24 September 2020 and the end of 2020, they estimated that the app was 'used regularly' by 28 percent of the population of England and Wales, and also prevented a significant number of infections (Wymant et al, 2021; Lyon 2022). By late 2021, however, almost 2 years into the pandemic, many governments had concluded that COVID-19 apps had not delivered on their promise. By the time Canada's COVID Alert app retired in June 2022, it had been rendered almost completely useless due to the decisions made by various Canadian health authorities (Wylie 2022).

Meanwhile, a report from the US Government Accountability Office (GAO) could not find evidence of the effectiveness of COVID-19 apps. This was partly because, for privacy reasons, officials and companies restricted the apps from collecting enough relevant information to assess their effectiveness. The GAO also noted the technological limitations of these Bluetooth-based apps affected their accuracy (2021, p 27), as well as the apps' low uptake and delays in receiving verification codes, a problem that was also noted in Canada. GAO argues that more data is needed to assess the effectiveness of these apps (United States Government Accountability Office, 2021, pp 27–33, 40).

Beyond ineffectiveness as measured in resource and time costs, and against unmet objectives, assessing the full impact of technological solutionism must also encompass a consideration of those paths not taken. The great flaw in technological solutionism is that it causes policy makers to overlook other viable options and fail to consider the potential harms that these technology-driven policies might cause. While the impact of the technology-driven policy can be measured, it is much harder to quantify what would have happened if a different policy had been chosen – though not impossible: in the case of manual contact tracing, as it can be assessed based on its long record as an established practice. In any case, the impact of a solutionist mindset is not just a waste of time, but, in the case of digital contact tracing, it could also have resulted in the loss of lives.

As van Dijck noted in her 2014 article, dataism's siren song is difficult to resist. Companies, governments, activists, and academics, to varying degrees, subscribe to the tempting notion that quantification via datafication provides a more neutral, superior form of knowledge. Similarly, the idea that digital technologies are necessarily superior to other forms of technology is treated as a given.

I am writing this chapter some 5 months into a 'generative AI' craze. This craze has led otherwise-intelligent people to believe that a pattern-recognition machine, which produces probability-based text from natural-language inputs, is on a par with human-written essays.[3] Meanwhile, stories about racist algorithms and algorithmic-driven welfare disasters remain all-too-common (Haggart and Tusikov, 2023).

Solutionism and dataism are not just a scourge in the health sector. In education, there is a pervasive belief that information and communication technologies are 'a panacea for solving educational problems,' despite the fact that these issues are 'wicked problems' and defy simple, reductionist solutions. 'Edtech', digital tools promoted by big companies, has surged, especially after COVID-19 pushed online learning activities. This follows a trend of relying on technology as a quick fix, seen across various sectors facing similar issues (Gràcia and Sancho-Gil, 2021, pp 1, 8–9). Another example is how the pursuit of autonomous and electric vehicles as a response to the climate emergency comes at the expense of developing public transit. This, despite public transit being the better option by almost every sustainable development measure: autonomous cars remain eternally 5 years away from deployment (Winton, 2022). Meanwhile, climate experts highlight that simply electrifying cars is not sufficient to meet countries' climate change obligations (Woodhouse and Mohsin, 2023). In both cases, as with the COVID-19 apps, focusing on technology as the progressive path forward ignores non-(digital) tech approaches, such as improving public transit, that can yield better results.

The root of these failures is not the technology, but the attitudes about the technology, specifically the unearned faith placed in data and the technicians who are seen as experts. Ideologies are by definition difficult to overcome, especially ones that have achieved the status of received wisdom. Still, there are several steps that policy makers can take to minimize their susceptibility to bad habits of mind such as dataism and technological solutionism.

First, policy makers should place data and technology, and technologists, in their proper place, as subordinate to subject-matter experts and the needs of the problem at hand. The pointless COVID-19 app detour could potentially have been avoided, or brought to a better end, had the app, as a form of policy, been judged according to healthcare needs and values, rather than those set by the technologists themselves. Starting with context-specific criteria provides a way to judge the utility (or not) of any proposed technological solutions. The question should not be, how can we adapt this digital tech to our current problem? Rather it should be, what is the best way to respond to this particular problem, and what are the range of options that are available to us?

Second, one must approach data, and the promises of tech companies and their acolytes, with a grain of salt. Presuming that the world, particularly the social world, is reducible to neutral data merely sublimates our existing biases, vested interests and prejudices into a machine. Data collection, even when done well, will not always capture what is most important about a process. This is also the same with algorithmic regulation. Something is always lost in translation. Most importantly, results will never be objective, for the very reason that data and algorithms are always human creations and will always reflect someone's ideologies, interests, and biases.

Algorithmic and data neutrality is a chimera. No matter how much data one collects, one will never escape human influences. This problem is especially challenging for policy makers who, when deploying algorithmic regulation, will be tempted to minimize accountability by hiding behind presumptions of data and algorithmic neutrality. App and algorithm-based processes change the process; it does not necessarily make it better. Even the promised efficiency often depends on how a problem has been redefined. In the case of COVID-19 apps, digital contact notification/tracing may have pinged some individuals more quickly (or efficiently), but at the cost of lowered efficiency at a systemic level (high number of false positives).

The COVID Alert app's failure is worth studying not simply because it failed, but also to acknowledge the public spirit that drove many people involved, who genuinely wanted to help fight, who genuinely wanted to help fight a dangerous pandemic. Just as failure alone does not constitute bad or structurally ineffective policy, good intentions alone do not excuse it. In this case, and in many other policy areas, dataism and technological solutionism, the leading ideologies of our age, stand in the way of thinking clearly about how to address the very real problems facing our societies. Without question, new technologies – new ways of manipulating and shaping our world – will play important roles in addressing these challenges, as they always have. But to use them effectively, we need to be cognizant of their limitations, and of the limitations inherent in data itself.

Notes

[1] Inevitable, and not just in hindsight. See, for example, Haggart (2020) for a critique of the app contemporaneous to its launch.

[2] This section is based on Haggart and Tusikov (2023, chapter 5).

[3] On essays and generative AI, and the implications for what we consider to be knowledge, see Haggart (2023).

References

Anderson, C. (2008) 'The end of theory: the data deluge makes the scientific method obsolete', *Wired* [online] 23 August 2008, Available from: https://www.wired.com/2008/06/pb-theory/

Berger, P.L. and Luckmann T. (1966) *The Social Construction of Reality: A Treatise in the Sociology of Knowledge*, London: Penguin.

boyd, D. and Crawford, K. (2012) 'Critical questions for Big Data: provocations for a cultural, technological, and scholarly phenomenon', *Information, Communication & Society*, 15(5): 662–79.

Eubanks, V. (2018) *Automating Inequality: How High-Tech Tools Profile, Police, and Punish the Poor*, New York: St. Martin's Press.

Ferretti, L., Wymant, C., Kendall, M., Zhao, L., Nurtay, A., Abeler-Dörner, L. et al (2020) 'Quantifying SARS-CoV-2 transmission suggests epidemic control with digital contact tracing', *Science*, 368:(6491).

Gerard, D. (2020) *Libra Shrugged: How Facebook Tried to Take Over The Money*, Independently published.

Gitelman, L. (ed) (2013) *Raw Data Is an Oxymoron*, Cambridge, MA: MIT Press.

Gràcia, X.G. and Sancho-Gil, J.M. (2021) 'Artificial intelligence in education: big data, black Boxes, and technological solutionism', *Seminar. Net*, 17(2).

Haggart, B. (2020) 'Canada's COVID alert app is a case of tech-driven bad policy design', *The Conversation* [online] 13 August, Available from: http://theconversation.com/canadas-covid-alert-app-is-a-case-of-tech-driven-bad-policy-design-144448

Haggart, B. (2023) 'ChatGPT strikes at the heart of the scientific world view', Centre for International Governance Innovation, Available from: https://www.cigionline.org/articles/chatgpt-strikes-at-the-heart-of-the-scientific-world-view/

Haggart, B. and Natasha Tusikov, N. (2023) *The New Knowledge: Information, Data and the Remaking of Global Power*, Washington, DC: Rowman & Littlefield.

Health Canada (2022) 'Statement from Health Canada on decommissioning COVID Alert' [online], Available from: https://www.canada.ca/en/health-canada/news/2022/06/statement-from-health-canada-on-decommissioning-covid-alert.html.

Johnson, R. (dir) (2017) *Star Wars: The Last Jedi*, San Francisco: Lucasfilm.

Lemos, A., Firmino, R.J., Marques, D., Matos, E., and Lopes, C. (2022) 'Smart pandemic surveillance? A neo-materialist analysis of the "Monitora Covid-19" application in Brazil', *Surveillance & Society*, 20(1): 82–99.

Loukissas, Y.A. (2019) *All Data Are Local: Thinking Critically in a Data-Driven Society*, Cambridge, MA: MIT Press.

Lyon, D. (2022) *Pandemic Surveillance*, Medford: Polity.

Mann, M. (2020) 'Technological politics of automated welfare surveillance: social (and data) justice through critical qualitative inquiry', *Global Perspectives*, 1(1): 1–12.

Mayer-Schönenberger, V. and Cukier, K. (2013) *Big Data: A Revolution That Will Transform How We Live, Work, and Think*, London: John Murray Publishers.

McDonald, S. (2020) 'COVID-19 lessons: building disaster-ready technologies', Centre for International Governance Innovation [blog] 12 October, Available from: https://www.cigionline.org/articles/covid-19-lessons-building-disaster-ready-technologies/.

Morozov, E. (2014) *To Save Everything, Click Here*, New York: Public Affairs.

Nissenbaum, H. (2004) 'Privacy as contextual integrity', *Washington Law Review,* 79(1): 119.

Noble, S.U. (2018) *Algorithms of Oppression: How Search Engines Reinforce Racism*, New York: New York University Press.

Sharon, T. (2018) 'When digital health meets digital capitalism, how many common goods are at stake?', *Big Data & Society*, 5(2): 1–12.

Sharon, T. (2020) 'Blind-sided by privacy? Digital contact tracing, the Apple/Google API and big tech's newfound role as global health policy makers', *Ethics and Information Technology*, 23(1): 545–57.

Taylor, L., Sharma, G., Martin, A., and Jameson, S. (eds) (2021) *Data Justice and Covid-19*, London: Meatspace Press.

United States Government Accountability Office (2021) *Exposure Notification: Benefits and Challenges of Smartphone Applications to Augment Contact Tracing*, GAO-21-104622, Washington, DC: United States Government Accountability Office, Available from: https://www.gao.gov/products/gao-21-104622.

van Dijck, J. (2014) 'Datafication, dataism and dataveillance: big data between scientific paradigm and ideology', *Surveillance and Society*, 12(2): 197–208.

Winton, N. (2022) 'Computer driven autos still years away despite massive investment', Forbes [online] 27 February, Available from: https://www.forbes.com/sites/neilwinton/2022/02/27/computer-driven-autos-still-years-away-despite-massive-investment/.

Woodhouse, S. and Mohsin, S. (2023) 'EV hype overshadows public transit as a climate fix', Bloomberg [online] 25 January, Available from: https://www.bloomberg.com/news/articles/2023-01-25/public-transit-gets-left-behind-in-us-climate-change-conversation.

Wylie, B. (2022) 'Canada's COVID alert app needs to be shut down. Here's Why', Medium [blog], 20 April, Available from: https://biancawylie.medium.com/canadas-covid-alert-app-needs-to-be-shut-down-here-s-why-dc5037ecdcf.

Wymant, C., Ferretti, L. Tsallis, D., Charalambides, M., Abeler-Dörner, L., Bonsall, D. et al (2021) 'The epidemiological impact of the NHS COVID-19 app', *Nature*, 594(7863): 408–12.

PART II

Ineffective policies, negative outcomes

8

Toxic growth in the circular economy: is the EU Plastics Strategy a bad policy?

Jacob Hasselbalch

Introduction

How does a good policy go bad? Even with good intentions, policies can sometimes become ineffective. For policy outcomes to turn truly bad, however, they must actively exacerbate the issues they aim to resolve. The story of the European Commission's (EC's) *A European Strategy for Plastics in a Circular Economy* (European Commission, 2018a), hereafter referred to as the Plastics Strategy, is a story of a good policy turning bad. Early engagements with plastics governance in the European Union (EU) from 2010 to 2014 correctly addressed the root of the plastics problem, namely its cheapness and its abundance as a byproduct of fossil fuel production. However, later engagements, from 2015 to 2019, shifted focus away from stringent regulatory measures, instead directing most of their attention towards turning plastic waste into a business opportunity. The Plastics Strategy is 'ineffective' in the sense that it is unlikely to do much to address the global problem of plastic pollution, and it is 'bad' in the sense that it is naturalizing conditions of 'toxic growth' in the plastics and petrochemicals sectors by viewing their continued expansion as compatible with environmental objectives in the face of evidence to the contrary (Persson et al, 2022; Tilsted et al, 2023). This compatibility rests on unrealistic expectations about fully closing material loops through a circular economy in plastics and petrochemicals.

Ample research has criticized the European circular economy policy program for becoming a technocratic and techno-optimistic perpetuation of the status quo, or at worst, a corporate capture of the policy agenda that facilitates capital accumulation while paying lip service to environmental goals (Blomsma and Brennan, 2017; Calisto Friant et al, 2021; Leipold, 2021; Mah, 2021; Palm et al, 2022). If we want to 'close the loops' in the circular economy, the circle cannot keep growing (Hobson, 2016). In this chapter, I contribute to such scholarship in two ways: first, by demonstrating the significant role played by the Plastics Strategy in stabilizing and legitimizing a business-friendly and light-touch version of the circular economy. Second, I trace the gradual disappearance of efforts to decouple plastics from fossil fuels. The Strategy marks the initial application of circular economy principles to an entire sector, serving as a blueprint for how the EC will make other industrial sectors 'circular' in the future (European Commission, 2020).

What we see when looking at the history of the Plastics Strategy is the emergence of a policy paradigm (Hall, 1993). Ten years ago, plastics did not receive much attention from EU policy makers – but today, the plastics sector represents the flagship initiative of European industrial policy informed by circular economy thinking (European Commission, 2019a, p 7). What has happened since then is the complete establishment of the 'plastics sector' as a distinct object of governance. This marks a shift especially from earlier tendencies to treat merely the externalities of the sector (harmful chemicals, waste, and so on), towards treating the sector holistically according to the principles of the circular economy. We can conceptualize this trajectory as a gradual yoking together of diverse elements (knowledge, ideas, actors, tools, and imperatives) that specifies the object, means, and ends of a policy, which Allan (2019) – extending Hall's (1993) classical definition of policy paradigms – defines as the assembling of a 'policy nexus'. A policy nexus emerges when such elements achieve a stable configuration and a discrete object of governance appears, in this case, a circular economy of plastics. The stability of a policy nexus is explained by an inherent complementarity between its constituent parts.

To show how a policy nexus is formed, Allan (2019, pp 188–9) suggests we must trace the 'relational histories' of actors, knowledge, and devices, which means showing how they come together in specific ways. I focus my relational history on the text corpus of the EC's policy documents, directing my attention to the links that are formed between the Plastics Strategy, documents preceding and following the strategy, and the ideas contained within them. These can be identified by examining the documents that are cited in the strategy, and then in turn examining the documents that are cited in those documents, and so on, until a full picture emerges of how each document and initiative led to the next. The timeline that thus emerges runs from the publication of the Europe 2020 Strategy in 2010 (European Commission, 2010a) up until the *Report on the Implementation of the Circular Economy Action Plan* in 2019 (European Commission, 2019b). During this decade, the concept of the circular economy emerged in high-level EU discourse, evolving from an earlier flexibility and open-endedness into a specific emphasis on business-friendly innovation and recycling. This emphasis continues to shape policy actions today. The goal of the chapter is to analyze this transformation through a relational history of the Plastics Strategy.

When relations within a policy nexus are reconfigured, the nexus itself undergoes change. The theoretical implication for the study of 'good' versus 'bad' policy is that policies which initially address their intended area effectively may become ineffective or worse when the relations between the elements of the policy nexus change, and not through any overt changes to the policies themselves. To understand how a good policy goes bad, the relational history of policies must be considered. As the analysis will show, changes in relations between the constitutive parts of plastics governance in the EU is what has led us to the current predicament of a circular economy that allows for toxic growth.

A relational history of the Plastics Strategy

To embark on a relational history, I begin by introducing the Plastics Strategy briefly, before tracing it back through time to uncover its deeper origins. This brings us back to the earliest discussions in 2010–12 on resource efficiency. We then observe a paradigm shift in circular economy discourse around 2014–15, which set the immediate background for the emergence of the Plastics Strategy. The relational history then advances slowly in time, looking into the aftermath of the strategy, and its central role in laying the groundwork for circular economy thinking in the EU in general. My core concern throughout the analysis is to trace the changing relations in the policy nexus between plastics, the circular economy, and the various policy problems and priorities to which they become connected.

On 16 January 2018, the EC presented their new *A European Strategy for Plastics in a Circular Economy* (European Commission, 2018a). According to the official press release, the aim of the strategy is to 'protect the environment from plastic pollution while fostering growth and innovation, turning a challenge into a positive agenda for the Future of Europe' (European Commission, 2018b). After emphasizing that there is a strong business case for European industries to take the lead in transforming the way plastic products are produced, designed, recycled, and used, the press release introduces the five overarching aims of the initiative. These include making recycling more profitable for business through developing new rules on packaging and standardizing the collection and sorting of waste; reducing plastic waste, particularly single-use plastics, fishing gear, and microplastics; stopping sea littering with new rules on port reception facilities; promoting investment and innovation with €100 million support for the development of smarter and more recyclable plastics materials; and fostering global change through developing international standards and liaising with partners around the globe.

The immediate background of the Plastics Strategy stems from the EC's adoption of the Circular Economy Action Plan in December 2015. This action plan identified plastics as a 'priority area', emphasizing that 'increasing plastic recycling is essential for the transition to a circular economy' (European

Commission, 2015). By following the document trail through the relational history, we can trace the genesis of the Plastics Strategy back to 2010's Europe 2020 Strategy (European Commission, 2010a). Written at a time of intense pressure on European economies, the 2020 Strategy emphasized the importance of dealing with the immediate demands of the financial and sovereign debt crisis, but also thinking further ahead and defining where the EU wanted to be in 2020. Three mutually reinforcing priorities were identified: smart growth, sustainable growth, and inclusive growth. These priorities were supported by several specific targets to measure progress, and by seven 'flagship initiatives' to catalyze progress on each theme. Under the sustainable growth priority, the flagship initiative of a 'resource-efficient Europe' was paramount.

Resource-efficient Europe

The aim of the 'resource-efficient Europe' initiative is to decouple economic growth from resource and energy use, reduce CO_2 emissions, enhance competitiveness, and promote greater resource and energy security. Most of the planned activities under this initiative would target the transport and energy sectors, but the strategy also mentions the importance of 'establishing visions of structural and technological changes required to move to a low-carbon, resource efficient, and climate resilient economy by 2050' (European Commission, 2010a, p 14).

As we will see, the policy nexus forming at this time was defined by close alignment and interaction between the EC's policy makers, Member States' interests in resource security, and transnational environmental concerns over marine pollution raised through the United Nations (UN) system.

In 2011, the EC published their *Roadmap to a Resource Efficient Europe* (European Commission, 2011), in which this flagship initiative under the Europe 2020 Strategy was fleshed out by determining a number of medium- and long-term objectives. Here is where the first explicit attention to plastics is found. First, in a section on supporting research and innovation, it is proposed that Horizon 2020 funding should, among other things, promote green chemistry and lower impact, biodegradable plastics. Second, in a section on marine resources, the EC brings attention to the negative environmental impact of plastic waste in the oceans, which needs to be addressed through the Marine Strategy Framework Directive. The *Roadmap* also notes the importance of turning waste into a resource through better recycling and management schemes, in a section that also discusses marine litter.

With growing international attention to marine plastic pollution in the wake of the UN Rio+20 Summit in 2012, the EC became acutely aware that plastic waste, as a distinct category, was not directly covered by existing EU legislation. In direct response to these concerns, the EC published the *Green Paper on a European Strategy on Plastic Waste in the*

Environment in 2013 (European Commission, 2013, p 3). The *Green Paper* points out the overlap with the aims of the 2011 Resource Efficiency Roadmap, in that better waste management through recycling could help reduce greenhouse gas emissions and imports of raw materials and fossil fuels. In this manner, the *Green Paper* very explicitly stands on two legs, addressing marine litter on one hand and resource efficiency on the other, but viewing these as complementary goals, in a way that foreshadows later circular economy initiatives.

With these links forwards and backwards in time, the *Green Paper* represents an important milestone in EU plastic politics. Arriving later in that same year, the 2013 *7th Environment Action Programme (EAP7)* (European Parliament and the Council of the European Union, 2013) encapsulated much of the thinking on plastics under its 'Priority objective 2: To turn the Union into a resource-efficient, green, and competitive low-carbon economy' (p 182). Under this objective, the *EAP7*, among other things, emphasizes the development of a framework to promote sustainable consumption and production, whole life cycle and circular thinking, as well as turning waste into a resource. The guiding vision for the *EAP7* in its entirety also bears clear traces of the prior discussions on plastics and resource efficiency:

> In 2050, we live well, within the planet's ecological limits. Our prosperity and healthy environment stem from an innovative, circular economy where nothing is wasted and where natural resources are managed sustainably, and biodiversity is protected, valued, and restored in ways that enhance our society's resilience. Our low-carbon growth has long been decoupled from resource use, setting the pace for a safe and sustainable global society. (European Parliament and the Council of the European Union, 2013, p 176)

The policy nexus emerging at this early stage of the EU's engagement with plastics was motivated by both internal and external pressures. Internally, to decouple production and growth from resource use and emissions, and externally, to address marine plastic pollution. Connections were being made between these pressures and a range of possible responses: bioplastics, waste management, recycling, and sustainable consumption and production. Whether and how to draw together these initiatives into a common circular economy framework was unclear at the time. But that changed with the publication of the *Zero-Waste Programme*.

From zero-waste Europe to circular Europe

To help solidify the circular economy as an overarching vision for plastics and environmental governance more broadly, the EC published a communication called *Towards a Circular Economy: A Zero Waste Programme for Europe* in 2014 (European Commission, 2014). Earlier mentions of 'circular economy' in EC policy documents were scattered and undetailed. For example, the 2011 *Resource Efficiency Roadmap* mentions the concept only in relation to minerals and metals, and in *EAP7* it is presented as a vision and ambition, but with few indications of what the circular economy entails. Meanwhile, the *Green Paper* and the Europe 2020 Strategy do not mention the concept at all. In contrast, the 2014 *Zero Waste Programme* very clearly explains the concept and reviews it in relation to different areas of EU legislation and policy making. Previously, plastics were considered mainly in the context of marine litter or the bioeconomy, but now plastics are explicitly identified as a challenge for waste management and an opportunity for the recycling industry (European Commission, 2014, p 12).

The 2014 *Zero Waste Programme* was the first of the policy documents to begin heavily emphasizing the business opportunities presented by the circular economy. The *EAP7* valorized the circular economy in terms of how it contributed to sustainable natural resource management, biodiversity, and low-carbon, decoupled growth. In contrast, the *Zero Waste Programme* argues in its first introductory paragraph that the linear economic model is a threat to 'European competitiveness'. A clear shift in relations within the policy nexus can be observed here, with the introduction of business interests, which played a much more marginal role in the earlier stage. As relations within the plastics policy nexus begin to congeal around the circular economy as its overarching framework, this simultaneously stabilizes the central framing of plastics governance as an opportunity for the private plastics, waste, and recycling sectors to capitalize on. This is the narrative that the 2015 *Action Plan for the Circular Economy* develops further: the plan was very clear in its aspiration to 'unlock the growth and jobs potential of the circular economy' (European Commission, 2015).

After its publication, the 2015 *Action Plan* became the guiding document in the EC's activities on the circular economy. Compared to earlier definitions of the circular economy, both the *Zero Waste Programme* and the *Action Plan* present much more business-oriented understandings of the concept. For example, the *Action Plan* states in its first sentence that in the transition to a circular economy, 'the value of products, materials, and resources is maintained in the economy for as long as possible' and 'the circular economy will boost the EU's competitiveness by protecting businesses against scarcity of resources and volatile prices, helping to create new business opportunities and innovative, more efficient ways of producing and consuming' (European Commission, 2015, p 2). The *Zero Waste Programme* and *Action Plan* represent EC's earliest references to the Ellen MacArthur Foundation's definitions of the circular economy. Its business orientation is not surprising given that the founding partners of the Ellen MacArthur Foundation are multinational companies (B&Q, BT, Cisco, Renault, and National Grid) and McKinsey & Co has been a constant co-author on the Foundation's reports (Ellen MacArthur Foundation, 2013, 2015, and 2016). As one indication of how the Foundation influenced the EC's thinking on circular economy, the foreword to the Foundation's 2013 report was written by Janez Potočnik, who was serving as European Commissioner for Environment at the time.

In the 2015 *Action Plan*, as previously mentioned, plastics were first defined as a priority area and key strategic concern for the circular economy (European Commission, 2015, p 13). This was the first time that a specific 'plastics strategy' was called for. In 2017, the EC provided an update on the development of the Plastics Strategy in their *Report on the Implementation of the Circular Economy Action Plan* (European Commission, 2017a). The report states that the purpose of the proposed Plastics Strategy is 'to improve the economics, quality and uptake of plastic recycling and reuse, to reduce plastic leakage in the environment and to decouple plastics production from fossil fuels' (p 13). These three stated goals cohere with the overall narratives emerging in the European plastics policy debate around this time, which have been identified by Palm et al (2022) as (a) resource inefficiency, (b) pollution, and (c) fossil feedstock dependency (to which they add a fourth narrative about toxicity).

The Plastics Strategy emerges

Together with the *Report on the Implementation of the Circular Economy Action Plan*, the EC also published a short roadmap document on the Plastics Strategy, communicating to stakeholders the progress of the ongoing work on the strategy (European Commission, 2017b). The document explains each of the three interrelated issues that were briefly defined in the 2017 report. Regarding point (a) on resource inefficiency, the EC highlights the problem of low recycling and reuse rates of plastics due to weak market incentives for secondary plastic materials and barriers to recyclability from design choices. On point (b), plastic pollution, the main issues are negative impacts on the marine environment, a lacking framework for biodegradable plastics, and low levels of consumer awareness regarding sustainable plastic use. Finally, on point (c), decoupling from fossil fuels, the EC notes the high dependence of plastics on fossil fuel feedstock and energy, a need to assess alternative feedstocks such as recycling, biomass, and CO_2, and a need to innovate in recycling and feedstock diversification.

When comparing the *Roadmap* document to the final published Plastics Strategy (European Commission, 2018a), the three priorities defined in the *Roadmap* have turned into four priority areas. These include improving the economics and quality of plastics recycling, curbing plastic waste and littering, driving innovation and investment towards circular solutions, and harnessing global action. Whereas the overlaps between the first two of these priority areas are clear when compared to the *Roadmap*, the point on global action is a new addition, and the emphasis on decoupling from fossil fuels has been reimagined around the focal point of 'circular solutions'. The types of circular solutions that are envisioned include innovations in sorting and recycling, improved polymer design, fully biodegradable plastics, and new business models (European Commission, 2018a, pp 3–14). Regarding alternative feedstocks, the strategy mentions several obstacles facing bio-based plastics, including their cost and uncertain life cycle environmental impact. The short message is that more research is needed on bio-based plastics, and that the EC is funding much of this through Horizon 2020.

There are clear changes happening to the EU's plastics policy nexus if we compare its form at this later stage around the time of the Plastics Strategy with the earlier form drawing mainly on *Roadmap to a Resource Efficient Europe* and the *Green Paper*. The links between bioplastics and decoupling have been severed, and instead we see new links being formed between recycling, 'circular solutions', and decoupling, which is strongly framed as a business opportunity. Rather than view the diversification of plastic feedstock as a switch to biomass, that role is now being played mainly by recycled plastics:

> Using more recycled plastics can reduce dependence on the extraction of fossil fuels for plastics production and curb CO_2 emissions ... Alternative types of feedstock (e.g. bio-based plastics or plastics produced from carbon dioxide or methane), offering the same functionalities of traditional plastics with potentially lower environmental impacts, are also being developed, but at the moment represent a very small share of the market. Increasing the uptake of alternatives that according to solid evidence are more sustainable can also help decrease our dependency on fossil fuels. (European Commission, 2018a, p 3)

Bioplastics are still understood to play a potential role in decoupling, but before scaling them up, we require 'solid evidence' as to their sustainability impact. Due to these issues, and because conventional plastics recycling is highly central to the understanding of the circular economy that is being advanced in the *Strategy*, bioplastics have receded further and further into the background over time. And as bioplastics receded, so did the components of the policy nexus focused on decoupling plastic production from fossil fuels and greenhouse gas emissions.

Aftermath of the Plastics Strategy

In 2019, the EC adopted a *Final Report on the Implementation of the Circular Economy Action Plan* (European Commission, 2019b), bringing the planned three years of regulatory activities to a close. Summarizing the central role of the Plastics Strategy in guiding their work, the EC brings attention to five areas: (1) industry engagement, (2) recycling targets, (3) economic and environmental synergies, (4) international partnerships, and (5) the Single-Use Plastics Directive. On point one, the report emphasizes how the Strategy spurred industry engagement through a voluntary pledging campaign that would create demand for 10 million tons of recycled plastics in the Single Market by 2025. However, the campaign fell short of its goal by approximately 4 million tonnes (European Commission, 2019b, p 7). In response, the EC has launched a multi-stakeholder platform called the Circular Plastics Alliance to collaboratively explore ways of bridging that gap. On point two, a 55 percent recycling target by 2030 for plastic packaging has been set. On point three, the report mentions the potential environmental and health impacts of microplastic pollution and biodegradable plastics. On point four, the Global Plastics Platform (with the UN Environment Programme) and the International Partnership on Plastic Waste (in the context of the Basel Convention) are highlighted. And finally, on point five, the report summarizes the main provisions of the directive targeting single-use plastics.

The report concludes with an intriguing suggestion:

> Building on the example of the *European Strategy for Plastics in a Circular Economy*, many other sectors with high environmental impact and potential for circularity such as IT, electronics, mobility, the built environment, mining, furniture, food, and drinks or textiles could benefit from a similar holistic approach to become circular. In none of them, the full potential of the EU's Single Market has yet been tapped into. (European Commission, 2019b, p 10)

What the EC is suggesting is that the Plastics Strategy may serve as a blueprint for how to target other industrial sectors with similar 'holistic approaches' to policy in pursuit of circularity. By 'holistic approach', the EC is referring to the fact that the Plastics Strategy is 'the first EU–wide policy framework adopting a material-specific life cycle approach to integrate circular design, use, reuse, and recycling activities into plastics value chains' (European Commission, 2019b, p 6). The holistic approach that was taken to plastics governance is becoming the blueprint for future regulatory packages targeting other sectors. The concept of the circular economy is emerging as the primary overarching industrial policy in general, as was already suggested in the 2017 *Industrial Policy Strategy* (European Commission, 2017c), and further underscored in the 2019 report:

> As suggested in the Reflection Paper *Towards a Sustainable Europe by 2030*, the circular economy should be made a backbone of the EU

industrial strategy, enabling circularity in new areas and sectors, life cycle assessments of products should become a norm and the eco-design framework should be broadened as much as possible. (European Commission, 2019b, p 10)

The rapid ascendance of the circular economy concept in EU industrial policy can be demonstrated by revisiting the 2010 industrial policy strategy, *An Integrated Industrial Policy for the Globalisation Era Putting Competitiveness and Sustainability at Centre Stage* (European Commission, 2010b), that was published in connection with the *Europe 2020 Strategy*. In the 2010 document, the 'circular economy' is not mentioned once. The Plastics Strategy has been instrumental in putting circularity front and center in EU industrial policy and beyond. Not only is the circular economy meant to define future industrial policy, it is also understood as a critical component in the construction of a low-carbon, sustainable economy. The 2019 report makes this clear:

As stated in the strategic long-term vision for a prosperous, modern, competitive, and climate-neutral economy by 2050, the transition towards a circular economy and a climate-neutral economy should be pursued together, based on a strong industrial ambition and reaping the EU businesses' first-mover advantage in these areas. New circular business models, recycling, energy and material efficiency, and new consumption patterns have a significant potential to cut global greenhouse gas emissions. (European Commission, 2019c, p 11)

The significance of the Plastics Strategy can now be fully appreciated. Where the circular economy used to be a fringe concept, it is now defining EU industrial, environmental, and climate policy. The Plastics Strategy has facilitated the ascendance of the circular economy concept by acting as a pilot and premier showcase of circular thinking applied to an entire industrial sector. It has done so in a way that has shifted attention away from the tough challenges of decoupling from fossil fuels towards emphasizing business-friendly opportunities in vertically integrating the sector with recycling. Reflecting back on the original vision of the European circular economy in 2050 as set out in *EAP7*, there has been a significant shift away from the environmental and low-carbon qualities of that definition. Today, there is only scant attention devoted within the EU institutions to the problem of continued growth in plastic production and the carbon impact of that.

All of this contributes to easing investor anxieties about plastic's long future. Current investments in the petrochemical sector are going towards a doubling of virgin plastic production globally from fossil fuels by 2040 (Ellen

MacArthur Foundation, 2016; Bauer and Fontenit, 2021), making it difficult to see how bioplastics or other novel plastic materials might dramatically upset the status quo of the sector. The EC recognizes this situation: 'The present-day chemical industry is geared to processing vast volumes of oil into fuel, with plastics as a side-stream product' (European Commission, 2019c, p 63). More importantly, those same investments will also challenge the market competitiveness of secondary (recycled) plastic materials, which will be forced to compete with abundant, cheap virgin plastic for many decades to come, in the absence of regulatory intervention. On this issue, the report suggests leveling the playing field through direct or indirect subsidies to recycled material (value-added tax reduction for recyclates or Extended Producer Responsibility schemes for virgin material are two options that are mentioned on p 138). The viability of the Plastics Strategy, and the European circular economy for plastics in general, depends on the ability of regulators at various levels (and the willingness of politicians) to counteract the toxic growth of fossil fuel production, which is otherwise investing heavily into maintaining and expanding the status quo of mass consumption and disposability of plastics – a situation that is directly legitimized by rhetorical and legislative commitments to the circular economy (Mah, 2021).

Discussion and conclusion

The story of the circular economy in the EU is essential to understanding how the approach to plastics governance changed over time. From 2010 to 2019, the formation of a policy nexus is observable (Allan, 2019). It initially begins in an unwieldy and loosely coupled form, spanning international obligations to combat marine litter with bioplastics, waste management, low-carbon innovation, and sustainable production/consumption. During the mid-2010s, the circular economy appears as the overarching framework that contains and connects this loosely coupled policy nexus into a tighter package. In the process of drawing tighter connections, however, the circular economy devolved into a less effective strategy for addressing the core problems of plastic pollution. This can be seen in how the meaning and connotations of a circular economy evolve.

In 2011, circularity was mentioned in relation to minerals and metals as a way to ensure European resource security of critical elements. In 2013, the *EAP7* contrasted the resource security angle with a radical, transformative environmental reading, highlighting biodiversity, natural resource management, low-carbon growth, and decoupling. When the Ellen MacArthur Foundation entered the stage in 2014, the priority for the circular economy became business opportunities, economic growth (see Kranke, this volume, for more on economic growth), and job creation – a direction that is cemented in the 2015 *Action Plan*. The influence of the

Ellen MacArthur Foundation – and its corporate sponsors – on the EU's circular economy program is well known to the literature (Leipold, 2021), but new dimensions come to light when we consider the role of the Plastics Strategy in this story.

The Plastics Strategy was instrumental in defining and testing the changing priorities of the EU's circular economy program. As the analysis demonstrated, the Plastics Strategy was seen as a litmus test of how to apply the growth-centric priorities of the refined 2015 *Action Plan* to an entire materials sector, and how to do so in a way that enrolled businesses in voluntary and light-touch regulatory initiatives. The exception to that paradigm might be the 2018 Single-Use Plastics Directive (European Commission, 2018c), which outright banned certain plastic products, but in the grander scheme of things, particularly considering the kinds of items banned, such as straws and cup lids and so on, it is looking more like the exception that proves the rule. This rule is basically a Faustian bargain with the petrochemical sector: in exchange for your commitments to increase the rate and volume of plastic recycling, continued expansion of fossil plastic production or the carbon impact of that will not be questioned.

This is what I mean by normalizing a situation of 'toxic growth' in the circular economy, which also pertains to sectors beyond petrochemicals. The utopian (and fundamentally unattainable) vision of a completely closed materials loop is giving industries *carte blanche* to expand production on the assumption that impacts can be contained within the loop. This is a far cry from the more radically transformative visions of circularity that emphasize reducing and slowing down the throughput of materials, while exploring new social and political implications of a circular economy (Calisto Friant et al, 2021, pp 338–9). In the latest 2020 update to the *Circular Economy Action Plan* (European Commission, 2020), it is evident that the experiences with plastics are informing the policy agendas for the sectors of textiles, electronics, batteries and vehicles, building and construction, as well as food and agriculture. In all cases, the background disposition of the EC is to advance 'regenerative growth' (European Commission, 2020, p 2), which they define as a 'growth model that gives back to the planet more than it takes', while 'keeping its resource consumption within planetary boundaries'. This entails, according to the text, reducing the footprint of European consumption and doubling the use rate of circular materials in the coming decade (European Commission, 2020, p 2).

All 'bad policies' can contain good things within them, and the sentiment here is certainly worth applauding. But there is nothing in the new plan which dares to contest the expansion of fossil fuel infrastructure, and the plan even works with a baseline assumption that plastics consumption will 'double in the coming 20 years' (European Commission, 2020, p 9). A more ambitious policy would directly contest this assumption and be willing to make tough regulatory decisions that impose much higher costs on polluters, rather than letting them off the hook with naïve win-win propositions. It would also question the rates of consumption and material use much more, asking not only for circularity, but also for reductions. When the planetary boundary on novel entities and plastic pollution is already overshot (Persson et al, 2022), 'good policies' must directly address the problem of toxic growth. In general, the lessons to take from the EU plastics story are to appreciate the relational configuration of policy nexuses, and how reconfigurations can lead to 'cognitive capture' of governance frameworks, as seems to be the case in the circular economy. Such cognitive capture can play out over the longer term, meaning we must also attend to the relational histories of policy outcomes, to ensure that good policies do not turn bad.

References

Allan, B.B. (2019) 'Paradigm and nexus: neoclassical economics and the growth imperative in the World Bank, 1948–2000', *Review of International Political Economy*, 26(1): 183–206.

Bauer, F. and Fontenit, G. (2021) 'Plastic dinosaurs – digging deep into the accelerating carbon lock-in of plastics', *Energy Policy*, 156: 112418.

Blomsma, F. and Brennan, G. (2017) 'The emergence of circular economy: a new framing around prolonging resource productivity', *Journal of Industrial Ecology*, 21(3): 603–14.

Calisto Friant, M., Vermeulen, W.J.V., and Salomone, R. (2021) 'Analysing European Union circular economy policies: words versus actions', *Sustainable Production and Consumption*, 27: 337–53.

Ellen MacArthur Foundation (2013) 'Towards the circular economy: economic and business rationale for an accelerated transition' [online]. Available from: https://www.ellenmacarthurfoundation.org/downloads/publications/Ellen-MacArthur-Foundation-Towards-the-Circular-Economy-vol.1.pdf.

Ellen MacArthur Foundation (2015) 'Growth within: a circular economy vision for a competitive Europe' [online], Available from: https://www.ellenmacarthurfoundation.org/assets/downloads/publications/EllenMacArthurFoundation_Growth-Within_July15.pdf.

Ellen MacArthur Foundation (2016) 'The new plastics economy: rethinking the future of plastics' [online], Available from: https://www.ellenmacarthurfoundation.org/assets/downloads/The-New-Plastics-Economy-Rethinking-the-Future-of-Plastics.pdf [Accessed 11 April 2019].

European Commission (2010a) *Europe 2020: A Strategy for Smart, Sustainable and Inclusive Growth* [online], Available from: https://eur-lex.europa.eu/legal-content/EN/TXT/?qid=1554895518427&uri=CELEX:52010DC2020.

European Commission (2010b) *An Integrated Industrial Policy for the Globalisation Era Putting Competitiveness and Sustainability at Centre Stage* [online], Available from: https://eur-lex.europa.eu/legal-content/EN/TXT/?qid=1554896031040&uri=CELEX:52010DC0614.

European Commission (2011) *Roadmap to a Resource Efficient Europe* [online], Available from: https://eur-lex.europa.eu/legal-content/EN/TXT/?qid=1554895723920&uri=CELEX:52011DC0571.

European Commission (2013) *Green Paper on a European Strategy on Plastic Waste in the Environment* [online], Available from: https://eur-lex.europa.eu/legal-content/EN/TXT/?uri=celex%3A52013DC0123.

European Commission (2014) *Towards a Circular Economy: A Zero Waste Programme for Europe* [online], Available from: https://eur-lex.europa.eu/legal-content/EN/TXT/?uri=celex%3A52014DC0398.

European Commission (2015) *Closing the Loop – An EU Action Plan for the Circular Economy* [online], Available from: https://eur-lex.europa.eu/legal-content/en/TXT/?uri=CELEX%3A52015DC0614.

European Commission (2017a) *Report on the Implementation of the Circular Economy Action Plan* [online], Available from: https://eur-lex.europa.eu/legal-content/EN/TXT/?qid=1554910065045&uri=CELEX:52017DC0033.

European Commission (2017b) *Roadmap: Strategy on Plastics in a Circular Economy* [online], Available from: http://ec.europa.eu/smart-regulation/roadmaps/docs/plan_2016_39_plastic_strategy_en.pdf.

European Commission (2017c) *Investing in a Smart, Innovative and Sustainable Industry. A Renewed EU Industrial Policy Strategy* [online], Available from: https://eur-lex.europa.eu/legal-content/en/TXT/?uri=CELEX%3A52017DC0479.

European Commission (2018a) *A European Strategy for Plastics in a Circular Economy* [online], Available from: https://eur-lex.europa.eu/legal-content/EN/TXT/?qid=1516265440535&uri=COM:2018:28:FIN.

European Commission (2018b) 'Plastic waste: a European strategy to protect the planet, defend our citizens and empower our industries', Press Release [online], Available from: http://europa.eu/rapid/press-release_IP-18-5_en.htm.

European Commission (2018c) *Proposal for a Directive of the European Parliament and of the Council on the Reduction of the Impact of Certain Plastic Products on the Environment* [online], Available from: https://eur-lex.europa.eu/legal-content/EN/TXT/?qid=1554895264204&uri=CELEX:52018PC0340.

European Commission (2019a) *The European Green Deal* [online], Available from: https://eur-lex.europa.eu/legal-content/EN/TXT/?qid=1576150542719&uri=COM%3A2019%3A640%3AFIN.

European Commission (2019b) *Report on the Implementation of the Circular Economy Action Plan* [online], Available from: https://eur-lex.europa.eu/legal-content/EN/TXT/?qid=1551871195772&uri=CELEX:52019DC0190.

European Commission (2019c) *A Circular Economy for Plastics: Insights from Research and Innovation to Inform Policy and Funding Decisions* [online], Available from: https://publications.europa.eu/en/publication-detail/-/publication/33251cf9-3b0b-11e9-8d04-01aa75ed71a1/language-en/format-PDF.

European Commission (2020) *A New Circular Economy Action Plan for a Cleaner and More Competitive Europe* [online], Available from: https://eur-lex.europa.eu/legal-content/EN/TXT/?qid=1583933814386&uri=COM:2020:98:FIN.

European Parliament and the Council of the European Union (2013) 'Decision No 1386/2013/EU of the European Parliament and of the Council of 20 November 2013 on a General Union Environment Action Programme to 2020 "Living well, within the limits of our planet"' [online], Available from: https://eur-lex.europa.eu/legal-content/EN/TXT/?uri=celex%3A32013D1386.

Hall, P.A. (1993) 'Policy paradigms, social learning, and the state: the case of economic policymaking in Britain', *Comparative Politics*, 25(3): 275–96.

Hobson, K. (2016) 'Closing the loop or squaring the circle? Locating generative spaces for the circular economy', *Progress in Human Geography*, 40(1): 88–104.

Leipold, S. (2021) 'Transforming ecological modernization "from within" or perpetuating it? The circular economy as EU environmental policy narrative', *Environmental Politics*, 30(6): 1045–67.

Mah, A. (2021) 'Future-proofing capitalism: the paradox of the circular economy for plastics', *Global Environmental Politics*, 21(2): 121–42.

Palm, E., Hasselbalch, J., Holmberg, K., and Nielsen, T.D. (2022) 'Narrating plastics governance: policy narratives in the European plastics strategy', *Environmental Politics*, 31(3): 365–85.

Persson, L., Carney Almroth, B.M., Collins, C.D., Cornell, S., de Wit, C.A., Diamond, M.L. et al (2022) 'Outside the safe operating space of the planetary boundary for novel entities', *Environmental Science and Technology*, 56(3): 1510–521.

Tilsted, J.P., Bauer, F., Deere Birkbeck, C., Skovgaard, J., and Rootzén, J. (2023) 'Ending fossil-based growth: confronting the political economy of petrochemical plastics', *One Earth*, 6(6): 607–19.

9

The environment, megacity growth, and ineffective policy: housing policy reform in Ontario

Mark Winfield and Madison Stirling

Introduction

The following chapter examines the package of land-use and planning reforms adopted by the Canadian Province of Ontario in the fall of 2022 as an example of bad or undesirable public policy. Major new legislation and policies were advanced by the province at that time in response to a housing affordability crisis. These measures included Bill 23, *The More Homes Built Faster Act, 2022* (Ontario, 2022a) and the removal of lands from the Greater Toronto Area (GTA) Greenbelt. These steps significantly weakened protections for agricultural and natural heritage lands, public participation in the planning process, and the capacity of local governments to address the impacts of climate change, with doubtful impacts on housing affordability.

For the purposes of this volume, 'bad' policy is defined as not merely being ineffective or inefficient in achieving its stated goals, but also making the problems the policy is intended to address worse, and carrying significant collateral negative externalities. We believe that the Government of Ontario's fall 2022 housing strategy meets these criteria for 'bad' policy.

Background on planning and development in Ontario

The Province of Ontario has a population of 14 million, encompasses an area of over 1 million square km, and has an annual gross domestic product of over US$800 billion per year. The province's population, area, and economy approximates that of the larger US states and is greater than most member states of the European Union. A large portion (70 percent) of Ontario's population (9.7 million) is concentrated in the Greater Toronto Region (Statistics Canada, 2021). As shown in Figure 9.1, the area encapsulates the City of Toronto, extending through what is often referred to as the Greater Golden Horseshoe region, ranging from Peterborough County in

Figure 9.1: Map of the Greater Golden Horseshoe planning area and greenbelt

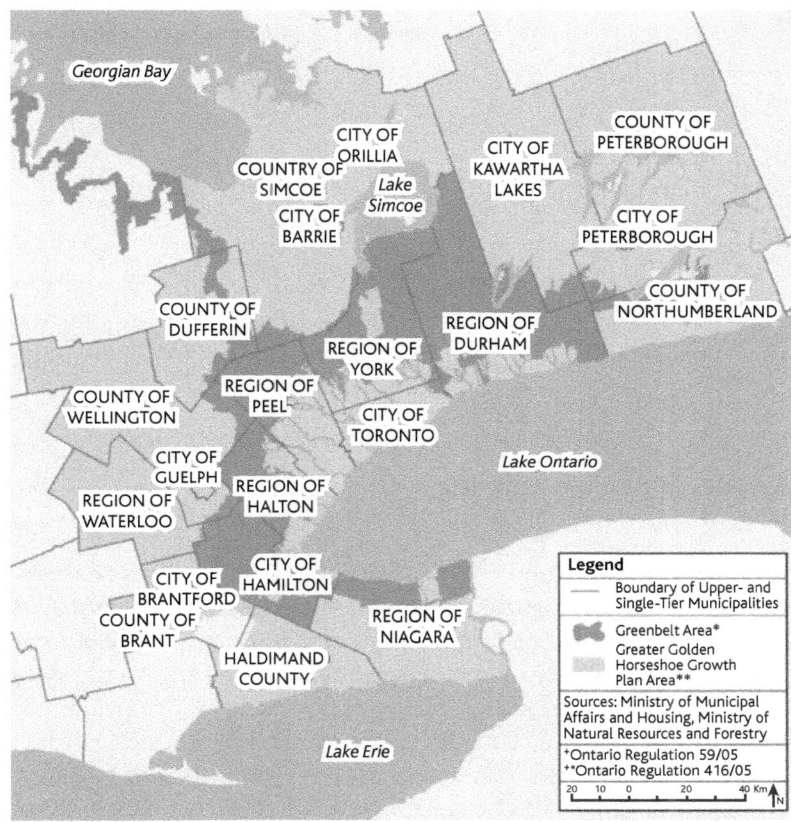

Source: Ontario Ministry of Municipal Affairs and Housing (MMAH) (2020). © King's Printer for Ontario, 2020. Reproduced with permission.

the east, through the western end of Lake Ontario, including the Waterloo Region. The region has long been a center for economic and population growth for the province and Canada as a whole (Toronto Global, 2023). The region's population and size places it in the category of a global scale urban agglomeration or 'megacity' (United Nations, 2019).

Over the past five decades the region's economy has transitioned significantly from a manufacturing base to one increasingly centered on service and knowledge-based activities (Blais and Neptis, 2018). In doing so, the region and province have followed a very different economic and demographic trajectory relative to urban areas in neighboring states around the Great Lakes. Many of these jurisdictions have seen significant declines in economic activity and population and are often referred to as a 'rust belt' (Gold et al, 2018; Hillson and Winfield, 2024).

Figure 9.2: Prime rate and Bank of Canada overnight rate (1935–2023)

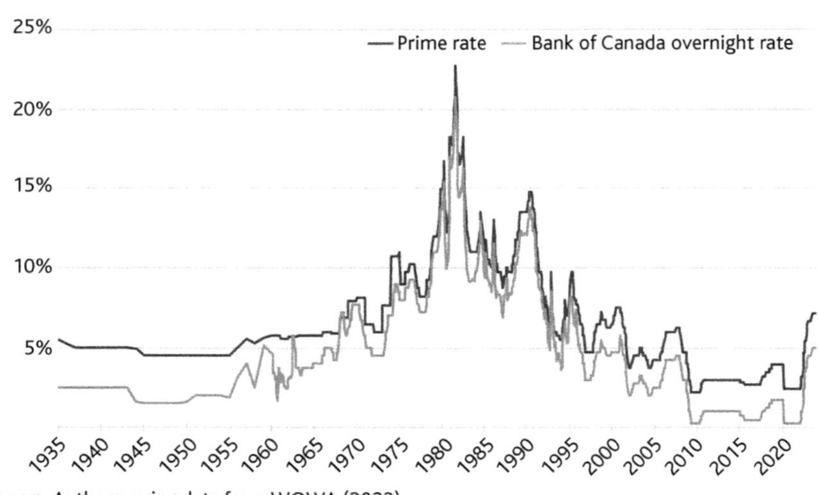

Source: Authors, using data from WOWA (2023)

The Greater Toronto region offers a case study of the tensions between the need to accommodate population growth within a globalizing urban area, as well as the protection of prime agricultural and natural heritage lands, development of responses to climate change, and maintenance of the livability and affordability of urban spaces. The region is the largest concentration of prime agricultural lands in Canada (Canada Land Inventory Class 1, 2, and 3) and specialty (that is, fruit and vegetable) croplands (Neptis Foundation, 2021, Figure 9.2). The GTA also contains ecological and hydrological features of internationally recognized importance, notably the Niagara Escarpment and the Oak Ridges Moraine, and biologically diverse Carolinian Zone forests (TRCA, 2023). All are threatened by increasing pressures for urban expansion in the region.

Municipal and regional governments have no status under Canada's constitution. Rather, the provincial legislatures are given exclusive jurisdiction over 'municipal institutions' (s.92(8)), 'property and civil rights' (that is, private land use) (s.92(13)), 'public lands' (s.92(5), s.109), and 'matters of a local or private nature' (s.92(16)). In practice, authority over urban land-use planning is delegated by provinces to local governments, but is ultimately subjected to provincial control. Municipalities and their powers and governance structures are often referred to as 'creatures of the provinces' in relation to which they have 'absolute and unfettered legal power to do with them (municipalities) as it (they) will(s)' (SCC, 2021). Direct federal authority over land use, outside of the Territorial North (that is, the Yukon and Northwest Territories and Nunavut) is limited to federal lands, such as national parks, defense installations, harbors, and airports.

Indigenous Peoples have been present in the region for many thousands of years. The processes of colonial occupation, settlement, and treaty making remain points of significant legal and political controversy. Provincial actions that affect Treaty or other rights of Indigenous Peoples may be subject to constitutional constraints, but the question has yet to manifest itself in a direct legal or constitutional conflict in relation to land use planning in the GTA region (ULI, 2020).

The efforts of successive provincial governments to manage urban growth pressures in the region led to the adoption of specific plans for the Niagara Escarpment (1985) and Oak Ridges Moraine (2002) areas. These initiatives culminated in 2005–06 through a series of major reforms to the land-use planning process for the region and province more generally. These included: the adoption of a plan and legislation to protect an 800,000 hectare Greenbelt of rural and agricultural lands in the region that would be off-limits to urban development; a regional Growth Plan intended to shape the regional patterns and form of urban development; and more general changes to the province's *Planning Act* and its accompanying Provincial Policy Statement (PPS), which are intended to regulate planning decisions made by local governments (Winfield, 2012, 158–65; Sandberg et al, 2013). The Growth Plan and PPS placed a strong emphasis on the intensification of development in existing urban areas over new greenfield development on prime agricultural or ecologically sensitive lands. The Growth Plan and PPS also emphasized the development of 'complete communities' (MMAH, 2020, p 67) which were defined as communities which provide: a variety of housing options, including those for low-income households; a mix of land uses to minimize the need for automobile travel; adequate infrastructures of all types; and which give serious attention to the livability and form of urban development. Accompanying multi-billion-dollar strategies were developed for public transit in the region, and a new agency – Metrolinx – was established to coordinate those efforts (Winfield, 2012, pp 158–63; Macdonald, Monstadt, and Friendly, 2021). The Growth Plan, in particular, garnered international acclaim for its efforts to manage the intensive growth pressures in the region (Ontario, 2007).

The emergence of the GTA housing 'crisis'

Although the province's efforts at growth management in the GTA were initially regarded as effective, a convergence of factors, starting with the global financial crisis of 2008, began to affect the region's housing market significantly. As shown in Figure 9.2, government efforts to respond to the financial crisis led to an extended period of historically low interest rates, a pattern dramatically reinforced by efforts to recover from the 2020–23 COVID-19 crisis.

Low interest rates coupled with a rising demand for housing led to rapid increases in housing prices, particularly for the middle- and upper-priced segments of the housing market are clear in the TRREB MLS Average Price chart of the Toronto Regional Real Estate Board (see TRREB, 2023, p 5). These developments encouraged speculative investment in the housing sector by both domestic and international buyers, further reinforcing the upwards trends in demand and prices (Gibson, 2021; Younglai, 2023). In Canada these trends were reinforced by the lack of capital gains taxes on sales of primary residences and favorable tax treatment of investment properties.

These demand factors were further strengthened by the federal government's post-2015 decision to double Canada's annual immigration targets, with a significant portion of the new arrivals settling in the GTA (Ontario, 2023). There have also been major increases in arrivals of temporary foreign workers and international students (Al Mallees, 2023). Net population growth in the region has been almost entirely attributable to immigration for the past two decades. Concerns were raised by federal officials over the impact of the increasing immigration rates on housing markets (Al Massees, 2024).

Housing affordability has been a long-standing crisis among lower-income households in the region, particularly across rental markets (Fung et al, 2020). The federal and provincial governments withdrew almost completely from the direct provision or financing of affordable rental housing in the 1980s and 1990s. This was despite the consideration that from the 1970s onwards, private capital was increasingly being invested into more lucrative condominium developments in lieu of dedicated rental housing. The province offloaded its publicly owned rental housing stocks to local governments following the 1995 provincial election and ended rent controls on new units in 2018. Federal tax rules around Real Estate Income Trusts (REITs) strongly reinforced the ongoing 'financialization' of rental housing as an asset held by large investors for the purpose of maximizing income and return on investment (August, 2021).

The weakening of rent controls by successive governments from 1995 onwards provided strong incentives to remove existing tenants to facilitate the raising of rents on units. A variety of pretenses, including the need for renovations (also referred to as reno-victions), have been employed for this purpose (Webber and Zigman, 2023). Strong investor interest in condominium development has also led to significant displacements of existing affordable rental housing to make way for new, largely investor-owned projects (also referred to as demo-victions), particularly in urban areas with good public transit connections (Harrison, 2023). The trend towards short-term Airbnb type rentals has put additional pressures on rental housing availability (Bartlett and Norman, 2023), as has the pricing-out of would-be middle-income buyers from the housing market, compelling them to seek rental housing.

All of these factors converged in the early 2020s into what was termed a housing crisis in the GTA region, particularly as economic activity increased in the aftermath of the COVID-19 pandemic (Üçoğlu et al, 2021). Extended periods of low interest rates were a global phenomenon, but the Toronto and Vancouver areas were particularly heavily affected in terms of real estate price increases and price growth in relation to income. Although the impacts on middle income buyers drew the greatest media attention, the challenges were most acute in terms of the availability of affordable rental housing, where demand was growing substantially faster than ownership households.

The fall 2022 housing 'package'

The Government of Ontario's Premier Doug Ford was first elected in June 2018, on the basis of a relatively thin, but clearly populist, electoral platform focused on reducing costs, particularly electricity costs, for consumers, framed as their 'respect for taxpayers', and facilitating economic development, deeming Ontario 'open for business' (Hillson and Winfield, 2024). The Progressive Conservative (PC) Party's close relationship to the land development industry was noted from the outset, as well as their disregard for the environment and climate change (Winfield, 2019).

During its first (2018–22) term in office, the government was repeatedly compelled to retreat on efforts to open the GTA Greenbelt to urban development, as it faced significant municipal and public opposition (Callan and D'Mello, 2023). Despite the backlash, provincial planning rules were more generally rewritten extensively in favor of development interests (Morgan, 2023). The use of Ministerial Zoning Orders (MZOs) and similar instruments, which allow the province to override municipal planning decisions, became commonplace, almost exclusively in response to development industry demands (Javed and Buist, 2021; Hristova, 2022; Gray, 2023).

Conservation Authorities, provincially mandated watershed-based agencies whose territories typically encompass multiple municipalities, found their roles within the planning process significantly constrained by the province, even in relation to areas subject to flooding or other hazards (TRCA, 2020). The authorities originated in the immediate post–Second World War era. They had become important actors in the land–use planning process across Ontario, playing key roles in the prevention of flooding, controlling development on hazardous lands, protecting the integrity of hydrological systems and biological conservation at the watershed scale, including the operation of parks and protected areas.

Following the government's retention of its majority in the provincial Legislature through the June 2022 election, it deepened its emphasis on accelerating private sector investments in housing by deregulating the development industry. A housing *affordability* crisis was subsequently framed as a crisis of housing *supply*, which would be resolved if the pace of construction could be increased. The inadequate pace of construction was attributed to the bureaucratic nature of municipal planning processes and timelines (that is, red tape). The government's approach was made clear in Ministry of Municipal Affairs and Housing's *Housing Supply Action Plan*, which stated that:

> We inherited a confusing and broken *housing development system* that is impossible for people and home builders to navigate and *this has led to a housing shortage* and *skyrocketing housing prices and rents*. The people of Ontario deserve better. We cannot fix the housing shortage on our own, but we can *cut red tape* to make it *easier to build new housing* for people to rent or own. We will give the people of Ontario more choice and *make housing more affordable*. (MMAH, 2019, p 17, emphasis in original)

Environmental and planning laws and policies, municipal implementation of these regulations and fees, and community-based critics of new development, labeled generically as NIMBYs (Not in My Backyard) regardless of income and context, were framed as the source of 'the bureaucratic costs and red tape that are delaying construction and pushing home prices even higher' (Ontario, 2022a). Municipalities and communities were portrayed as the villains behind the crisis and developers as the heroic victims who were trying to respond, but were weighed down by red tape. All of this fit well with the Ford government's 'market populist' orientation (Hillson and Winfield, 2024) – that increasing the freedom of action for the development industry would serve the general desire of 'the people' for more affordable housing.

The government's fall 2022 housing plan consisted of several major components. These included Bill 23, the *More Homes Built Faster Act*; the removal of 3,000 hectares from the GTA Greenbelt, established in 2006, to permit housing development; and an arbitrary series of urban boundary expansions covering thousands of hectares of agricultural lands, over the objections of the affected municipalities. Further legislation (Bills 3 (*The Strong Mayors, Building Homes Act, 2022*) and 39 (*The Better Municipal Governance Act, 2022*)) was adopted to give mayors extraordinary powers when implementing provincial policies, including the ability to pass measures with the support of only one third of council members.

A Toronto law firm, trying to explain the changes contained in Bill 23, summarized the situation by suggesting their readers 'forget everything you thought you knew about planning in Ontario' (Barnett et al, 2022).

The legislation further limited the authority of the province's Conservation Authorities in the planning process, proposed to remove upper tier (that is, regional or county governments, whose roles include the provision of major infrastructure) from certain types of planning approvals, and curtailed the ability of municipalities to impose development changes on new developments to finance the required infrastructures. Additionally, it provided authority to remove requirements that rental units lost or demolished to facilitate new development be replaced, reduced the amount of land at new development sites that had to be dedicated to parkland, and weakened the rules around built heritage conservation. The natural heritage conservation provisions within the planning process were significantly constrained as well. The 2006 Growth Plan for the region was to be repealed.

The provisions of Bill 23 had their roots in the February 2022 report of the Housing Affordability Task Force Report established by the province. The Task Force was mandated to provide 'actionable, concrete solutions to help Ontarians' within a 2-month time frame (Housing Affordability Task Force, 2022, p 3). Nine people were selected to be on this task force: Lalit Aggarwal, president of a real estate development company; David Amborski, urban planner and university professor; Andrew Garrett, real estate executive; Tim Hudak, CEO of the Ontario Real Estate Association; Jake Lawrence, CEO of Global Banking and Markets; Julie Di Lorenzo, operator of a real estate development company; Justin Marchand, CEO of Ontario Aboriginal Housing Services; Ene Underwood, CEO of Habitat for Humanity; and Dave Wilkes, president and CEO of BILD (Housing Affordability Task Force Report, 2022, pp 27–8). The overpowering presence of real estate interests and a tokenization of other groups (one Indigenous representative, one planner, two female representatives vs. six private industry CEOs and real estate executives) was noteworthy.

The task force's report concluded that 'Canada has the lowest amount of housing per population of any G7 country' (2022, p 7), and that Ontario was 1.2 million homes short of that average. The answer to solving the supply crisis was therefore to build *more* than the 1.2 million homes required to meet the average G7 home-population ratio. Instead, the province needed to build 1.5 million homes over the next decade to meet the future demands of a growing population.

In pursuit of this goal, the task force report made 55 high-level recommended actions across six themes for the Ontario government to pursue in increasing the housing supply. The first theme was to create the 'bold goal of adding 1.5 million homes over the next 10 years' (p 4). The second focused on increasing density and land-use efficiency across the province, although the government had actually reduced the Growth Plan density requirements for new developments at the urban periphery.

The third theme was to weaken urban design rules and standardize design guidelines across all municipalities and neighborhoods. The fourth sought to 'depoliticize the process and cut red tape' by limiting public consultation in the planning process, restricting, and overriding municipal decision-making processes, as well as preventing the 'abuse of the heritage process' (p 5). The fifth theme was to limit public appeals to the Ontario Land Tribunal in order to accelerate development. The final element centered on rewarding municipalities who complied with the recommendations with provincial funding, and decreasing funding for those who did not.

All 55 recommendations made by the task force were accepted by the government, along with 19 additional recommendations in the appendix of the report. The recommendations provided the foundations for Bill 23 (Ontario, 2023b).

The task force's recommendations were criticized as representing a 'wish list for developers' (Winfield, 2023) and for having been produced without adequate levels of consultation (Pothen, 2022). Negative comments on the task force's approach, recommendations, and the resulting legislation came from municipal governments (AMO, 2022; City of Toronto, 2022; County of Brant, 2022), conservation authorities (Conservation Ontario, 2022), civil society organizations (Ontario Public Health Association, 2022; Canadian Environmental Law Association, 2022) and the Indigenous Chiefs of Ontario (2022). The task force's conclusions were challenged as having greatly overestimated the region's actual future housing needs (Doucet, 2022; Winfield and Castrilli, 2023), and for failing to provide any analyses of the different types of housing that were required, particularly for lower-income households (ALO, 2023).

The second major component of the Housing Supply Action Plan, the removal of lands from the Greenbelt and the imposition of involuntary urban boundary expansions, proved to have an even weaker evidentiary base than Bill 23. The Housing Affordability Task Force itself had acknowledged that an adequate supply of land was already designated for urban development to meet the 1.5 million homes target (Housing Affordability Task Force, 2022), noting that: 'a shortage of land isn't the cause of the problem, land is available both inside the existing built-up areas and on undeveloped land outside greenbelts' (p 10).

Subsequent analyses confirmed that adequate land was designated for development to support over 2 million housing units in the region (Eby, 2023, p 3). Investigations by the province's Auditor General and Integrity Commissioner around the Greenbelt removals concluded that the process by which the lands had been identified for removal had been 'improper' and 'madcap' (Integrity Commissioner, 2023, p 142) and 'biased' in favor of certain well-connected development interests (Ontario, 2023b, p 32).

Evaluation: does the provincial government's housing strategy qualify as 'ineffective' or even 'bad' policy?

The Ford government's approach to the housing issue is potentially a very strong candidate not merely for 'ineffective' policy but for 'bad' or 'undesirable' policy. The government's housing supply plan was grounded on weak or non-existent evidentiary bases for action. The land supply limitation and red tape/NIMBY rationales for the government's strategy have been found to be unsupported by evidence by a variety of authoritative sources, including the province's Auditor General (2023, p 31), regional planning commissioners (RPCO, 2023), local governments (Toronto, 2022), as well as professional and academic observers (Doucet, 2022; Fallis, 2022; Eby, 2023). At the same time, the government offered little or no meaningful analysis of the actual drivers of the housing crisis, which might have informed more effective policy responses.

Instead, the government's responses seemed grounded, at best, in either a blindness to or deeply naïve understanding of the nature and motives of the private development industry, and their likely behavior if given free reign through the types of policy measures embodied in Bill 23 and other elements of the government's housing supply package (Winfield, 2022a). Development interests represent capital, and can reasonably be expected to seek to maximize their profits and return on investment, rather than ensuring affordability in the housing supply. Indeed, they may be willing to game the development system to achieve these ends. Properties may be purchased with the intention of obtaining planning approvals for redevelopment and then 'flipping' them onwards to new buyers for substantial profit, or landowners may hold properties approved for housing development without building, in anticipation of future increases in their value (Crawley, 2023; Javed, 2023). These types of behavior can be especially prevalent where the planning rules are very permissive.

Other, less generous, interpretations would suggest that the government's housing strategy was the product of a long-term strategic communications and lobbying agenda designed to promote the interests of well-connected developers under the guise of responding to the housing crisis (Doyle, 2023). The Ford government's responsiveness to certain types of interests, including the building and land development sector, throughout its first term in office, had been noted by numerous observers (Winfield, 2019; Warnica and Bailey, 2021). The theme was central to the reports of the Auditor General (2023) and Integrity Commissioner (2023) on the Greenbelt episode as well.

More broadly, the government's disregard for long-established democratic norms in local government and in the municipal–provincial relationship was well known. The pattern began to emerge early on in the government's first term, with the involuntary restructuring of the City of Toronto's council from 44 to 25 members in the midst of the fall 2018 municipal election campaign (Mahoney, 2019). The pattern continued with the increasing marginalization, and in many cases, direct provincial ministerial overrides of the decisions of local governments in the planning process through MZOs and other instruments (Javed and Buist, 2021). In some cases, these overrides had removed municipal requirements that portions of new developments be affordable to lower-income households (Gray, 2023).

All of these elements: a willful ignorance of the actual drivers of the housing crisis; a disregard for evidence; a willingness to provide exceptional levels of access and responsiveness to certain well-connected development-oriented interests; and a disregard for democratic norms in local government, public participation and the municipal–provincial relationship, would seem to provide a perfect storm of conditions for making bad policy.

In that context, the following section considers whether the Ontario government's Fall 2022 housing plan qualifies as 'bad' policy as defined for the purposes of this volume. To qualify as bad policy, a strategy must not only be ineffective in addressing the problem to which it was intended to respond; it must also have the potential to make the problem worse; and carry with it the potential for substantial collateral damage or negative externalities as well.

Effectiveness/ineffectiveness

The Ford government's fall 2022 housing strategy was grounded in the assumption that the housing *affordability* crisis was rooted in a housing *supply* crisis. Increasing the housing supply would eventually result in lower housing prices. Removing 'red tape' from the housing approval and development process should accelerate housing construction and solve the problem.

The problem with this 'trickle down' (Chappel and Burda, 2022) strategy to address housing affordability was that it failed to recognize the complex and variegated range of factors driving the housing issue. These have included an extended period of historically low interest rates, the increasing financialization of housing, and accelerating population growth, as well as capacity and supply chain limits in the construction sector (Kennedy, 2019).

Despite the government's claims that red tape was stifling development, the pace of construction was already at a point where the supply of dwellings was increasing faster than population growth (Fallis, 2022), and as noted earlier, adequate supplies of land and housing planning approvals were already in place or in process (RPCO, 2023). But contrary to conventional expectations, housing prices continued to rise.

The problem was less about the volume of construction and more about the nature and location of what was being built (Morgan, 2023). In the deregulated space created by the Ford government's policies, development in urban areas focused on single-use, high-rise condominium development, particularly around certain urban transit hubs, with more than 50 percent of units bought by investors (Younglai, 2023), and often displacing existing rental housing in the process (that is, gentrification). Low-density sprawl continued to define the urban periphery (Griffin, 2022). These directions reflected the impact of the increasing financialization (Belec, 2022) of housing as an investment vehicle. Multi-property-owning investors came to constitute the largest (> 25 percent) category of homebuyers in the province (Merali, 2021).

The province's strategy failed to respond to these drivers of rising costs in the housing market. Moreover, the planning environment created by the province invited widespread speculation by developers, particularly the purchase of properties in anticipation of being able to obtain relatively easy approvals for development or redevelopment.

The most effective measures in reducing housing prices appear to have been the Bank of Canada's increases in interest rates (Figure 9.2), which reduced the incentives for borrowing to bid up prices and for speculative investments. Taxes on non-resident purchasers imposed by the province (Ontario, 2022) and restrictions on non-resident buyers imposed by the federal government through its 2022 budget (CMHC, 2023), may have further reduced speculative activities of non-resident investors. Substantial declines in house prices in the region have occurred relative to the spring 2022 peak (TRREB, 2023) particularly in middle and upper segments of the market, correlating closely with the Bank's interest rate increases. No effective measures have been taken to address affordability for lower-income households, particularly renters.

Given that the province's housing strategy was based on a fundamental misdiagnosis of the problem, and that the reductions in housing prices which have occurred in some segments of the market can be attributed to other factors, it can be judged that the province's fall 2022 housing supply 'package' was ineffective in addressing the problem of housing affordability in the GTA. In fact, the province itself was compelled to reverse key elements of its housing initiatives, notably the Greenbelt withdrawals and involuntary urban boundary expansions, admitting that they were unnecessary to meet housing needs (CBC News, 2023). The province was also compelled to replace the infrastructure funding lost to municipalities through the Bill 23 restrictions on development charges through general provincial revenues (The Canadian Press, 2022; Ontario, 2023a).

Does the policy make the problem worse?

In addition to being ineffective at reducing housing costs, the government's approach to the housing crisis had the potential to make the problem worse.

As noted earlier, the government's 'anything you ask for' approach to planning, where development interests with the right access and connections were involved, strengthened the speculative dynamics of the land development industry, driving costs and prices higher (Winfield, 2022b).

Bill 23 had further negative effects. The legislation introduced a degree of chaos into the planning process by legislating fundamental changes to the land-use planning framework across the province. Noteworthy among these changes is the removal of upper tier municipalities from certain types of approval processes, with no consultation and no clear explanation of how the new processes would work in practice (Jeffords, 2022). Similarly, the curtailment of the ability of municipalities to impose development charges to pay for the infrastructures needed to support new development undercut municipal capacity to support that development (AMO, 2022; Warren et al, 2023).

With respect to rental housing, Bill 23's weakening of the ability of municipalities to require replacements of rental housing units displaced by new development is likely to accelerate the tenant demo-/reno-viction phenomena in areas subject to high development pressures. This will further reduce the existing stock of affordable rental housing in the region.

Taken as a whole, the government's fall 2023 housing supply plan can be said to not only have been ineffective in addressing the problem it was supposed to address – the shortage of housing and specifically of affordable housing – it can also be seen to have made important aspects of the problem worse. This is particularly true with respect to the encouragement of speculative activity in the housing market, and the availability of affordable rental housing.

Substantial negative externalities/collateral damage

Beyond failing to address, and in some cases exacerbating, the key drivers of upwards price pressures in the housing market and having negative effects on the availability of affordable rental housing, the government's housing reform package carried with it a range of wider adverse effects, particularly with respect to the environment, and democratic norms in local government.

These impacts are most pronounced with respect to the role of the province's Conservation Authorities. Bill 23 significantly curtailed their capacity and authority to intervene in planning matters, particularly in relation to watershed management. This has been seen to increase the risk of development being approved in areas subject to flooding and other hazards. The legislation also weakened the authorities' capacity to identify and protect natural heritage features and lands important to biological conservation, such as the habitat of endangered species, and to deal with the impacts of a changing climate more broadly (Syed, 2023).

Other aspects of the housing supply package significantly altered the province's policies around wetlands and other ecologically significant features. The concept of wetland complexes (that is, a network of wetlands and minor waterways whose connectivity is important to their hydrological and ecological functions) was eliminated, and rules were introduced that allow for the destruction and then later replacement of wetlands and other ecologically important features, including habitats of endangered species, of doubtful equivalent ecological value (Hevenor, 2022).

More directly, the Greenbelt removals and involuntary urban boundary expansions contained in the government's housing plan would have made prime agricultural lands available for urban development, even though the lands were widely regarded as unnecessary to meet the government's housing goals (McClaren, 2022). Consistent with the House Affordability Task Force's recommendations, the rules around built heritage (that is, buildings and sites of historical, architectural or cultural importance) were also significantly weakened, putting these buildings and sites at risk in the face of development pressures (Latif, 2023).

The government's approach to the housing affordability problem also had negative effects on norms of local democratic governance. These impacts are most prominently visible with respect to the 'strong' mayor powers contained in Bills 3 and 39, allowing not only for the veto of majority decisions of municipal councils, but also the adoption of measures with the support of less than majorities of council members (Taylor and Horak, 2022). Significant steps were also taken to limit opportunities for public participation in the planning process, and to raise major barriers to the participation of individuals and community organizations in the Ontario Land Tribunal (OLT) appeal process (Nadarajah and Lindgren, 2021).

In summary, the government's fall 2023 housing plan failed to improve the housing affordability situation in the province, and likely made several aspects of the problem worse. Perhaps most notably, the plan also carried with it very substantial indirect negative effects, particularly with respect to ecological conservation, watershed management and flood prevention, protection of prime agricultural lands, climate change adaptation, built heritage conservation, and long-established democratic norms in local governance.

Conclusion

For the purposes of this volume, to qualify as 'bad' as opposed to merely ineffective policy, a policy or strategy must demonstrate three characteristics: ineffectiveness in addressing the problem it is intended to resolve; having the potential to make the initial problem worse; and carrying with it the risk of significant negative externalities.

Applying these criteria to the Government of Ontario's fall 2022 housing supply plan, the findings of our assessment are summarized in Table 9.1.

Table 9.1: Assessing Ontario's fall 2022 housing strategy as bad policy

Criteria	Addresses problem (effectiveness)?	Makes problem worse?	Negative externalities
Assessment	Policy is likely ineffective, focused on wrong factors (land supply, public participation, 'red tape') causing housing affordability problem; fails to address need for affordable rental housing.	Policies encourage further speculation and financialization in the land and housing markets, accelerate gentrification and losses of existing affordable rental housing.	Significant negative externalities in relation to: • ecological conservation; • climate change impacts and adaptation; • prime agricultural lands; • built heritage; and • democratic norms and public participation in local governance.

The Government of Ontario's fall 2022 housing supply package is found to meet all three criteria for a 'bad' policy. It is likely to be ineffective in addressing the housing affordability problem, particularly in relation to affordable rental housing; it has the potential to make certain aspects of the problem, especially with respect to affordable rental housing, worse; and it carries significant negative externalities across a range of dimensions from climate change impacts and adaptation to democratic governance. On this basis we conclude that the Government of Ontario's fall 2022 housing supply package meets the criteria for being a 'bad' policy as defined for the purposes of this volume.

Paths forward

The Government of Ontario's fall 2022 Housing Supply Plan was the product of a deeply flawed policy-making process. The process failed to develop a meaningful understanding of the drivers of the housing affordability crisis in the GTA. The province then relied on a very narrow range of well-connected and self-interested development industry voices in the formulation of its responses. A more effective process would have been grounded in a meaningful appreciation of the factors driving the crisis and would have drawn on a much wider range of interests and expertise in developing a strategy in response. The resulting case of 'bad' policy comes as no surprise in this context.

A more effective response would have sought to address the increasing financialization of the housing supply, and to remove incentives for inflationary speculation. Among other things this would have required stabilizing the decision-making process around land-use planning. The process needed to be led by public institutions, not the development industry, and to be grounded in policy and reliable evidence. The planning and decision-making processes need to emphasize transparency, accountability, and democratic values, and not access, connections, and political whim.

The land-use planning framework needs to protect prime agricultural and ecologically significant features from development pressures. New developments should emphasize the development of complete communities with a mix of housing types geared to different household structures and incomes, incorporating a mix of land uses to facilitate active (that is, walking and biking) transportation and transit, and give attention to urban form and public spaces. Development charges and similar fees should reflect the actual costs of providing the infrastructures needed to facilitate new development, with provisions to support non-profit and affordable rental housing.

Development approvals should only be valid for limited time periods, and lapse if the approved development does not occur. Municipalities should have the right to reject proposals that are incomplete, obviously flawed, or clearly speculative in nature. These measures would reduce incentives for prospective land acquisitions and planning applications, reducing inflationary pressures and meritless demands on municipal planning and approval capacity.

Specific steps need to be taken to mandate affordable housing within new developments, to protect existing affordable housing, especially rental housing, and prevent the displacement of low-income vulnerable households and communities (Anguelovski and Connolly, 2022). This will require the establishment of a more effective rent control regime, and much stronger rules to prevent reno- and demo-victions. At the federal level, the rules around REITs need to be reviewed to understand their impacts on the affordable rental housing market.

Public investments and subsidies for affordable housing should be focused on cooperative and non-profit housing development, not the subsidization of for-profit developments. Finally, federal immigration policies need to be better aligned with the capacity of communities to provide housing and other required infrastructures.

The Ontario housing policy experience is a case study in how bad policy making can lead to bad policy. The case provides important lessons about the importance of understanding the root causes of a problem before implementing a response, and of giving consideration to the potential for significant collateral damage associated with different alternatives in choosing pathways through which to respond to the original challenge.

These problems were reinforced by a discourse of 'crisis' around housing, which was used to justify pushing aside evidentiary, procedural, and democratic norms. The crisis framing also provided the means of avoiding more fundamental questions around the underlying drivers of the crisis, or about what pace of growth and development in the region was actually feasible, environmentally and economically sustainable, or desirable.

References

Alliance for a Liveable Ontario (ALO) (2023) 'New data provides a snapshot of Ontario's affordable housing needs – and it's bad', Press release, 21 November [online], Available from: https://drive.google.com/file/d/1Tu69suc9aQofAVZCM6hbNRG3-gt11s9N/view

Al Mallees, N. (2023) 'Temporary residents helped drive record growth in Canada's population in the third quarter', *The Globe and Mail* [online] 20 December, Available from: https://www.theglobeandmail.com/canada/article-statistics-canada-reports-record-population-growth-in-third-quarter/

Al Mallees, N. (2024) 'Government was warned two years ago high immigration could affect housing costs', *Winnipeg Free Press* [online] 11 January, Available from: https://www.winnipegfreepress.com/business/2024/01/11/government-was-warned-two-years-ago-high-immigration-could-affect-housing-costs

Anders Sandberg, L., Wekerle, G.R., and Gilbert, L. (2013) *The Oak Ridges Moraine Battles: Development, Sprawl, and Nature Conservation in the Toronto Region*, Toronto: University of Toronto Press.

Anguelovski, I. and Connolly, J. (2022) *The Green City and Social Injustice: 21 Tales from North America and Europe*, London: Taylor & Francis.

Association of Municipalities of Ontario (AMO) (2022) 'AMO's submission to consultations related to the more homes built faster plan' [online], Available from: https://www.amo.on.ca

August, M. (2021) 'The rise of financial landlords has turned rental apartments into a vehicle for profit', *Policy Options* [online] 11 June, https://policyoptions.irpp.org/magazines/june-2021/the-rise-of-financial-landlords-has-turned-rental-apartments-into-a-vehicle-for-profit/

Barnett, C., Barz, E., and Rintoul, A. (2022) 'Forget everything you thought you knew about planning in Ontario', *Oster* [online] 26 October, Available from: https://www.osler.com/en/resources/regulations/2022/forget-everything-you-thought-you-knew-about-planning-approvals-in-ontario%E2%80%A6

Bartlett, R. and Norman, K. (2023) 'Could restricting short-term rentals help alleviate Canada's housing crisis?', *Desjardins Economic Viewpoint* [online] 3 December, Available from: https://www.desjardins.com/qc/en/savings-investment/economic-studies/short-term-rentals-dec-4-2023.html

Belec, J. (2022) 'We're going to hear a lot more about the financialization of housing this year', *The Globe and Mail* [online] 6 January, Available from: https://www.theglobeandmail.com/opinion/article-were-going-to-hear-a-lot-more-about-the-financialization-of-housing/

Blais, P. and Neptis Foundation (2018) *Planning the Next GGH*, Toronto: Neptis Foundation.

Callan, I. and D'Mello, C. (2023) 'What did Doug Ford say about the Greenbelt? A timeline of the premier's promises', *Global News* [online] 12 May, Available from: https://globalnews.ca/news/9694836/ontario-greenb elt-promise-timeline/

Canada Mortgage and Housing Corporation (CMHC) (2023) 'Prohibition on the Purchase of Residential Property by Non-Canadians Act' [online], Available from: https://www.cmhc-schl.gc.ca

Canadian Environmental Law Association (2022) 'Written Submission to Standing Committee on Bill 23 – More Homes Built Faster Act, 2022' [online] 15 November, Available from: https://cela.ca/written-submission-to-standing-committee-on-bill-23-more-homes-built-faster-act-2022/

CBC News (2023) 'Ford apologizes for "wrong" Greenbelt decision, vows to reverse land swap', *CBC News* [online] 21 September, Available from: https://www.cbc.ca/news/canada/toronto/ford-stag-and-doe-integr ity-commissioner-1.6974058

Chappel, K. and Burda, C. (2022) 'The province is setting a housing affordability trap for Toronto', *The Toronto Star* [online] 26 October, Available from: https://www.thestar.com/opinion/contributors/the-provi nce-is-setting-a-housing-affordability-trap-for-toronto/article_823f8447-250a-53a4-8b02-2cff8aac11bc.html

Chiefs of Ontario (2022) 'Chiefs of Ontario and First Nations Oppose Bill 23: More Homes Built Faster Act', News release, 23 November, Available from: https://chiefs-of-ontario.org/chiefs-of-ontario-and-first-nations-oppose-bill-23-more-homes-built-faster-act/

City of Toronto (2020) 'Condominiums: two decades of new housing', Available from: https://www.toronto.ca/wp-content/uploads/2020/05/ 8f4f-City-Planning-Condominiums-Two-Decades-of-New-Housing.pdf

City of Toronto (2022) 'City of Toronto Review of Provincial Housing Affordability Task Force', Available from: https://www.toronto.ca/legd ocs/mmis/2022/ex/bgrd/backgroundfile-222958.pdf

Conservation Ontario (2022) 'Submission on Bill 23 the More Homes Built Faster Act' [online], Available from: https://conservationontario.ca/fileadmin/ pdf/policy-priorities_section/CA_Act_2022/Bill_23_Standing_Committee_ Submission_Conservation_Ontario_Angela_Coleman_FINAL.pdf

County of Brant (2022) 'Bill 23 summary and implications' [online], Available from: https://www.brant.ca/en/planning-and-Development/ bill-23-summary-and-implications.aspx

Crawley, M. (2023) 'What should Doug Ford's government do about developers who go years without building homes?' *CBC News* [online] 30 November, Available from: https://www.cbc.ca/news/canada/toronto/ ontario-housing-doug-ford-developers-approvals-new-homes-1.7039776

Doucet, B. (2022) 'Ontario's "affordable housing" task force report does not address the real problems', *The Conversation* [online] 10 February, Available from: https://theconversation.com/ontarios-affordable-housing-task-force-report-does-not-address-the-real-problems-176869

Doyle, V. (2023) 'Plan Canada: Ontario government relegates smart growth to the dust bin', *Plan Canada* [online] 31 October, Available from: https://friendsofgh.ca/plan-canada-ontario-government-relegates-smart-growth-to-the-dust-bin/

Eby, K. (2023) *Review of Existing Housing Unit Capacity Identify in Municipal Land Needs Assessments Prepared for Upper- and-Single Tier Municipalities in the Greater Golden Horseshoe*, Toronto: Alliance for a Liveable Ontario/ Environmental Defense Canada.

Fallis, G. (2022) 'A shortage of homes isn't the main reason house prices keep rising', *The Globe and Mail* [online] 14 March, Available from: https://www.theglobeandmail.com/opinion/article-a-shortage-of-homes-isnt-the-main-reason-house-prices-keep-rising/

Fung, C., Parikh, S., and Zulauf, P. (2020) 'The crisis of affordable rental housing in Ontario', Ryerson (TMU) University [online], Available from: https://www.torontomu.ca/content/dam/social-innovation/Progr ams/Affordable_Housing_Visual_Systems_Map_Oxford.pdf.

Gibson, V. (2021) 'This investor owns 17 homes. He and other multiple-property owners are now the largest slice of Toronto homebuyers', *The Toronto Star* [online] 23 October, Available from: https://www.thestar.com/ news/gta/this-investor-owns-17-homes-he-and-other-multiple-prope rty-owners-are-now-the-largest/article_5936d490-9492-5ae1-afbd-ce482 789e0cf.html

Gold, A., Pendall, R., and Treskon, M. (2018) *Demographic Change in the Great Lakes Region*, Washington DC: The Urban Institute.

Gray, J. (2023) 'Developers propose taller towers for Toronto's Midtown', *The Globe and Mail* [online] 7 April, Available from: https://www.theg lobeandmail.com/canada/article-developers-propose-taller-towers-for-torontos-midtown/

Griffon, T. (2022) 'Ontario rapidly losing farmland amid urban sprawl, provincial agriculture group says', *CBC News* [online] 18 June, Available from: https:// www.cbc.ca/news/canada/toronto/ont-farmland-loss-1.6493833

Harrison, L. (2023) 'Demovictions are on the rise in Toronto. Some fear they'll make the rental market worse for everyone', *CBC News* [online] 3 October, Available from: https://www.cbc.ca/news/canada/toronto/ demovictions-rights-for-tenants-1.6984622

Hevenor, D. (2022) 'Bill 23 could cause irreparable harm to wetlands', *Newmarket Today* [online] 21 November, Available from: https://www. newmarkettoday.ca/columns/opinion/opinion-bill-23-could-cause-irre parable-harm-to-wetlands-6124279

Hillson, P. and Winfield, M. (2024) 'Understanding the political durability of Doug Ford's market populism', *Studies in Political Economy*, 105(1): 69–93.

Hristova, B. (2022) 'MZOs have been a trump card for the Ford government – here's why it's a serious Ontario election issue', *CBC News* [online] 31 March, Available from: https://www.cbc.ca/news/canada/hamilton/mzo-election-2022-1.6399276

Javed, N. (2023), 'Doug Ford's government issued dozens of special orders designed to fast-track LTC homes and housing. That hasn't happened, a Star analysis reveals', *The Toronto Star* [online] 6 November, Available from: https://www.thestar.com/news/gta/doug-ford-s-government-iss ued-dozens-of-special-orders-designed-to-fast-track-ltc-homes/article_c 7b479ca-8521-52bf-b809-aa49de0a0714.html

Javed, N. and Buist, S. (2021) 'How the Ford government's love of MZOs is increasingly benefiting private developers with ties to PC and local politicians', *The Toronto Star* [online] 14 June, Available from: https:// www.thestar.com/news/investigations/how-the-ford-government-s-love-of-mzos-is-increasingly-benefiting-private-developers-with-ties/article_1 5e8c443-f348-5e98-88f5-98a3d5af9aee.html

Jeffords, S. (2022) 'Ford's controversial housing bill could have "major unintended consequences," planners warn', *CBC News* [online] 26 November, Available from: https://www.cbc.ca/news/canada/toronto/planners-ford-housing-bill-1.6665015

Kennedy, D. (2019) 'Construction capacity among major concerns for Ontario as it plans four-line $28.5B transit expansion', *On-Site* [online] 20 November, Available from: https://www.on-sitemag.com/infrastruct ure/construction-capacity-among-major-concerns-for-ontario-as-it-plans-four-line-28-5b-transit-expansion/1003965964/

Latif, A. (2023) 'Thousands of heritage properties risk losing protection under Bill 23, including more than 300 in Cambridge', *CBC News* [online] 26 January, Available from: https://www.cbc.ca/news/canada/kitchener-waterloo/bill-23-heritage-properties-impact-cambridge-1.6728343

Macdonald, S., Monstadt, J., and Friendly, A. (2021) 'Towards smart regional growth: institutional complexities and the regional governance of Southern Ontario's Greenbelt', *Territory, Politics, Governance*, 11(8): 1727–47.

Mahoney, J. (2019) 'Doug Ford government started work on cuts to Toronto City Council a day after election win', *The Globe and Mail* [online] 17 October, Available from: https://www.theglobeandmail.com/canada/arti cle-doug-ford-government-started-work-on-cuts-to-toronto-city-coun cil-a/

McClearn, M. (2022) 'Areas to be removed from Ontario's Greenbelt include prime farmland, wetlands and floodplains', *The Globe and Mail* [online] 26 December, Available from: https://www.theglobeandmail.com/business/article-ontario-greenbelt-farmland-wetlands-floodplains/

Merali, F. (2021) 'Investors now make up more than 25% of Ontario homebuyers, pushing prices higher, experts warn', *CBC News* [online] 23 November, Available from: https://www.cbc.ca/news/canada/toronto/investors-in-ontario-real-estate-market-1.6258199

Morgan, R. (2023) 'Experts say PC's Bill 97 a sprawl inducing "full frontal assault" on Ontario agriculture', *The Pointer* [online] 24 April, Available from: https://thepointer.com/article/2023-04-24/experts-say-pcs-propo sed-bill-97-is-a-sprawl-inducing-full-frontal-assault-on-ontario-agriculture

Nadarajah, R. and Lindgren, R.D. (2021) 'Analysis of Ontario Bill 245: Accelerating Access to Justice Act, 2021', *Canadian Environmental Law Association*, Available from: https://cela.ca/wp-content/uploads/2021/03/CELA-Brief-Bill-245-March-2-2021.pdf

Neptis Foundation (2021) 'Where are significant agricultural lands located?' [online], Available from: https://neptis.org/publications/chapters/where-are-significant-agricultural-lands-located

Office of the Auditor General of Ontario (2023) Special Report on Changes to the Greenbelt [online], Available from: https://www.auditor.on.ca/en/content/specialreports/specialreports/Greenbelt_en.pdf

Office of the Integrity Commissioner (2023) *Report of J. David Wake, K.C., Integrity Commissioner, Re: The Honourable Steve Clark, Minister of Municipal Affairs and Housing and Member of Provincial Parliament for Leeds – Grenville – Thousand Islands and Rideau Lakes* [online] 30 August, Available from: https://www.oico.on.ca/web/default/files/public/Commission ers%20Reports/Report%20Re%20Minister%20Clark%20-%20August%20 30%2C%202023.pdf

Ontario Housing Affordability Task Force (2022) Report of the Ontario Housing Affordability Task Force [online] 8 February, Available from: https://files.ontario.ca/mmah-housing-affordability-task-force-rep ort-en-2022-02-07-v2.pdf

Ontario Public Health Association (2022) 'Submission to the Legislative Assembly of Ontario, Standing Committee on Heritage, Infrastructure and Cultural Policy RE: Bill 23, More Homes Built Faster Act, 2022', Available from: https://opha.on.ca/wp-content/uploads/2022/11/Ontario-Public-Health-Assn-submission-to-the-Standing-Committee-on-Heritage-Infrast ructure-and-Cultural-Policy_Bill-23_Nov_2022.pdf?ext=pdf

Ontario (2007) 'Ontario celebrates second major award for growth plan', Press release, 24 April, Available from: https://news.ontario.ca/en/release/86986/ontario-celebrates-second-major-award-for-growth-plan-

Ontario (2022) 'Non-resident speculation tax' [online], Available from: https://www.ontario.ca/document/non-resident-speculation-tax

Ontario (2022a) More Homes, Built Faster: Ontario's Housing Supply Action Plan 2022–2023 [online], Available from: https://www.ontario.ca/page/more-homes-built-faster

Ontario (2023) 'Ministry of Finance, Ontario Demographic Quarterly: highlights of first quarter' [online], Available from: https://www.ontario.ca/page/ontario-demographic-quarterly-highlights-first-quarter

Ontario (2023a) 'To build more homes, Ontario launching building faster fund and expanding strong mayor powers', News release [online] 21 August, Available from: https://news.ontario.ca/en/release/1003397/to-build-more-homes-ontario-launching-building-faster-fund-and-expanding-strong-mayor-powers

Ontario (2023b) *Housing Affordability Task Force Report* [online] Available from: https://www.ontario.ca/page/housing-affordability-task-force-report

Ontario Ministry of Municipal Affairs and Housing (MMAH) (2019) More Homes, More Choice: Ontario's Housing Supply Action Plan [online], Available from: https://www.ontario.ca/page/more-homes-more-choice-ontarios-housing-supply-action-plan

Ontario Ministry of Municipal Affairs and Housing (MMAH) (2020) *A Place to Grow: Growth Plan for the Greater Golden Horseshoe*, Toronto: Queen's Printer [online], Available from: https://files.ontario.ca/mmah-place-to-grow-office-consolidation-en-2020-08-28.pdf

Pothen, P. (2022) 'Ontario's housing bill is actually a trojan horse for environmentally catastrophic rural sprawl', Environmental Defense [online] 31 October, Available from: https://environmentaldefence.ca/2022/10/31/ontarios-housing-bill-is-actually-a-trojan-horse-for-environmentally-catastrophic-rural-sprawl/

Regional Planning Commissioners of Ontario (RPCO) (2023) 'News release and media package: Regional Planning Commissioners of Ontario issue inventory of Ontario's unbuilt housing supply' [online] 7 March, Available from: https://yourstoprotect.ca/wp-content/uploads/sites/3/2023/03/RPCO-News-Release-Inventory.pdf.

Statistics Canada (2021) 'Census of population' [online], Available from: https://www12.statcan.gc.ca/census-recensement/index-eng.cfm

Supreme Court of Canada (SCC) (2021) – *Toronto (City) v. Ontario (Attorney General)*, 2021 SCC 34 (CanLII) [online], Available from: https://scc-csc.lexum.com/scc-csc/scc-csc/en/item/19011/index.do

Syed, F. (2023) 'While you were on holiday, Ontario stripped conservation authority powers', *The Narwal* [online] 10 January, Available from: https://thenarwhal.ca/ontario-strips-conservation-authority-powers/

Taylor, Z. and Horak, M. (2022) 'Strong mayor powers in Ontario are a gross violation of democratic principles', *Policy Options* [online] 16 December, Available from: https://policyoptions.irpp.org/magazines/december-2022/strong-mayor-powers-in-ontario-are-a-gross-violation-of-democratic-principles/

The Canadian Press (2022) 'Ontario promises to make municipalities "whole" if they can't fund infrastructure due to new housing law', *CBC News* [online] 30 November, Available from: https://www.cbc.ca/news/canada/toronto/toronto-bill-23-reaction-1.6669428

Toronto Global (2023) 'Toronto region quick facts' [online], Available from: https://torontoglobal.ca/why-toronto-region/toronto-region-quick-facts/

Toronto Region Conservation Authority (TRCA) (2020) 'TRCA calls for the immediate removal of Schedule 6 from Bill 229', News release, 4 December [online], Available from: https://trca.ca/news/trca-calls-for-immediate-removal-of-schedule-6-from-bill-229/

Toronto Region Conservation Authority (TRCA) (2023) 'Natural Heritage System' [online], Available from: https://trca.ca/conservation/terrestrial-ecosystems/natural-heritage-system/

Toronto Regional Real Estate Board (TRREB) (2023) 'TRREB housing market charts, November' [online], Available from: https://trreb.ca/wp-content/files/market-stats/housing-charts/TREB_Housing_Market_Charts-November_2023.pdf

Üçğolu, M., Keil, R., and Tomar, S. (2021) 'Contagion in the markets? Covid-19 and housing in the Greater Toronto area', *Built Environment*, 47(3): 355–66.

United Nations (2019) *World Urbanization Prospects: 2018 Revision*, New York: Department of Economic and Social Affairs.

Urban Land Institute (ULI) (2020) '13,000 years of Indigenous history in the GTA – and why it matters to Planning & Development' [online], Available from: https://www.youtube.com/watch?v=jmy9BFR8dwc

Warnica, R. and Bailey, A. (2021) 'Several of Doug Ford's key pandemic decisions were swayed by business interests, Star analysis suggests', *The Toronto Star* [online] 15 July, Available from: https://www.thestar.com/business/several-of-doug-ford-s-key-pandemic-decisions-were-swayed-by-business-interests-star-analysis/article_0c21f657-537e-50a0-97b7-e8f57369f9f0.html

Warren, M., Spurr, B., and Gibson, V. (2023) 'City warns its long-awaited housing plan is "at high risk" in latest report', *The Toronto Star* [online] 14 March, Available from: https://www.thestar.com/news/gta/city-warns-its-long-awaited-housing-plan-is-at-high-risk-in-latest-report/article_efed5dab-7c58-567e-8d10-cf730d58d032.html

Webber, C. and Zigman, P. (2023) 'Renovictions are fuelling Toronto's housing crisis', *Canadian Dimension* [online] 17 April, Available from: https://canadiandimension.com/articles/view/renocitions-are-fueling-torontos-housing-crisis

Winfield, M. (2012) *Blue-Green Province: The Environment and Political Economy of Ontario*, Vancouver: University of British Columbia Press.

Winfield, M. (2019) 'Doug Ford's Ontario: who's winning, and what it means for the province's future', *The Conversation* [online] 24 February, Available from: https://theconversation.com/doug-fords-ontario-whos-winning-and-what-it-means-for-the-provinces-future-112127

Winfield, M. (2022a) 'Giving developers free reign no solution to the GTHA's housing challenges', *The Conversation* [online] 3 February, Available from: https://theconversation.com/giving-developers-free-rein-isnt-the-solution-to-the-gtha-housing-challenges-176128

Winfield, M. (2022b) 'Missing the mark on housing', *The Hamilton Spectator* [online] 17 April, Available from: https://www.thespec.com/opinion/contributors/missing-the-mark-on-housing/article_2646ccd7-b591-59d7-9ca6-9b07db4274f5.html

Winfield, M. (2023) 'Bill 23, planning reform and the future of the GTA and Hamilton region', Toronto: York University [Lecture], Available from: https://www.youtube.com/watch?v=3qqljI_mBx4

Winfield, M. and Castrilli, J. (2023) 'Has Ontario's housing "plan" been built on a foundation of evidentiary sand?', *The Conversation* [online] 22 January, Available from: https://theconversation.com/has-ontarios-housing-plan-been-built-on-a-foundation-of-evidentiary-sand-198133

WOWA.ca (2023) 'Prime rate and Bank of Canada overnight rate (1935 – 2023)' [online], Available from: https://wowa.ca/banks/prime-rates-canada

Younglai, R. (2023) 'Investors own big chunk of Ontario's condo market', *The Globe and Mail* [online] 6 February, https://www.theglobeandmail.com/business/article-investors-own-big-chunk-of-ontarios-condo-market/

10

Death by a thousand clarifications: how the Volcker Rule's inevitable ambiguity makes it easy to erode and hard to defend while leaving the power of banks unchecked

Erin Lockwood

Introduction

The 2008 global financial crisis set in motion the first major increases in banking regulation since the 1930s, culminating in the Dodd-Frank Wall Street Reform and Consumer Protection Act 2010 in the US. A core provision of this Act, known as the Volcker Rule, represents one of the most substantive attempts to change the universal banking model, which involves the merging of investment and commercial banking. The universal model had taken hold since the 1980s and received official sanction since the Clinton-era deregulatory reforms. The Volcker Rule banned proprietary trading by commercial banks, based on the perception that excessive risk-taking with customer deposits had been a core cause of the wave of bank solvency and liquidity crises in 2008–09, incentivized by public backstopping of banks deemed too big to fail. Widely lauded in the early 2010s by supporters of banking reform and widely opposed by bankers, the Volcker Rule has been characterized by a glacially slow rollout. The implementation was delayed by years of administrative efforts to pin down definitions of terms like 'near-term investments' and 'market-making activities'. By 2020, core provisions of the Rule, which had only come into effect 5 years before, had already been substantively weakened by regulatory agencies under the Trump administration. How did such a landmark piece of post-2008 financial regulation come to be so bogged down and vulnerable to repeal?

This chapter examines the Volcker Rule through this volume's conceptual focus on 'bad policy,' arguing that the Volcker Rule's many definitional ambiguities both weakened the Rule's impact and gave fuel to its opponents. The very scrupulousness with which rule makers attempted to proscribe acceptable banking practices has made the Rule a lightning rod for deregulatory forces. This has rendered any effort to roll back the rollbacks costly, unpopular, and lacking support from both internal and external constituencies.

The Volcker Rule is certainly not unique in being ultimately subject to a high degree of regulatory interpretation for its enforcement, and regulatory discretion does not inherently make policy 'bad' – ineffective, prone to unintended consequences, or ill-suited to the problem it attends to address. Nor is the Volcker Rule unique in the gap between its grand initial ambition and anemic present form: this dynamic characterizes large swaths of post-crisis financial regulation, especially in the realm of macroprudential regulation (for example, Baker, 2013; Moschella, 2013; see also Patashnik, 2008). However, it is distinctive in both the scope of its initial ambition – to fundamentally alter the prevailing structure of banking practices – and the exceptionally protracted and complicated rulemaking that has followed in its wake. As such, it represents a useful empirical case for this book's central task of making sense of ineffective policies: those that are developed, adopted, and sustained even though they can be shown to be ineffectual and generate undesirable or unanticipated negative outcomes.

This chapter argues that the Volcker Rule is ineffective for two reasons: first, because of a lack of clarity regarding what problem, exactly, it was trying to solve; and second, because from the beginning, the Rule was characterized by exceptions and exemptions that blunted its potential to restructure banking and finance. The goals of constraining banks' risk-taking, limiting systemic risk, eroding the presumption of public backstopping for private losses are certainly desirable ones. However, I argue that the lack of clarity regarding its purpose meant that the Volcker Rule fundamentally takes for granted the structure of contemporary financial markets and, via its many exceptions and exemptions, safeguards the right (and perceived necessity) of banks to use capital markets to manage the risks associated with taking short-term deposits and making longer-term loans. As such, it was bound from the beginning to rely on a series of tenuous conceptual distinctions, making it an easy target for critics and difficult to both defend and implement by its supporters. The unwillingness to risk US banks' global competitiveness constrained what was possible and tempered what was ultimately enacted. In brief, the muddiness concerning what problem the Rule was intended to address that plagued the initial policy debate over the Volcker Rule has shadowed this process from the beginning.

My argument here has strong resonances with political scientist Eric Patashnik's (2008) thesis about the reversal and unraveling of general interest reforms. Patashnik argues that non-incremental policy reforms intended to produce broad public benefits tend to be unsustainable when they fail to reconfigure political dynamics and leave intact the basic power structures that they are intended to reform. In such cases, policy reforms suffer from what he terms 'agency slippages' between the citizenry and the government, which is unwilling or unable to bind its successors to effective implementation of the policy. Although Patashnik is looking primarily at cases of *de*regulatory policy, his framework is a useful one for examining the erosion of the Volcker Rule both in the legislative and rulemaking phases of its implementation. In particular, Patashnik (2008, p 32) finds that policy erosion ('death by a thousand cuts') is most likely when the investments of beneficiaries of the policy is modest and those groups are loosely organized with low levels of cohesion. This dynamic is particularly acute in financial regulation where the constituency which benefits from regulation is diffuse and poorly organized (broad consumer interests vs. highly organized and resourced banks).

This chapter proceeds in four sections, beginning with a discussion of the historical regulatory context out of which the Rule emerged. The second section traces the process through which the 2008 financial crisis catalyzed support for the Volcker Rule, culminating in a lengthy period of agency rulemaking and implementation that followed its passage into law. The choices that were made during this period – and, in particular, the (non-)decision to not risk undermining the global competitiveness of the US financial sector – help explain why the resulting policy became overburdened with ambiguities. In the third section, I analyze the Rule, focusing on its weaknesses and limitations that expose it to criticism as 'ineffective policy', ultimately concluding that these weaknesses stem from the Rule's attempt to define and curb excessive risk-taking, rather than structurally change the financial sector – a thin reed on which to support what began as an effort to transform the dominant banking model of the 1990s and first decade of the 21st century. The chapter concludes with some reflections on potential alternatives to the Volcker Rule and the necessity of reckoning more seriously with the consequences of a financialized economy for the ability of public actors to transform banking and capital markets.

US banking regulation: the Volcker Rule in context

Deposit-taking institutions face a problem known as 'maturity mismatch': they issue short-term liabilities (deposits) to finance long-term assets (loans). Short-term deposits are transformed into long-term credit by borrowing short and lending long, and banks have long looked to underwriting and securities markets to perform this maturity transformation. The risks associated with this practice became evident during the lead-up to the financial crash of the 1930s, resulting in over 1,100 bank failures. In response, as part of the New Deal, Congress enacted the Banking Act of 1933. This legislation established the Federal Deposit Insurance Congress (FDIC) to insure deposits and, under the Glass-Steagall Act, imposed strict operations: commercial banks with deposit insurance were prohibited from trading securities, and investment banks were barred from accepting deposits.

However, by the early 1990s, this structural separation between investment, deposit-taking, and loan-making had begun to erode substantially. Banned from trading securities, banks turned instead to the novel financial products unleashed at the end of the Bretton Woods monetary order and fueled by advances in financial economics, investing in swaps and other derivatives, many of them traded over-the-counter (OTC) and wholly outside regulatory scrutiny, to hedge their risks – and to make a profit (a fuzzy distinction that will continue to be central to the Volcker Rule story).

In response to the specter of a regulatory crackdown on this new, trillion-dollar market in swaps and derivatives, the Clinton administration steered hard in the opposite direction. It declared the OTC derivatives market outside the scope of both the Securities and Exchange Commission (SEC) and the Commodity Futures Trading Commission (CFTC) regulation – and, via the Financial Modernization Act 1999, repealing Glass-Steagall's restrictions on speculative investments (see Lockwood, 2020). This legal certainty led to massive growth in the swaps market and dramatic increases in proprietary trading by banks; by 2010, 10 percent of Goldman Sachs's – one of the ten largest banks in the US at the time – revenue was from proprietary trading (Gary, 2012, p 1345).

In 2007, the US housing bubble burst, resulting in huge losses among banks who had issued, underwritten, and securitized risky mortgages. The resulting contagion throughout the financial sector spilled over into the real economy, resulting in a downturn in economic growth, widespread job losses, and, in 2008, the Troubled Assets Relief Program (TARP) which enabled the Treasury Department to purchase US$700 billion[1] of troubled assets from banks and other financial institutions. TARP and the implicit guarantee of public backstopping it granted to future risk-taking by private financial firms was a central motivation for financial reform to mitigate this moral hazard and make future bailouts less likely.

A return to Glass-Steagall was briefly considered, as proposed by Senators McCain and Cantwell in 2009,[2] but quickly ruled out on the logic that would come to dominate the regulatory and policy-making community's approach to post-crisis banking regulation: a return to Glass-Steagall's strict separation of investment and commercial banking was widely understood to reduce the US financial sector's global competitiveness. Indeed, a hallmark part of the US government's crisis response – facilitating Bank of America's acquisition of Merrill Lynch and the sale of Bear Stearns to JPMorgan – turned precisely on the kind merging of investment and deposit-taking institutions that Glass-Steagall had proscribed. The system was widely seen as both too complex and too profitable for a return to Glass-Steagall to be thinkable, reflecting both the structural power of finance in the US economy and the capture – both cultural and material – of lawmakers and regulators by the financial industry (Johnson and Kwak, 2011; Kwak, 2014).

This unwillingness to consider a regulatory response that would jeopardize the profitability and competitiveness of the US financial sector is at once obvious and remarkable. Indeed, I argue that it is behind the subsequent trajectory of the regulatory reform that did emerge: the so-called Volcker Rule.

The Volcker Rule and its implementation

In 2009, the Group of 30 (G30), an international group of bankers and central bankers, chaired by former Fed Chair Paul Volcker, produced a report on the 2008 crisis which called for heightened regulation across a range of areas from credit rating to liquidity and capital requirements. The G30 report cited banks' proprietary trading, sponsorship of hedge funds, and exposure to structured credit as contributing to the financial crisis, and recommended restrictions on systemically important financial institutions (so-called SIFIs) to prevent risky trading and conflicts of interest between bank and customer interests.

Although the G30 report did not call for an outright ban on proprietary trading, in 2010, President Obama issued a call for restrictions on proprietary trading and hedge fund investing (Obama, 2010). This was formalized as a somewhat belated addition to the sweeping Dodd-Frank Act: the Merkley-Levin Amendment, often known as the Volcker Rule, which banned proprietary trading by systemically important insured depository institutions and their affiliates.

The amendment immediately became a target for lobbying by the banking and financial sector; Gary (2012) notes that 15 percent of the total active lobbyists in Washington in 2009 were lobbying on behalf of Wall Street interests. Support for the amendment generally split along predictable partisan lines, though Republican Scott Brown's special election win complicated the political bargaining over the Rule (Beutler, 2010). Balancing his reelection campaign against Elizabeth Warren with the significant contributions mutual funds like Fidelity had made to his campaign, Brown broke with his party to become the 60th (filibuster-proof) vote for the bill. However, before doing so, he secured a loophole in the bill, allowing banks to make 'de minimis' investments in hedge funds (Lavelle, 2014). Not surprisingly, given the weakness and diffuseness of consumer interests (the famously 'inattentive public') and the strength of well-organized, exceptionally well-funded financial interests who kept a revolving door for regulators propped wide open, the version of the amendment that was ultimately enacted was weaker than that proposed by Senators Merkley and Levin (Gary, 2012), particularly filled with a series of loopholes, which will be discussed later in this chapter.

The final version of the Volcker Rule, section 619 of the Dodd–Frank Act, was the first major banking reform since the Glass–Steagall Act. The Rule places two main restrictions on commercial banks' investment activities. These restrictions apply to entire banking groups: banks, their parent companies, and any subsidiaries. First, it prohibits banks from engaging in proprietary trading. Understanding what this means entails unpacking a series of nested definitions. Specifically, it prohibits banking entities (that is, insured depository institutions) from 'engaging as a principal for a trading account' (that is, any account used for acquiring and taking positions in securities and instruments for the purpose of selling in the near term or otherwise with the intent to resell in order to profit from short-term price movements) in 'any transaction to purchase, sell, or otherwise acquire or dispose of any security, any derivative, any contract of sale of a commodity for future delivery, any option, or any other security or financial instrument'.

Second, the Rule bans depository institutions from acquiring equity, partnership, or ownership interest in hedge funds with certain, significant exemptions[3]: specifically, market-making activities to meet the near-term demands of clients; risk-mitigating hedging; small business investment; and Brown's crowning achievement: permitting bank ownership of hedge funds and a de minimis investment defined as no more than 3 percent of the fund's capital 1 year out and 3 percent of the bank's Tier I capital – a substantial amount of money given how highly capitalized the biggest banks are. Gary (2012) argues that this exception allows banks to structure hedge funds in a way that meets the Rule but still exposes the bank to the risks associated with hedge fund failure. Volcker himself decried the many exemptions as weakening the Rule.

As enacted, the Volcker Rule left many crucial definitional issues subject to regulatory rulemaking: defining hedge funds, 'near term' profits, hedging, and market-making, among other terms. Five regulatory agencies – the Office of the Comptroller of the Currency (OCC) the Fed Board of Governors, the Federal Deposit Insurance Corporation (FDIC), the SEC, and the CFTC were involved in the rulemaking process, which presented a second (and arguably more consequential) opportunity for lobbying. As a result, there was an exceptionally long period between the Rule's passage in 2010 and its implementation (Baker, 2015; Krawiec and Liu, 2015). In her analysis of this process, Baker (2015) identifies multiple potential 'regulatory collisions' among the multiple agencies responsible for implementation, and indeed, the absence of a single decision maker to implement the Volcker Rule and the dependence on informal coordination mechanisms among agencies with a history of turf wars was raised in a 2014 congressional hearing. The initial document resulting from the period of public comment and the inter-agency consultation process was 963 pages long (Morgan and Sheehan, 2015, p 706).

The length of both the rulemaking process and the agencies' interpretation of the rules itself are rooted in a legalistic and fundamentally conservative approach to financial regulation: one that attempts to build ever more finely grained specifications of permitted and prohibited investment practices, while leaving unchecked the structural power of US financial institutions within the global political economy. This approach to regulatory policy responds to the complexity of the financial system and its constituent parts with equally complex regulation, rather than enacting the kind of structural reforms that characterized the Glass-Steagall era. Ultimately, the complexity of the Volcker Rule's final rulemaking meant that the agencies tasked banks' internal compliance systems with the burden of implementing much of the Volcker Rule's monitoring for purposes of enforcement.

The Volcker Rule finally came into effect in 2015, following years of delays and lawsuits pushing the compliance deadline out. Even then, banks continued to receive extensions to offload illiquid investments that could not be immediately shed. The Rule had only been in effect for 3 years before Congress, in response to bank industry lobbying, passed the Economic Growth, Regulatory Relief, and Consumer Protection Act 2018, which, among other deregulatory policies,[4] also eliminated the Volcker Rule's applicability to banks with less than US$10 billion in assets. While this was a fairly modest reform, it set the stage for a much more ambitious rollback of the Volcker Rule 2 years later.

In 2020, the Federal Reserve under Trump, and with the approval of the FDIC, OCC, SEC, and CFTC, rolled back the Volcker Rule's limitations on bank investment in venture capital funds and securitized loans. The rules change eliminated the 3 percent cap on ownership and allowed banks to own stakes in and operate venture capital funds and credit funds. Fed Chair Jerome Powell cited the complexity of the Volcker Rule, claiming that the rules change represented 'a simpler, cleaner approach to implementing the rule [that] makes [it] easier for banks and regulators to carry out the intent of the rule' (Cheung, 2020). Fed Governor Randal Quarles likewise supported the rules change, while Governor Lael Brainard opposed it, contending that the language of the change made venture capital funds indistinguishable from private equity funds, opening the door to banks' direct investment in those. Dennis Kelleher of the consumer advocacy non-profit Better Markets concurred, calling the resulting form of the rule 'Swiss cheese, full of expansive loopholes that Wall Street will exploit' (Merle, 2020).

Although the Biden administration has taken a tougher stance toward regulating markets and Sarah Bloom Raskin has taken over from Randal Quarles as vice chair for supervision at the Fed, the likelihood of reversing the Trump-era changes to the Volcker Rules appears slim. Doing so would require substantial time and resources from regulatory agencies that are understaffed, overburdened, and facing the pressing issues of the climate crisis and emerging fintech issues (Schroeder, 2021). Major changes require a public comment period and the agreement of the five regulatory agencies. Moreover, even Congressional Democrats are far from united around prudential regulation; several Democrats voted for the Trump-era weakening of the Volcker Rule in 2018.

Evaluating the Volcker Rule

In its evaluation of the Volcker Rule as 'bad policy', this chapter intentionally sidesteps a discussion of the economic impacts of the Volcker Rule which are notoriously difficult to measure and calculate, in no small part due to the very complexity that the Rule targets (Schiff, 2020). From the beginning, banks contended that the costs of complying with the Volcker Rule would be intolerably high. As discussed in Lavelle's (2014, p 115) analysis of the implementation and comment periods, bank lobbyists frequently cited claims that the rule would shrink banks' balance sheets and decrease lending, making banks less profitable overall. Piasio's (2013) objections to the Rule also come from the perspective of the profitability of the banking industry.

Rather than attempt to measure whether the compliance costs and ban on proprietary trading have increased the cost of capital or eroded bank profits (which stood at US$22.3 billion for the three largest US banks in the first quarter of 2023), this discussion instead focuses on two questions: the extent to which the Rule has fulfilled its intended purposes and the extent to which the ambiguities and exemptions discussed weaken the Rule.

What was the Volcker Rule intended to solve?

Central to the Rule's proposal was the perception that proprietary trading was to blame for the 2008 crisis. However, while ending proprietary trading may well be desirable in its own right, the role played by proprietary trading in fueling the crisis is contested. On the one hand, the collapse of a bank-owned hedge fund did impose massive losses on Bear Stearns, leading the parent bank to bail it out due to reputational concerns – an indirect subsidy of a hedge fund by taxpayers (Duffie, 2010). Goldman Sachs and Citigroup also bailed out hedge funds prior to their collapse. Additionally, banks' pre-crisis trading desks were a massive source of value – and losses. Chatterjee (2011, p 47) notes that 75 percent of Goldman's 2004 pre-tax revenue came from trading investments. Merrill Lynch lost close to US$20 billion on proprietary collateralized debt obligation (CDO) bets and was eventually sold to Bank of America; Citigroup lost US$15 billion and received a bailout. Indeed, a Government Accountability Office report (2011) found that proprietary trading accounted for US$15.8 billion in losses at six of the biggest bank holding companies during the five quarters spanning the depth of the financial crisis. Many observers at the time identified proprietary trading as 'a major cause of the recent crisis' (Crotty et al, 2010; see also Richardson et al, 2010). Paul Krugman (2010) cited the repeal of Glass–Steagall as contributing to a 'dangerously unstable' financial system.

On the other hand, while banks did sustain major losses from risky assets held by their hedge funds, most of their losses came from traditional extensions of credit: securitized packages of real estate loans, which fell sharply in value when the housing market collapsed. These were long-term investments, held to maturity: precisely the kind of asset the Volcker Rule encourages banks to hold. Moreover, Lehman Brothers, the collapse of which set the crisis in motion, was an investment bank, not a deposit-taking institution – a category of institution that the Volcker Rule's provisions would not have applied to. At the same time, banks' losses were not limited to the mortgage-backed securities on their balance sheets; banks also sustained significant losses from CDO written on those loans which were repurchased from off-balance-sheet trading (Rajan, 2011, p 173). Critics of the Volcker Rule also point out that proprietary trading by Goldman Sachs and Merrill Lynch had already resulted in the SEC filing fraud charges, suggesting the regulatory regime was already adequately scrutinizing proprietary trading, though these charges had little to do with the implicit public backstopping of risky trades targeted by the Rule.

Would a ban on proprietary trading have prevented or significantly mitigated trading losses and contagion during the 2008 crisis? Answering this question is surprisingly difficult. As Whitehead (2011, p 42 footnote) observes, 'Part of the discrepancy may turn on what is meant by proprietary trading. Short-term trading, which is what the Volcker Rule addresses, may have been less of a concern than longer-term holdings of risky asset-backed securities.' Of course, a policy need not be sufficient to have stopped the 2008 crisis for it to be desirable and effective in its own right; that is a very high bar for any policy to clear. However, I do want to suggest that the lack of clarity about the precise role proprietary trading played in the 2008 crisis helped set the stage for the loopholes and exemptions that eventually resulted. While it was clear that banks' hedge funds had sustained huge losses, the impact of these losses was difficult to disaggregate from losses incurred from conventional bank lending, given that the trading book losses resulted, in no small part, from derivatives written on the badly performing bank loans, enmeshing banks and non-bank financial institutions in a dense web of counterparty losses, write-downs, and illiquid, difficult-to-value assets. While the Volcker Rule would have impacted some of these dynamics, it would not have altered others, making the Rule challenging to defend and strengthen, given the lack of clarity of the overall impact on systemic risk of stronger versus weaker versions of the Rule.

In the following section, I analyze how the ambiguities and exemptions that have plagued the Rule from the beginning undermine even a more modest set of goals than preventing a repeat of a 2008-style crisis.

Loopholes and ambiguities

According to Nabilou (2017, p 301), while motivated by financial crisis prevention, the Rule had three more specific goals: managing and containing systemic risk by preventing contagion between commercial banking and investment/private funds; addressing conflicts of interest when depository institutions engage in proprietary trading and the investment or sponsorship of private funds[5]; and limiting the transfer of government subsidies from depository institutions to private funds. As we have seen from the history of the policy, the devil is in the details regarding the ability of the policy to move the needle on those goals, and this section will discuss some of the exemptions and loopholes and associated ambiguities in greater detail. But more fundamentally, the Rule is at odds with the structure of contemporary global finance. Once regulators made the decision to not jeopardize banks' ability to remain globally competitive, they ensured that bank connections with and reliance on the shadow banking sector and systemic importance would remain intact, meaning that the Rule would have limited power to constrain banks' power and public backstop.

A major and frequently referenced (Piasio, 2013; Whitehead, 2011; Chatterjee, 2011; Nabilou, 2017) challenge to both the Volcker Rule's efficacy and its resilience against deregulatory rollbacks lies in the subjectivity of separating prohibited speculative investment from permitted market-making and hedging activities. Because significant exemptions[6] were built into the Rule from the beginning, interpreting when these exemptions hold has been of central interest to the banking lobbying and regulators alike. As Lehmann (2016, p 178) writes: 'Details that appear, at first sight, to be of a merely technical nature often reflect underlying assumptions about the social values of various financial services, about "right" and "wrong" banking activities, and about the appropriate amount of risk-taking for an economy.' These are fundamentally both normative and interpretive questions, and their slipperiness leads critics of the Rule from both the pro-regulatory and de-regulatory sides to term the rule 'ineffective' (Chatterjee, 2011) and 'unworkable' (Piasio, 2013). There is no objective bright line dividing speculation from hedging and market-making,[7] and legislators left much of the work of distinguishing the two to the protracted agency rulemaking process. As Lehmann (2016, p 180) notes, the Volcker Rule's prohibition on proprietary trading is quite limited compared to a return to Glass-Steagall style separation of investment and commercial banking. Banks can still trade US Treasury bonds and government-sponsored enterprises (GSE) securities, underwrite securities, engage in market making and risk mitigating hedging, buy and sell securities on behalf of their customers, as well as invest in small businesses. The ban is on what are perceived as the riskiest investment activities, not investment activities per se, leaving the post-Glass Steagall universal banking model, in which deposit-taking institutions also participate in investment banking, more or less intact (Lehmann, 2016).

In attempting to pin down which transactions were prohibited by the Volcker Rule, regulators appealed to the time horizons of the transactions, identifying short-term transactions as particularly likely to be for proprietary purposes. However, even this is far from a clear standard as what constitutes a short-term transaction varies significantly by markets, assets, and customer needs; banks may need to sell long-term assets quickly if they fall sharply in value. In its initial study, the Financial Stability Oversight Council (2011), the federal organization established by the Dodd-Frank Act to monitor risk-taking in the financial system, advised regulators to consider a range of indicators that were written into the rulemaking: limited liquidity, low trading volumes, rapidly growing new products, embedded leverage, historical volatility, Value-at-Risk, hard-to-value assets, and assets whose exposure cannot be quantified are all markers of high-risk, prohibited assets and trading strategies. But who determines whether a given transaction meets the criteria? The final rulemaking tasks internal bank compliance desks with this determination, abdicating core supervisory responsibilities to internal risk monitoring.

This fundamental ambiguity is problematic for further reasons: if standards are applied unevenly across banks, they may lead to regulatory arbitrage opportunities. Moreover, as Whitehead (2011, p 51) observes, because there is no objective distinction between permitted and prohibited activities, this Rule becomes gameable by banks: they can implement technically compliant trading strategies that may nonetheless place the bank at significant risk. Finally, the difficulty of separating holding assets for customers as part of market-making activities from holding assets on the books for purposes of bank profits makes the Rule an easy target for criticism and rollbacks, as we learned in 2020. For these reasons, many observers – including Volcker himself – have concluded that the exemptions introduced into the Rule weaken and undermine the Rule's efficacy (Nabilou, 2017).

Banking and finance are social activities, whose practices and legitimacy are dependent on a host of normative beliefs, social processes, and taken-for-granted assumptions about the relationship between states and markets. Therefore, it should not come as a surprise that banking regulation is plagued with irreducibly interpretive questions. These interpretive questions do not render the Volcker Rule ineffective – my argument is instead that such ambiguities are the inevitable result of choosing to leave the universal banking model intact, prioritizing US banks' arguments about their global competitiveness over competing goals related to paring down bank strength and systemic risk. Moreover, these interpretive challenges *are* a problem to the extent that their resolution is outsourced to banks themselves and that they give fuel to opponents looking to weaken even the Rule's limited prohibition on proprietary trading and investment activities.

The Volcker Rule vs. the financial system

In this sub-section I turn to a final, more fundamental way in which the Volcker Rule's efficacy is constrained: its reluctance to fully sever ties between depository institutions and the broader financial system. As discussed in the first section, the late 20th century saw a blurring of the lines between traditional banking activities and financial investment. By the end of the 20th century, banks, which had initially turned to capital markets to offload the risks associated with maturity transformation, quickly realized that they could use these markets to trade for their own account via syndicated loans and secondary loan trading. Credit default swaps (CDS), in particular, represented a powerful tool that banks used for both risk transfer and profit-making purposes. Bank of America estimated that 13 percent of the CDS market in 2006 involved the net transfer of credit risk away from banks' loan portfolios (Whitehead, 2011, p 64).

Even as banks were turning to capital markets, capital markets were increasingly taking on core traditional banking functions, with market-making increasingly taking place in securities markets via non-bank intermediaries who used derivatives and structured securities to bridge the maturity gap between investors and borrowers. The so-called shadow banking sector began acquiring and securitizing debt instruments financed with short-term external debt. Crucially, however, because shadow banking relies on credit markets, rather than deposits, for funding, there is no public insurance provision to back short-term liabilities nor access to a discount window to provide emergency liquidity such as FDIC-insured banks have enjoyed since 1933, making trading in this sector much riskier. Banks' shadow banking special investment vehicles are particularly vulnerable to liquidity crises, as a result: their trading strategy relies on high levels of leverage which must be unwound quickly, resulting in fire sales of long-term assets to meet short-term demands.

The shadow banking sector is not separate from the conventional banking sector: the liquidity spirals that shadow banking is particularly vulnerable to, can rapidly spread to the banking sector due to the tight linkages between the two.[8] As Morgan and Sheehan (2015) have observed, the Volcker Rule does not remove banks from financial networks including shadow banking. Moreover, an immediate result of the Volcker Rule's enactment was the exit of proprietary trading desks' financial activities to hedge funds, which are less regulated than banks, potentially leading to an overall increase in risk-taking. While US banks are no longer as directly exposed to these risks as when their own hedge funds and proprietary trading desks were directly involved in capital market investment, banks continue to rely on CDS for hedging and market-making purposes, exposing them to market-based risks associated with hedge funds' solvency and the possibility of highly correlated investment strategies or performance (Whitehead, 2011, p 70). In the aftermath of the crisis, hedge fund investments and numbers rapidly surpassed their pre-crisis peak and remain central to banks' activities.

The riskiness of this relationship was illustrated by the London Whale Trade – a US$6.2 billion trading loss incurred by J.P. Morgan, at the hands of a trader who worked at the bank's Central Investment Office, which was supposed to provide hedging for the bank, offsetting balance sheet risks. This loss did not involve proprietary trading, illustrating that even arguably permissible hedging can put banks at substantial risk of loss and that continued speculation in CDS markets remains intact.

Morgan and Sheehan (2015, p 696) identify a core neo-classical economic logic to the Volcker Rule: one that aims to make markets function better via curbing excesses and limiting losses rather than fundamentally altering the power and purpose of a crisis-prone system. The Volcker Rule, they write, attempts to:

> tame and stabilize entities that retain their significance within the system. As such, success can be an ever-present potential for failure because financial organizations remain powerful as actors with political influence and remain integrated into a market system that is vulnerable precisely because of the significance of finance as part of that system. (p 700)

Their critique, which is broadly shared by this chapter, is that the Volcker Rule does little to rein in the central dynamic of the too-big-to-fail dynamic: the entrenched political power of private firms whose individual and especially systemic risk-taking is backstopped by public resources.

Conclusion

The Volcker Rule's many exemptions and ambiguities are illustrative of its reluctance to risk erode the practices and relationships at the heart of the US banking sector's competitiveness and exceptional profitability. Rather than ban position-taking outright (floated in Bloomberg by prominent financial writer Michael Lewis in 2010) or reinstate a divide between commercial and investment banking as the frequently defeated McCain-Warren-Cantwell bill would attempt, regulators instead have spent years and literally thousands of pages attempting to clarify which transactions are permissible and which are not. Critics of banking regulation are quick to point out the potentially significant economic costs associated with doing away with the universal banking model and its permissiveness to deposit-taking institutions' profitable investments entirely and to dismiss as unthinkable or impossible a return to Glass–Steagall. As financial lawyer Rex Chatterjee writes:

> because of globalization, the financial services industry as we know it has crossed that Rubicon. Many of the large firms that function as both commercial and investment banks – the so-called 'banking entities' – are too vital to the health of the US and global economies to cleave them into separate parts: commercial bank from investment bank, or client-servicing firm from trading firm. (2011, p 60)

Chatterjee's argument is that because banks were allowed to grow so big and powerful throughout the end of the 20th and early 21st centuries, we are now unable to regulate them strongly, is a bleak conclusion. We need not – and should not – as Chatterjee does, accept this conclusion on normative grounds or regard the inability to regulate big banks as final or inevitable in order to appreciate the extent to which this argument has animated the history of the Volcker Rule's rulemaking, implementation, and subsequent weakening. From the moment legislators and regulators, who were all to easily swayed by the banking industry's claims to systemic importance and centrality to the US economy, decided that commercial and investment banking was too tightly enmeshed to ever fully sever, the resulting policy was destined to be characterized by a host of ambiguous exceptions and a failure to end banks' exposure to the risks of unregulated shadow banking. As Patashnik (2008, p 32) writes of policy erosion more generally, 'All the political compromises and administrative complexities that were denied or papered over during the adoption phase will show themselves, sooner if not later'.

In addition to contributing to our understanding of ineffective policy by highlighting the consequences of lack of clarity surrounding what a given policy is intended to accomplish, this analysis of the Volcker Rule also has profound implications for the public, the intended beneficiaries of this policy. Outrage at the public backstopping of private financial firms provided much of the initial motivation for the Volcker Rule, but there is little reason to think that the Volcker Rule reforms have made banks any less systemically important and therefore likely to bailed out or backstopped in the next crisis. While the ban on proprietary trading was intended to make banks' investment activities less risky and therefore less likely to bring about the kinds of solvency and liquidity crises the sector saw in 2008, there has been surprisingly little effort to analyze whether this is in fact the case, especially given the many exemptions and exceptions introduced into the Rule. More generally, the processes documented in this chapter reflect just how weak the public is vis-à-vis the financial sector: from the beginning, regulators sided with banks' argument (sometimes made explicitly, sometimes taken for granted) that their competitiveness and profitability hinged on their investment activities, resulting in a form of policy making that targeted particular kinds of investment activities rather than the structure of banking more generally. The public's interest, to the extent that it was represented in this process at all, was reduced to preventing excessive risk-taking by banks, while the disproportionate privilege and influence these private institutions enjoy in the policy landscape remains fundamentally unaltered.

Notes

[1] Only about US$428 billion were actually disbursed and later repaid, but the magnitude of both the authorization and the actual spending was central to public opposition to what was widely perceived as a bail-out of the private sector with taxpayer funds.

[2] This bill, or variants of it, have been introduced in 2013, 2015 (co-sponsored by Senators Warren and McCain) and 2017 (co-sponsored by McCain, Warren, Cantwell, and King) without success.

[3] Gary (2012) notes that not all the changes hashed out in the legislative process weakened the final version of the amendment. Language about 'facilitating customer relationships' was omitted from the market-making exemption and the language describing risk-mitigating hedging was tightened. Nonetheless, the balance of the changes added exemptions and loopholes.

[4] The bill also eliminated the Federal Reserve's ability to fail banks on stress tests on the basis of subjective concerns and decreased capital, leverage, and liquidity rules for all but the largest banks.

[5] For example, a conflict of interest that arises when a bank acts as a customer's agent and dealer on the same transaction, producing an incentive to potentially advise clients to buy low quality securities if the bank is also underwriting an IP. Supporters of the Rule also point to conflicts of interest when banks trade on non-public information acquired through knowledge of financial condition of borrowing institutions or exploitation of non-public information.

[6] Even otherwise exempt transactions are still prohibited if they would materially expose a bank to conflicts of interest with clients, but in practice, those conflicts can be very challenging to identify in the context of complex, highly structured, opaque, illiquid, or hard-to-value assets.

[7] For a genealogical look at how legitimate financial practices have been normatively and legally separated from illegitimate ones, see de Goede (2005).

[8] Shadow banking institutions are more vulnerable to liquidity spirals than conventional banks, but they are also better capitalized, possibly due to not enjoying a government guarantee (see Admati and Hellwig, 2014).

References

Admati, A. and Hellwig, M. (2014) *The Bankers' New Clothes: What's Wrong with Banking and What to Do About It*, Princeton, NJ: Princeton University Press.

Baker, A. (2013) 'The gradual transformation? The incremental dynamics of macroprudential regulation', *Regulation & Governance*, 7(4): 417–34.

Baker, C.M. (2015) 'Regulatory reforms and unintended collisions: the case of the Volcker Rule and the over-the-counter derivative markets', *Capital Markets Law Journal*, 10(4): 433–46.

Beutler, B. (2010) 'Scott Brown winning fight for loophole in Volcker Rule,' *TPM* [online] 23 June, Available from: https://talkingpointsmemo.com/dc/scott-brown-winning-fight-for-loophole-in-volcker-rule.

Chatterjee, R.R. (2011) 'Dictionaries fail: the Volcker Rule's reliance on definitions renders it ineffective and a new solution is needed to adequately regulate proprietary trading', *Brigham Young University International Law & Management Review*, 8(1): 33–62.

Cheung, B. (2020) 'Fed to pare back "Volcker rule" to expand bank investment in venture capital, securitized loans', *Yahoo!Finance* [online] 30 January, Available from: https://finance.yahoo.com/news/federal-reserve-volcker-rule-covered-funds-capital-securitized-loans-150332315.html.

Crotty, J., Epstein, G., and Levina, I. (2010) 'Proprietary trading is a bigger deal than many bankers and pundits claim', 18 February, Economists' Committee for Stable, Accountable, Fair, and Efficient Financial Reform. Policy Note No. 15.

DeGoede, M. (2005) *Virtue, Fortune, and Faith: A Genealogy of Finance*, Minneapolis, MN: University of Minnesota Press.

Duffie, D. (2010) 'The failure mechanics of dealer banks', *The Journal of Economic Perspectives*, 24(1): 51–72.

Financial Stability Oversight Council (2011) *Annual Report*, Available from: https://home.treasury.gov/system/files/261/FSOCAR2011.pdf.

Gary, A.K. (2012) 'Creating a future economic crisis: political failure and the loopholes of the Volcker rule', *Oregon Law Review*, 90(5): 1339–88.

Government Accountability Office (2011) 'Proprietary trading: regulators will need more comprehensive information to fully monitor compliance with new restrictions when implemented', GAO-11–529 [online] Available from: https://www.gao.gov/assets/gao-11-529.pdf.

Johnson, S. and Kwak, J. (2011) *13 Bankers: The Wall Street Takeover and the Next Financial Meltdown*, London: Vintage Books.

Krawiec, K.D. and Liu, G. (2015) 'The Volcker Rule: a brief political history', *Capital Markets Law Journal*, 10(4): 507–22.

Krugman, P. (2010) 'Bankers without a clue', *New York Times* [online] 14 January, Available from: https://www.nytimes.com/2010/01/15/opinion/15krugman.html.

Kwak, J. (2014) 'Cultural capture and the financial crisis', in D. Carpenter and D.A. Moss (eds) *Preventing Regulatory Capture: Special Interest Influence and How to Limit It*, New York: Cambridge University Press.

Lavelle, K.C. (2014) 'Implementing the Volcker Rule in national and international politics', in T. Porter (ed) *Transnational Financial Regulation after the Crisis*, New York: Routledge.

Lehmann, M. (2016) 'Volcker Rule, ring-fencing or separation of bank activities – comparison of structural reform acts around the world', *Journal of Banking Regulation*, 17: 176–87.

Lockwood, E. (2020) 'From bombs to boons: changing views of risk and regulation in the pre-crisis OTC derivatives market', *Theory and Society*, 49: 215–44.

Merle, R. (2020) 'Federal Reserve proposes weakening Volcker Rule, key post-financial crisis regulation', *Washington Post* [online] 30 January, Available from: https://www.washingtonpost.com/business/2020/01/30/volcker-rule-fed/.

Morgan, J. and Sheehan, B. (2015) 'Has reform of global finance been misconceived? policy documents and the Volcker Rule', *Globalizations*, 12(5): 695–709.

Moschella, M. (2013) *Great Expectations, Slow Transformations: Incremental Change in Post-Crisis Regulation*, Colchester: ECPR Press.

Nabilou, H. (2017) 'Bank proprietary trading and investment in private funds: is the Volcker Rule a panacea or yet another Maginot Line?', *Banking and Finance Law Review*, 32(2): 298–341.

Obama, B. (2010) 'Remarks by the President on financial reform' [online] 21 January, Available from: https://obamawhitehouse.archives.gov/the-press-office/remarks-president-financial-reform.

Patashnik, E.M. (2008) *Reforms at Risk: What Happens After Major Policy Changes Are Enacted*, Princeton, NJ: Princeton University Press.

Piasio, C.A. (2013) 'It's complicated: why the Volcker Rule is unworkable', *Seton Hall Law Review*, 43(2): 737–71.

Rajan, R.G. (2011) *Fault Lines: How Hidden Fractures Still Threaten the World Economy*, Princeton, NJ: Princeton University Press.

Richardson, M., Smith, R.C., and Walter, I. (2010) 'Large banks and the Volcker Rule', in V.A. Acharya, T.F. Cooley, and M.P. Richardson (eds) *Regulating Wall Street: The Dodd-Frank Act and the New Architecture of Global Finance*, New York: John Wiley & Sons.

Schiff, J. (2020) 'The Volcker Rule in practice: its impact, reception, and evolving profile', *Columbia Business Law Review*, 2: 743–800.

Schroeder, P. (2021) 'Analysis: Biden's new Fed regulation chief faces dilemma over Trump rules rewrite', *Reuters* [online] 16 December, Available from: https://www.reuters.com/markets/us/bidens-new-fed-regulation-chief-faces-dilemma-over-trump-rules-rewrite-2021-12-16/.

Whitehead, C.K. (2011) 'The Volcker rule and evolving financial markets', *Harvard Business Law Review*, 1(1): 39–74.

11

Borrowing money from the fringes: the problematic regulation of payday loans in Canada and the US

Heather McKeen-Edwards

Payday lending is a highly contested issue in North American society. The industry's association with claims of financial insecurity, over-indebtedness, and poverty encourage continuous discussions on its role in both consumer finance and social welfare. Policy decisions on how it should be regulated can significantly impact both harm and opportunity for individuals. This chapter examines the policies that have emerged to address payday lending in Canada and the US, arguing that this is ineffective policy. Both countries have adopted regulatory policy tools guided by ideas of responsible lending. However, policies have been built within an uncoordinated policy system, particularly between jurisdictions, which has led to an ineffective regulatory patchwork. This chapter argues that this framework is ineffective for two reasons. First, regulatory arbitrage undermines the efficacy of individual policies by creating gaps within each country, while also generating additional challenges for borrower financial literacy. Second, there is a disproportionate focus on regulation, with little systematic interest in policies encouraging the development of alternative financial solutions. These realities are more than abstract issues as they allow income and financially vulnerable borrowers to continue to be exposed to harm.

Consumer finance and the rise of payday lending

The past 35 years have been marked by the explosive increase in the consumer credit market and its increasing centralization into economic life around the world. Conventional liberal economic analysis argues that this development has expanded economic opportunities and well-being overall, highlighting its connection to credit playing 'an important role in life cycle budgeting, balancing saving and spending and income smoothing' (Ramsay, 2012, p 26). Many critical scholars, however, link the growth of consumer credit to larger negative economic trends, particularly the stagnation of wages, changing employment system, and the constriction of the welfare state.

These changes increase credit demand as individuals struggle to address financial shortfalls in their everyday lives.

As the need for consumer credit expanded, however, mainstream banks increasingly left the small amount lending market and closed branches in low-income areas across North America (Ramsay, 2000; Elliehausen and Lawrence, 2001; Marsh et al, 2010; Buckland, 2012). This left a gap and the need for credit is increasingly met by loans from alternative financial actors, like payday lenders in what is broadly called fringe financial services.[1] In the US, Americans borrow nearly US$29 billion dollars a year collectively (Confessore and Cowley, 2020) and every year more than 12 million borrowers take out payday loans in states where it is legal (Consumer Financial Protection Bureau, 2022b). In the much smaller Canadian market, the sector is still estimated to issue loans with a face value between C$2.3 to 2.7 billion per year (Buckland and Spotton Visano, 2018, p 4).

However, as they are companies who do not take deposits, fringe finance is subject to different regulations than banks and credit unions. Payday lending is one of the most widely known forms of non-bank lending, focusing on providing small value loans to individuals over a short term, traditionally a single payday ranging from a few weeks to a month. These loans are well-known for being particularly high-cost, with their interest and fees often reaching triple-digit annual percentage interest rates (APR). This combination of demand, supply, and regulatory policy system has arguably created an ideal environment for over-indebtedness (Montgomerie, 2006, p 109) and financial harm for individuals. As such, they have been subject to longstanding policy debates.

It is important to recognize that as the industry has grown over the years, payday loan markets are increasingly dominated by large corporations and online lenders that operate in multiple jurisdictions. This is a significant change from the early forms of lenders and the conceptualization of the industry as populated by small localized storefront businesses within the community, such as 'mom and pop' shops. Today's payday lending markets are also part of a significant globalized financial industry (Packman, 2014), adding another dimension of geographic breadth. Therefore, payday lending is best conceptualized as a 'mature industry with chronic challenges' (Consumer Financial Protection Bureau, 2022b).

Payday lending, vulnerability, and harm

When considering if payday lending is bad policy one can first look to whether the lending process itself creates harm. The impact of this kind of lending on borrowers has received considerable attention over the past 20 years and various researchers have come up with different results. A number of studies have argued against a universal link to exclusion and harm, finding that some payday borrowers choose to take on this type of loan for factors like convenience or an aversion to mainstream banks (Ramsay, 2000, p 17; Rowlingson et al, 2016). Others argue that payday lending and other fringe finance can be useful in certain circumstances like unexpected financial emergencies (Elliehausen and Lawrence, 2001; Morse, 2011) and may reduce the need to undertake personal bankruptcy (Barth et al, 2020). Some also assert that the higher interest rates and fees charged can be justified because of high fixed costs and risk of default assumed by the lender (Flannery and Samolyk, 2005).

However, many other analyses highlight the connection of this high-cost lending to larger social ills of poverty, economic precariousness, and financial exclusion. Buckland (2012) has developed an extensive and comprehensive argument on the inherent connection between financial exclusion and the use of fringe banking. Other studies also raise concerns about the impact of the very high interest rates/fees on income (Kempson et al, 2004; Buckland and Thibault, 2005) and the potential role of frequent or chronic use by borrowers (Stegman and Faris, 2003). Questions about choice are raised by findings that consumers are likely to borrow from fringe lenders, regardless of warnings about the high costs, due to economic and/or social constraints and perceptions of few alternatives (Wilson et al, 2009).

Therefore, it is hard to argue in a universal way that this kind of short-term lending is universally 'bad'. Even if one accepts the argument of exclusion and precariousness, there is reasonable concern that curtailing payday lending without developing viable lending alternatives could lead to more hardship (Zinman, 2008), particularly for those who use loans to cover basic needs. As Ben-Ishai et al (2021) assert, 'banning payday loans is not much of a solution. There is a need that payday loans respond to for those who are disenfranchised from traditional financial products and services. An access issue here creates justice issues elsewhere' (p 208). This situation presents a proverbial regulatory needle for the government to be thread.

Regulating payday lending

The existence of this industry at the edges of legitimate financial governance,[2] and research that ties it to financial exclusion and rising personal debt, has meant the legitimacy of payday loans has been questioned since it emerged (Caskey, 2004; Buckland et al, 2018; Hembruff and Soederberg, 2019). In order to understand why payday lending policies in Canada and the US are ineffective, it is necessary to explain how each country has approached it in more detail.

Canadian regulatory environment

Canada is a federal country with some powers allocated to ten subnational provinces. However, since 1980, the cost of lending has been covered nationally under Section 347 of the Criminal Code of Canada which criminalizes excessive interest rates. This law made it illegal for a lender to charge above 60 percent APR on a loan. In essence, this would make payday lending with its triple digit APR rates illegal. Yet by the 1990s, payday lending was growing in every province other than Quebec. Enforcement of these violations of the criminal code were rare (Kobzar, 2012) as the consent of a provincial Attorney General was required to prosecute. This inconsistency in enforcement created a window for avoidance (Banks et al, 2015) and eventually led to the filing of class-action lawsuits against lenders in the early 2000s. In response to the specter of the class-action suits, the industry pushed for a solution and the government created a federal/provincial Consumer Measures Committee Working Group on the Alternative Consumer Credit Market to discuss the issue (Irving, 2010). When a British Columbia provincial judge on one of these lawsuits found that a payday loan company was violating the Canadian Criminal Code (*Kilroy v. A OK Payday Loans Inc*, 2007), this jumpstarted regulatory policy change (Kitching and Starky, 2006). The federal government introduced Bill C-26, which amended Section 347 of the Criminal Code to exempt payday lenders from the usury cap if their province regulated the industry through their constitutional jurisdiction for contract law, in 2006. This regulation centered around creating a licensing system, setting limits on the cost of borrowing, and ensuring adequate consumer protections in provincial regulation (Ben-Ishai, 2008). The exemption was specific to payday lenders as it was limited to loans that were under C$1500 and less than 62 days in duration (Government of Canada, 2007, p c9). This intentional choice by the federal government is the source of the payday lending regulatory patchwork in Canada up to this day.

In the aftermath of Bill C-26, the provinces reacted in very different ways. In Quebec, all lending over a 35 percent APR was already prohibited in the 1970s and they chose to maintain this provincial rate (Ben-Ishai, 2008). This meant there was no exception made for payday loans. All lenders in the province remain licensed by the *Office de la Protection du Consummator* and are required to offer loans at rates that do not exceed the provincially mandated APR. The historical presence of this stricter interest rate cap meant that the industry never really emerged in the province.

The other nine provinces, however, have moved over the years to introduce payday loan specific regulations but at different paces. Manitoba and Nova Scotia were the first provinces to introduce regulation for this type of lending.[3] They were followed relatively quickly by Ontario, British Columbia, and Alberta. In these provinces regulatory systems were in effect by 2009[4] and they have been updated over time to make interest rate and fee caps more strict and introduce other regulatory requirements. In Saskatchewan, Prince Edward Island (PEI), and New Brunswick, payday regulations were also introduced within a few years but took many years to come into effect. In Saskatchewan, the Payday Loans Act was passed in 2007 but its subsequent regulations only began in January 2012. PEI passed its relevant law in 2009, with related regulations only effective in 2015. Meanwhile, New Brunswick did not implement regulations until 2018, which was approximately a decade later (Dilay and Williams, 2018, p 189).

Finally, the province of Newfoundland and Labrador was the late mover in regulating payday loans. It initially made the choice to leave the Criminal Code in effect with the government reaffirming this in 2010, 'we could not in good conscience implement regulations that potentially could result in annual interest rates equating to nearly 550 per cent' (Newfoundland, 2010). However, the window of avoidance also remained. In 2014 a 3-year police investigation revealed that payday lenders were active in the province but the prosecutor's office declined to lay charges (Antle, 2014). It was only in 2019 that the province finally enacted provincial regulations within its *Consumer Protection and Business Practices Act*[5] (Government of Newfoundland, 2019).

US regulatory environment

In the US, regulation of payday lending began and has largely remained at the subnational (state) level. To bring some order to an assessment of 50 states, the framework proposed by the Pew Trusts is useful. It categorized payday regulation approaches into four categories: restrictive, reformed, some safeguards and few safeguards (Pew Charitable Trusts, 2022). In 2022, 18 states, as well as Washington DC, fall into the 'restrictive' category having enacted interest rate caps or strong laws that severely limit or outright ban licensed payday lending. North Carolina, for example, put in place a usury limit of 36 percent APR for payday loans in 2001 and by 2006 the lenders had left the state (Wolff, 2015). These regulatory policies serve to essentially stunt the growth of the legal industry like in Quebec.

The other three categories of regulation capture states that allow payday loans. Most states have brought in more regulations over time but there is still significant variation in the amount and type of safeguards provided. The 'reformed' category covers the four states that have built comprehensive legislation to lower the cost of payday loans, while also requiring 'loans be repayable in affordable installments, and preserve consumers' access to credit' (Pew Charitable Trusts, 2022). There are five states that fall into the 'some safeguards' category. These states have lower than average prices and limited protections in place. These rules are generally more permissive than comprehensive regulations mentioned earlier, but they do provide some stronger protections to consumers. However, the majority of states, 23 overall, fall into the 'few safeguards' category with permissive payday lending structures. In this category states have no 'meaningful protections to ensure affordable payments; APRs above 250 percent; and [allow] single-payment loans' (Pew Charitable Trusts, 2022). Unsurprisingly, they have substantially larger amounts of payday lending and higher costs. For example, Florida averaged 5.4 loans per borrower a year with a total of 3,605,089 loans issued in the state, while much smaller Iowa averaged 11 loans per borrower, with 340,776 loans issued in the state (Glottmann et al, 2023).

Until recently, there was little national regulation in the US. Regulatory action was limited to the Military Lending Act passed in the 2000s which essentially prohibited payday lending to active service members by establishing a 36 percent APR cap. A push for a broader national level regulatory framework emerged in 2010 following the financial crisis. Furthermore, after significant policy contestation, the Consumer Financial Protection Bureau (CFPB) announced in June 2016 that it would create regulations for payday lending. The CFPB's regulation for payday, vehicle title, and certain high-cost installment loans was announced in November 2017 and was specifically aimed at preventing debt traps for borrowers (Consumer Financial Protection Bureau, 2016; Government of the United States, 2017). However, like with the Volcker Rule in the previous chapter, it was weakened and challenged from day one and generally efforts were shifted by the Trump Administration. One of the most prominent aspects of the regulation was the requirement of an 'ability to pay test' for borrowers focusing on affordability (Dilay and Williams, 2018). However, by 2019 the government was looking to eliminate this aspect, and when 'the Bureau issued a final rule in 2020 that effectively limited the pathway forward for regulatory protections through CFPB rulemaking' (Glottmann et al, 2023, p 5). What remains of the regulation also faces significant effectiveness problems. A 2018 industry-led lawsuit that challenges the jurisdiction of the CFPB is currently under consideration in the Supreme Court in 2023. According to the *Washington Post*, this legal maneuver has been effective in stalling ongoing CFPB investigations and punishments of the industry (Romm, 2023). In essence, it can be argued that the efforts of the CFPB have 'largely fallen short' (Macfarlane and Thrasher, 2021, p 1) and the regulatory patchwork continues.

Regulatory policy tools

In most states and provinces, legitimation of payday lending is provided if they meet a defined range of 'acceptable' practices that are laid out in regulation. This is communicated through the requirement that a lender should be licensed to provide loans,[6] and then connecting the license to more specific policies and regulatory tools. The regulatory practices of different jurisdictions can be deconstructed using the discourse of responsible lending in consumer finance more broadly. The International Financial Consumer Protection Organization (FinCoNet, 2014) has identified three main categories of regulatory practices in responsible lending:

- Consumer engagement: this refers to practices that encourage consumers to choose suitable products. These include additional or specific disclosure requirements, protections from misleading advertising, guaranteed 'cooling off' periods allowing consumers to withdraw from the loan contract, or requirements related to provide or support broader financial literacy initiatives, programs, or funds.
- Industry-based requirements: this refers to practices focused on proper business conduct. These include requirements for lenders to assess ability to repay or other affordability assessments of borrowers, as well as things like limits on harmful collection practices.
- Regulatory controls: this refers to practices focused on altering or limiting product design. These include financial instrument specific limitations like interest rate and fee caps, bans on rolling over loans, limits on the amount of money that can be borrowed, maximum payback (total cost) caps, and so on.

After a detailed examination of regulatory documents in the different jurisdictions in Canada and the US, it is clear each of these practices are incorporated into payday lending regulation. Table 11.1 looks at the main features in Canadian jurisdictions, while Table 11.2 focuses on the US.

Turning to Canada, common regulatory tools are evidently used, drawing from all of the areas of responsible lending. All provinces with payday regulation have explicit disclosure requirements, particularly for indicating the maximum cost of credit on the loan and other terms to borrowers.[7] A similar overarching agreement on the policy tools related to the cost of borrowing and features like rollovers is also clear. However, looking more closely, the strength and specifics of different tools vary between provinces. The maximum cost allowed ranges between C$14 and C$17 per C$100 loan, which are still triple-digit APRs. The cooling off periods to cancel a loan are 2 days in many provinces, but only 24 hours in Nova Scotia and Saskatchewan. Furthermore, borrowing limits range between 30 percent of net pay in Manitoba and a C$1500 fixed limit that is not income sensitive (Dilay and Williams, 2018, p 189). The monitoring of payday lending also varies, so comparable statistics from the provincial regulators are not generally available.

Turning to look at the regulations in the US, all states have disclosure components related to lending, particularly in terms of what information needs to be presented in the loan contract. Beyond this, many assessments are quite focused on the cost of borrowing regulation. Unsurprisingly, once

Table 11.1: Regulatory tools used in Canadian payday lending regulations

	Consumer engagement				Industry requirements	Primary regulatory controls			
	Licensing system	General disclosure and advertising rules	APR explicit in contract	Financial literacy information or education tool	Borrowing limit (maximum loan amount) based on borrower's net monthly income	Limits on interest and charges (per $100)	Maximum interest cap on arrears	Rollover ban	Installment or extended payment plan option
Alberta	Yes	Yes	Yes	Yes		$15	Yes	Yes	Yes
British Columbia	Yes	Yes	Yes		Yes	$17	Yes	Yes	
Manitoba	Yes	Yes	Yes		Yes	$17	Yes	Yes	
New Brunswick	Yes	Yes	Yes	Yes	Yes	$15	Yes	Yes	
Newfoundland	Yes	Yes	Yes		Yes	$14	Yes	Yes	
Nova Scotia	Yes	Yes	Yes			$15	Yes	Yes	*
Ontario	Yes	Yes			Yes	$15	Yes	Yes	Yes
PEI	Yes	Yes				$15	Yes	Yes	
Quebec									
Saskatchewan	Yes	Yes	Yes		Yes	$17	Yes	Yes	

Note: * Nova Scotia has recommended this option but it is not currently in effect

Table 11.2: Key regulatory tools used in US payday lending regulations

	Pew classification	Average cost to borrow $500 or the max loan for 4 months (1)	Most common form of loan (installment or single payment) (1)	Rollover loans restrictions (2)	Extended repayment options (3)
Alabama	Few limitations	$521	Single	Limited	Yes
Alaska	Few limitations	$640	Single	Limited	Yes
Arizona	Restricted				
Arkansas	Restricted				
California	Few limitations	$360	Single	Prohibited	Yes
Colorado	Reformed	$110	Installment	Limited^	
Connecticut	Restricted				
Delaware	Few limitations	$390	Installment	Limited	Yes
Florida	Few limitations	$430	Single	Prohibited	Yes
Georgia	Restricted				
Hawaii	Reformed	$158	Installment	Prohibited	
Idaho	Few limitations	$1,000	Single	Limited	Yes
Illinois	Restricted				
Indiana	Few limitations	$536	Single	Prohibited	Yes
Iowa	Few limitations	$440	Single	Prohibited*	
Kansas	Few limitations	$600	Single	Prohibited*	
Kentucky	Few limitations	$712	Single	Prohibited	
Louisiana	Few limitations	$435	Single	Limited^	Yes
Maine	Some restrictions	$200	Single	Prohibited^	
Maryland	Restricted				
Massachusetts	Restricted				
Michigan	Few limitations	$525	Single	Prohibited	Yes
Minnesota	Some restrictions	$251	Single	Prohibited	
Mississippi	Few limitations	$324	Installment	Prohibited	
Missouri	Few limitations	$445	Installment	Limited	
Montana	Restricted				
Nabraska	Restricted				

(continued)

Table 11.2: Key regulatory tools used in US payday lending regulations (continued)

	Pew classification	Average cost to borrow $500 or the max loan for 4 months (1)	Most common form of loan (installment or single payment) (1)	Rollover loans restrictions (2)	Extended repayment options (3)
Nevada	Few limitations	$924	Single	Limited	Yes
New Hampshire	Restricted				
New Jersey	Restricted				
New Mexico	Restricted				
New York	Restricted				
North Carolina	Restricted				
North Dakota	Few limitations	$543	Single	Limited	
Ohio	Reformed	$159	Installment		
Oklahoma	Some restrictions	$204	Installment	Prohibited	
Oregon	Some restrictions	$157	Single	Limited	
Pennsylvania	Restricted				
Rhode Island	Few limitations	$360	Single	Limited	
South Carolina	Few limitations	$603	Single	Prohibited	Yes
South Dakota	Restricted				
Tennessee	Few limitations	$600	Single	Prohibited	
Texas	Few limitations	$645	Installment		
Utah	Few limitations	$850	Single	Limited	Yes
Vermont	Restricted				
Virginia	Reformed	$138	Installment	Prohibited	Yes
Washington	Some restrictions	$210	Single	Prohibited	Yes
West Virginia	Restricted				
Wisconsin	Few limitations	$395	Installment	Limited	Yes
Wyoming	Few limitations	$361	Single	Prohibited	Yes

Notes: * Iowa and Kansas restrict loans from being repaid with the proceeds of another, functionally a rollover restriction.

^ Author addition taken from assessing state regulation.

Sources: Author, using (1) information from Center for Responsible Lending (2023); (2) Office of the Federal Register (2019); (3) Consumer Financial Protection Bureau (2022a).

attention is shifted here, the patchwork nature of the system becomes clear but with even more pronounced differences than in Canada. For example, average APRs range from 36 percent in a restrictive state like North Carolina, to 114 percent in the reformed state of Colorado, and up to 652 percent in Idaho. Given this, payday loans cost four times more in states that have fewer protections (Pew Charitable Trusts, 2022). Table 11.2 highlights how these result in a wide range of costs for borrowing across states. Similar variations can be seen in whether states allow rollover loans or provide extended repayment options.

Payday policy as ineffective policy

State and provincial regulatory policies are assessed individually for their ability to address the problems associated with payday lending. It can already be seen from the two tables how some policy mixes provide more protection for borrowers than others. Returning to the spectrum presented in the introduction, these policies fall in the moderately effective or moderately ineffective categorization. However, regulatory policy does not exist in a vacuum and it is how these policies interact with each other and the larger policy system that further enhances their ineffectiveness. By looking at the whole policy subsystem, two additional significant challenges to the effectiveness of these policies become visible.

Implications of regulatory arbitrage

Regulatory policy for payday lenders is in the jurisdiction of the provinces and states in what is aptly described by Dilay and Williams (2018, p 13) as a 'decentralized regulatory patchwork' of different rules and levels of protection across each country. While federal powers explain why decision making happens in these subnational spaces, the amount of harmonization between actors can be improved by having greater informal coordination between actors to harmonize rules. One can see this in multiple sectors where concerns span beyond state boundaries. There are indications that regulators are aware of actions in other states and provinces, however, there is no formal coordination or explicit indication of interest in harmonizing rules in Canada or the US.

The variation across jurisdictions decreases the efficacy of the payday lending policies in two ways. First, even in states and provinces that have sought to limit the harm of payday lending, their efforts are partly undermined by the decisions of their neighbors. A US study found that there are 14 percent more payday lender branches in areas that border prohibitive states than in more central parts of their home state (Ramirez and Harger, 2020). This implies that potential borrowers in prohibitive states are willing to cross a border to access loans. Some payday lenders have also engaged in partnerships with banks to evade state restrictions in the US, a process better known as rent-a-bank lending. These partnerships are sought as national and state-charter banks have the right to use their home state laws in transactions with consumers in other states under federal law (Nehf, 2022). As borrowers have access to loans offered through other more lenient jurisdictions in border regions or online, it also creates increased pressures on enforcement capacity and monitoring for these states.

This concern can be seen in the recent interest toward more national regulation. A discussion of the ineffectiveness of the initiative of the CFPB in the US has already been discussed earlier. Furthermore, in late 2023 the Canadian federal government introduced legislation to harmonize the maximum charge to C$14 on each C$100 lent – an APR of 336 percent – on payday loans (Galea, 2023). This move has promise and some poverty advocates highlight it as an important step forward in addressing concerns with high-cost credit. However, the focus is exclusively on price/cost regulation, leaving the other regulatory tools and overall licensing still varying across provinces (Dobby, 2023).

Second, regulatory arbitrage is also a significant challenge to the effectiveness of regulatory policy because of its effects on borrowers' financial literacy. The variety within the regulatory tools arguably places some people who utilize payday loans in an even more precarious position vis-à-vis lenders. When there are different rules within a single country, it can be harder for people to know the legal limits in their state or province, and what they are in the jurisdiction of the lender. This is particularly important given the increasingly interconnected national and international marketplace, with the same corporate lenders in different jurisdictions, and the broad reach of payday lending advertising in media/social media. In the case of payday lending, the real or perceived power imbalance between lenders and borrowers is a key part of the justification for regulation as there are concerns of procedural unfairness in lending in general (Schwartz and Robinson, 2018). For example, Aldohni (2013) argues, 'vulnerable consumers will presume that short-term lenders are safe to use because they are licensed. It is that badge of legitimacy that vulnerable consumers rely on, often without understanding the implications of the high interest rate' (p 444). Considering that there are different levels of protection and obligation depending on the state or province, the presumption of what licensing guarantees may not be accurate, not to mention any variations in the fine print of loan agreements.

This challenge to literacy becomes even more problematic when considered in the context of studies that raise questions about whether borrowers can identify their interests (Ben-Shahar and Schneider 2011). Lusardi and de Bassa Scheresberg (2013) find 'most high-cost borrowers display very low levels of financial literacy, that is, they lack numeracy and do not possess knowledge of basic financial concepts. Most importantly, we find that those who are more financially literate are much less likely to have engaged in high-cost borrowing'. A US National Financial Capability Study (NFCS) reinforced this, showing that payday loan users scored lower in five financial capability variables than other borrowers (O'Neill and Xiao, 2015).

The explosion of online lenders and related fintech options also poses a significant opportunity for regulatory arbitrage in payday and other forms of lending.[8] The common emphasis in online lenders is the 'speed, ease, and convenience of obtaining a loan' through the Internet (Chen, 2020), highlighting access to a loan in minutes or guaranteed. A simple Google search of the words loan and a state/province name results in pages and pages of links and advertisements for potential lenders. Online payday loans follow the same process as store fronts, but all communication and transactions are virtual from the loan application through the direct deposit of the money borrowed. It may also include an authorization for automatic electronic withdrawal from the borrower's account for repayment (Bennett, 2019). These lenders are increasingly common in the lending space. A 2023 news report of a Canadian licensed insolvency firm, Hoyes, Michalos and Associates Inc., said it has records of nearly 1,000 different websites running payday lending schemes in their insolvency files administered since 2020 (Alini and Galea, 2023). More problematically, despite the lack of storefront costs, early results from a study by Correia et al (2022) have found that the prices are about 100 percent higher for online loans in the US. These issues are further exacerbated by the emergence of lead generators, as they are not actual lenders despite looking like it to potential borrowers.[9]

The Center for Responsible Lending in the US asserts that Internet lending is a 'burgeoning' sector, often unmonitored by the consumer finance regulatory agencies in states (Glottmann et al, 2023, p 2). In Canada, similar concerns can be observed, particularly as the lack of harmonization in payday lending regulation is magnified with the growth of online payday lenders (Ben-Ishai et al, 2021, p 188). There is an added level of difficulty for regulators as challenges to jurisdiction and enforcement of legislation that 'arise when lenders are located outside the province or the country' (Dilay and Williams, 2018, p 188). Yet, the abstractness of the virtual world also makes it harder for borrowers to identify legal actors and to ensure the presence of warning and disclosure protections.

Focus on regulation with little systematic attention on alternatives

The second challenge relates to the fact that payday lending has largely been addressed by the government through regulatory policies. This makes sense in the context that banning these loans may cause greater harm. At the heart of the payday lending debate there is a conundrum as 'borrowing from payday lenders exacerbates poverty, yet many low-income households rely on these loans' (Banks et al, 2015, p 37). When one looks at the regulation and other policy documents that the governments in Canada and the US produce, there is consistent language that without these loans (or similar fringe lending options), individuals and households will be left even more vulnerable as other mainstream lending options may not be available to them. In this reading, the lack of access to payday loans may become a further point of financial exclusion by removing a credit option from those who are assumed to have very few options. These missing 'viable' alternatives or options language create a perception of 'supply vulnerability', that is 'the lack of options that vulnerable consumers could resort to if they were not going to use payday lenders' (Aldohni, 2013).

This means that to build a 'good' policy that addresses the larger problems that payday lending can exacerbate requires a broader policy toolbox, particularly to encourage different alternative small amount lending options. However, this supply side of the problem has not been the consistent policy focus, as decision makers have primarily concentrated on regulatory tools. There has been very little consistent government policy attention on supporting or developing alternatives. While there are some alternative schemes and tools in different states and provinces, they represent a relatively small and limited market. Instead, the alternatives that exist have emerged in an ad hoc way from civil society groups and other financial actors, like credit unions or banks themselves.

From ineffective policy to bad policy making

Returning to the overall frame of the book, what pushes these ineffective policies into 'bad policy' territory is that they allow, and even increase, harm for some individuals. This is definitely the case here. It is true that payday borrowers do come from a range of socioeconomic classes and some borrowers are capable of utilizing payday loans like any other financial tool. However, these loans are disproportionately utilized by vulnerable individuals. Vulnerability is a contested term, but in this context, it refers to a mixture of income and financial vulnerability, two interconnected but distinct circumstances. Income vulnerability is a lack of funds and resources needed for everyday life. Financial vulnerability connects more to a lack of savings or over-indebtedness. For example, the regulatory justifications of the Public Utilities Board of Manitoba (2013) concluded, 'the common denominator of the majority of payday loan customers is their financial vulnerability. They have insufficient savings, insufficient cash flow and, more than likely, exhausted regular low-cost consumer credit options (assuming they qualify for consumer credit options through main line institutions)' (pp 43–4). This vulnerability is related to possession of funds and access to funding. It is also important to remember that,

> 'Vulnerable consumers' do not form a static separate group in the population. In reality consumer vulnerability can be a transient state that affects people at different periods of time, or it can be long-term in effect. It may be triggered by events such as loss of a job, the onset of disability, or becoming a carer. (George et al, 2014, pp 5)

It is also important to realize that these vulnerabilities do not affect populations within each country consistently. Similar to other poverty statistics, minority groups tend to be overrepresented. A 2016 Financial Consumer Agency of Canada (FCAC) study found 53 percent of payday loan borrowers in Canada earned less than C$55,000 annually. The agency has also estimated that 'by September 2022, 4.52 percent of Canadians had used a payday loan in their lifetime to manage daily expenses [and] Indigenous peoples, recent immigrants, Canadians with low income, and women are over-represented in these results' (Government of Canada, 2023). In the US, similar breakdowns occur, with payday lending utilized in higher proportions by people to lower incomes, recent migrants, and racial minorities (see Charron-Chénier, 2020).

This connection to vulnerable borrowers makes the connection between ineffective policy and harm more significant. Despite continuous industry claims that these loans are primarily used for discretionary spending or an emergency across all socioeconomic classes, studies have shown that the most cited reasons for use have been to cover basic needs, particularly by those with lower income levels. These needs generally include everyday expenses such as food, bills, rent, and other necessities rather than one-time emergency shortfalls (Pew Charitable Trusts, 2012; Banks et al, 2015). Therefore, the potential for harm with this kind of lending is high, it concerns the everyday lives of individuals and families, particularly those with lower and/or more precarious incomes. The connection to harm of an improperly regulated industry is also clear in the rationale for the regulations that prohibits this type of lending to current military members in the US as military leaders testified these high interest loans were exploitative and weakened readiness and morale (Carpenter et al, 2023).

Conclusion

This chapter has focused on payday lending policy and reasons as to why it is a good example of ineffective policy. It has shown that the regulatory frameworks in Canada and the US are intentionally creating regulatory patchworks with distinct rules in each province and state. This structure accepts that there is variation in regulatory requirements, but also creates regulatory gaps across jurisdictions encouraging ineffectiveness. This also increases the potential harm on borrowers as it places additional burdens on them about what products and practices are legal, and which lenders are licensed, in their home state or province. To develop effective payday lending regulatory policy, there should be further debate on how to best address the potential harm of this kind of lending that not only focuses on the regulations themselves, but also considers harmonization between jurisdictions and the need to further develop alternatives to protect vulnerable borrowers. Given that the harm of ineffective policy in this area is greater on groups in society that already face disadvantages and potential exclusion, it is necessary to create 'good' policies that protect citizens better.

Acknowledgments

The author would like to express her appreciation for the research assistance of Michael Chuang, Emily Prangley Desormeaux, Jennifer Rooney, and Regan Simpson as well as the helpful comments from the panel at International Public Policy Association (IPPA) conference in July 2023.

Notes

[1] Fringe financial sector is populated by private incorporated or limited liability companies who offer some basic retail financial services to consumers – including check cashing, payday lending, rent-to-own loans, tax refund anticipation loans, auto title loan services, and pawn shop lending among others.

[2] For more nuanced discussion on the notions of borders and 'fringe' in mainstream finance, see Aitken (2010).

[3] Manitoba quickly moved to introduce payday legislation with regulation coming into effect in 2007 (Payday Loans Regulation, Regulation 99/2007). Nova Scotia amended its Consumer Protection Act in November 2006 and the Payday Lenders Regulations (N.S. Reg. 248/2009) which came into effect in 2009.

[4] Ontario passed specific payday lending legislation in 2008 (Payday Loans Act, S.O. 2008, c. 9) and its related general regulations (Ontario regulation 98/09) have gone through multiple iterations since 2009. In British Columbia, the legislation was passed in 2007 and the Payday Loans Regulations (B.C. Reg. 57/2009) came into effect in 2009. Furthermore, Alberta also passed their payday loans regulation (Alberta Regulation 157/2009) in 2009.

[5] The regulations were amended to be even stricter in 2022 (Strickland, 2022).

[6] Licensing processes include a set of required business practices and other rules, which serve to create a clear dividing line between lenders demarcating some as legitimate and others as illegitimate. If the licensee does not follow these rules, they can be penalized either through fines or through revocation of the license.

[7] Even with the interest and fee maximums, Buckland and Spotton Visano (2018) point out that for the same amount of money, payday loans costs remain over ten times that of a line of credit or credit card cash advance.

[8] While not discussed in this chapter, the emergence of online earned wage advances have been highlighted by some legal scholars to be a new form of payday loan (Hirota, 2020; Nehf, 2022).

[9] Lead generators (including pingtree operators, directory listing, or database lead generators, affiliates, and fee-charging brokers) identify potential borrowers and direct them to payday lenders for a fee. A Canadian study found they are important intermediaries between borrowers and worldwide lenders (Consumers Council of Canada, 2015). In the US, a 2014 report found that lead generators and marketing sites were the source of 75 percent of applications for online payday loans (Pew Charitable Trusts, 2014).

References

Aitken, R. (2010) 'regul(ariz)ation of fringe credit: payday lending and the borders of global financial practice', *Competition and Change*, 14(2): 80–99.

Aldohni, A.K. (2013) "Loan sharks v. short-term lenders: how do the law and regulators draw the line?", *Journal of Law and Society*, 40(3): 420–49.

Alini, E. and Galea, I. (2023) 'The rise of illicit online payday lenders: non-stop collection calls, no licence and no address', *The Globe and Mail* [online] 29 May, Available from: https://www.theglobeandmail.com/investing/personal-finance/household-finances/article-illicit-online-pay day-lenders-consumers/.

Antle, R. (2014) 'Prosecutors opt against N.L. payday loan criminal charges: RNC, RCMP wrapped up 3-year probe in December 2013', *CBC News* [online] 22 December, Available from: http://www.cbc.ca/news/canada/newfoundland-labrador/prosecutors-optagainst-n-l-paydayl oan-criminal-charges-1.287342.

Banks, M., Marston, G., Russell, R., and Karger, H. (2015) 'In a perfect world it would be great if they didn't exist': how Australians experience payday loans', *International Journal of Social Welfare*, 24: 37–47.

Barth, J.R., Hilliard, J., Jahera, J.S., Lee, K.B., and Sun, Y. (2020) 'Payday lending, crime, and bankruptcy: is there a connection?', *Journal of Consumer Affairs*, 54(4): 1159–77.

Ben-Ishai, S. (2008) 'Regulating payday lenders in Canada: drawing on American lessons', *Comparative Research in Law & Political Economy*, Research Paper No. 16/2008.

Ben-Ishai, S., Schwartz, S., Butt, A., and Linton, M. (2021) 'Bankruptcy lessons for payday lending regulation', *University of New Brunswick Law Journal*, 72(January): 173–209.

Bennett, J.N. (2019) 'Fast cash and payday loans', *Page One Economics*, April. https://doi.org/10/fast-cash-and-payday-loans_SE.pdf.

Ben-Shahar, O. and Schneider, C.E. (2011) 'The failure of mandated disclosure', *University of Pennsylvania Law Review*, 159: 647–749.

Buckland, J. (2012) *Hard Choices: Financial Exclusion, Fringe Banks, and Poverty in Urban Canada*, Toronto: University of Toronto Press.

Buckland, J. and Thibault, M. (2005) 'Two-tier banking: the rise of fringe banks in Winnipeg's inner city', *Canadian Journal of Urban Research*, 14(1): 158–81.

Buckland, J. and Visano, B.S. (2018) 'Introduction' in: J. Buckland, C. Robinson, and B.S. Visano (eds) *Payday Lending in Canada in a Global Context: A Mature Industry with Chronic Challenges*, New York: Palgrave Macmillan US, pp 1–40.

Buckland, J., Robinson, C., and Visano, B.S. (eds) (2018) *Payday Lending in Canada in a Global Context: A Mature Industry with Chronic Challenges*, New York: Palgrave Macmillan US.

Carpenter, C.W., Deming, K., Anders, J., Lotspeich-Yadao, M., Tolbert, C.M., and Ingrao, A. (2023) 'Do payday lending bans protect or constrain regional economies? Evidence from the Military Lending Act's final rule', *Contemporary Economic Policy*, 42(2): 1–17.

Caskey, J. (2004) *Fringe Banking: Check-Cashing Outlets, Pawnshops, and the Poor*, New York: Russell Sage Foundation.

Center for Responsible Lending (2023) 'Red alert rates: annual percentage rates on $400, single-payment payday loans in the United States' [online], Available from: https://www.responsiblelending.org/research-publicat ion/red-alert-rates-annual-percentage-rates-400-single-payment-payday-loans-united.

Charron-Chénier, R. (2020) 'Predatory inclusion in consumer credit: explaining black and white disparities in payday loan use', *Sociological Forum*, 35: 370–92.

Chen, V. (2020) 'Online payday lenders: trusted friends or debt traps?', *University of New South Wales Law Journal*, 43(2): 674–706.

Confessore, N. and Cowley, S. (2020) 'Trump appointees manipulated agency's payday lending research, ex-staffer claims', *New York Times* [online] 29 April, Available from: https://www.nytimes.com/2020/04/29/busin ess/cfpb-payday-loans-rules.html.

Consumer Financial Protection Bureau (2016) 'Consumer financial protection bureau proposes rules to end payday debt traps', Consumer Financial Protection Bureau [online] 2 June, Available from: https://www. consumerfinance.gov/about-us/newsroom/consumer-financial-protect ion-bureau-proposes-rule-end-payday-debt-traps/.

Consumer Financial Protection Bureau (2022a) 'Market snapshot: consumer use of state payday loan extended payment plans', Consumer Financial Protection Bureau [online], Available from: https://files.consumerfinance. gov/f/documents/cfpb_market-snapshot-payday-loan-extended-paym ent-plan_report_2022-04.pdf.

Consumer Financial Protection Bureau (2022b) 'CFPB finds payday borrowers continue to pay significant rollover fees despite state-level protections and payment plans', Consumer Financial Protection Bureau [online] 6 April, Available from: https://www.consumerfinance.gov/ about-us/newsroom/cfpb-finds-payday-borrowers-continue-to-pay-sign ificant-rollover-fees-despite-state-level-protections-and-payment-plans/.

Consumers Council of Canada (2015) '2015. Consumer experiences in online payday loans, Denise Barrett Consulting' [online], Available from: https://canadiancfa.com/wp-content/uploads/2016/10/consumers-council-canada-online-loans_2015-study.pdf.

Correia, F., Han, P., and Wang, J. (2022) 'The online payday loan premium', Preliminary paper, Economics of Financial Technology Conference, January 2022 [online], Available from: https://www.eftconference.business-school.ed.ac.uk/sites/eft_conference/files/2022-06/Correia%20paper.pdf.

Dilay, K. and Williams, B. (2018) 'Payday lending regulations', in J. Buckland, C. Robinson, and B.S. Visano (eds) *Payday Lending in Canada in a Global Context: A Mature Industry with Chronic Challenges*, New York: Palgrave Macmillan US, pp 177–218.

Dobby, C. (2023) 'The government is finally lowering the maximum interest rate on loans – to 35% – and the alternative loan industry isn't happy', *The Toronto Star* [online] 30 March, Available from: https://www.thestar.com/business/2023/03/30/finally-theyre-listening-to-us-activists-hail-federal-budget-move-to-cut-interest-rate-on-predatory-loans.html.

Elliehausen, G, and Lawrence, E.C. (2001) 'Payday advance credit in America: an analysis of customer demand', *Monograph No. 35*, Georgetown University: Credit Research Center [online], Available from: http://www.msb.edu/prog/crc/publications.html.

FinCoNet (International Financial Consumer Protection Organization) (2014) 'FinCoNet report on responsible lending: review of supervisory tools for suitable consumer lending practices' [online] July, Available from: http://www.finconet.org/FinCoNet-Responsible-Lending-2014.pdf

Flannery, M. and Samolyk, K. (2005) 'Payday lending: do the costs justify the price?', Working Paper No. 2005–09, Arlington, VA: FDIC Center for Financial Research.

Galea, I. (2023) 'New rules to curb predatory lending still leave many vulnerable', *The Globe and Mail* [online] 29 March, Available from: https://www.theglobeandmail.com/business/article-payday-loans-lending-rates-budget/

George, M., Graham, C., Lennard, L., and Scribbins, K. (2014) 'Tackling consumer vulnerability: regulators' powers, actions and strategies', Research Paper No. 15–06, Citizens Advice [online], Available from: https://www.citizensadvice.org.uk/global/migrated_documents/corporate/tackling-consumer-vulnerability.pdf

Glottmann, S., Rios, C., and Constantine, L. (2023) *The Debt Trap Drives the Fee Drain: Payday and Car-Title Lenders Drain Nearly $3 Billion in Fees Every Year*, Center for Responsible Lending [online], Available from: https://www.responsiblelending.org/sites/default/files/nodes/files/research-publication/crl-debt-trap-fee-drain-jun2023.pdf

Government of Canada (2007) 'An Act to Amend the Criminal Code (Criminal Interest Rate)', S.C. 2007, c. 9. [online], Available from: http://lawslois.justice.gc.ca/eng/annualstatutes/2007_9/page-1.html.

Government of Canada (2023) 'Regulatory impact analysis statement', *Canada Gazette, Part I*, 157:51 [online], Available from: https://www.gazette.gc.ca/rp-pr/p1/2023/2023-12-23/html/reg3-eng.html.

Government of Newfoundland (2019) 'NLR 10/19 – payday loans regulations under the Consumer Protection and Business Practices Act' [online], Available from: https://assembly.nl.ca/Legislation/sr/Regulations/rc190010.htm.

Government of the United States (2017) 'Payday, vehicle title, and certain high-cost installment loans' [online], Available from: https://www.gpo.gov/fdsys/pkg/FR-2017-11-17/pdf/2017-21808.pdf.

Hembruff, J. and Soederberg, S. (2019) 'Debtfarism and the violence of financial inclusion: the case of the payday lending industry', *Forum for Social Economics*, 48(1): 49–68.

Hirota, L. (2020) 'Tomayto, tomahto: the cunning new face of payday lending', *University of the Pacific Law Review*, 52(1): 185–205.

Irving, N. (2010) 'Bill 14: the Consumer Protection Amendment Act (payday loans)', *Manitoba Law Journal*, 34(3): 159–82.

Kempson, E., Atkinson, A., and Pilley, O. (2004) *Policy Level Response to Financial Exclusion in Developed Economies: Lessons for Developing Countries*, Bristol: The Personal Finance Research Centre (University of Bristol).

Kilroy v. A OK Payday Loans Inc. (2007) 240 B.C.A.C. 151 (CA); 398 W.A.C. 151 [online], Available from: https://ca.vlex.com/vid/kilroy-v-ok-payday-681203077.

Kitching, A. and Starky, S. (2006) 'Bill C-26: an act to amend the criminal code (criminal interest rate)', Legislative Summary, Ottawa: Library of Parliament.

Kobzar, O. (2012) *Networking on the Margins: The Regulation of Payday Lending in Canada*, Thesis [online], Available from: https://tspace.library.utoronto.ca/handle/1807/34771.

Lusardi, A. and de Bassa Scheresberg, C. (2013) 'Financial literacy and high-cost borrowing in the United States' NBER Working Paper 2013-1, Global Financial Literacy Excellence Center [online] 31 January, Available from: https://gflec.org/wp-content/uploads/2014/12/WP-2013-1-Financial-Literacy-and-High-Cost-Borrowing.pdf.

Macfarlane, E. and Thrasher, K. (2021) 'The Fed of the future: a framework to optimize short-term lending practices', *University of Michigan Journal of Law Reform*, 55: 517.

Marsh, S., Dildar, Y., and Janzen, R. (2010) 'Payday lending: in search of a local alternative', Centre for Community Based Research [online], Available from: http://www.wellesleyinstitute.com/wp-content/uploads/2010/05/Payday_loan_final_report.pdf.

Montgomerie, J. (2006) 'Giving credit where it's due: public policy and household debt in the United States, the United Kingdom and Canada', *Policy and Society*, 25(3): 109–41.

Morse, A. (2011) 'Payday lenders: heroes or villains?', *Journal of Financial Economics*, 102(1): 28–44.

Nehf, J.P. (2022) 'Fintech, payday loans and the changing landscape of cash-advance consumer credit in the United States', *International Journal on Consumer Law and Practice*, 10: 1.

Newfoundland (2010) 'Provincial government will not regulate payday loan companies', Press release, Government Services [online], Available from: http://www.releases.gov.nl.ca/releases/2010/gs/0616n11.htm.

Office of the Federal Register (2019) '84 FR 4252 – Payday, Vehicle Title, and Certain High-Cost Installment Loans' [online], Available from: https://www.federalregister.gov/documents/2019/02/14/2019-01906/payday-vehicle-title-and-certain-high-cost-installment-loans.

O'Neill, B. and Xiao, J.J. (2015) 'Payday loan usage, state law, and financial capability', *Journal of Financial Service Professionals*, 69(6): 89–98.

Packman, C. (2014) *Payday Lending: Global Growth of the High-Cost Credit Market*, New York: Palgrave Macmillan US.

Pew Charitable Trusts (2012) 'Payday lending in America: who borrows, where they borrow, and why', Pew Safe Small-Dollar Loans Research Project, Washington, DC: Pew Charitable Trusts [online], Available from: https://www.pewtrusts.org/-/media/legacy/uploadedfiles/pcs_assets/2012/pewpaydaylendingreportpdf.pdf.

Pew Charitable Trusts (2014) 'Fraud and abuse online: harmful practices in internet payday lending', Pew Charitable Trusts [online], Available from: https://www.pewtrusts.org/-/media/assets/2014/10/payday-lending-report/fraud_and_abuse_online_harmful_practices_in_internet_payday_lending.pdf.

Pew Charitable Trusts (2022) 'Payday loans cost 4 times more in states with few consumer protections', Briefing paper [online] 5 April, Available from: https://pew.org/3tRtkOg.

Public Utilities Board of Manitoba (2013) *Report of the Public Utilities Board of Manitoba in respect of the 2013 Payday Loans Review* [online] 23 September, Available from: https://www.pubmanitoba.ca/payday_loan/final_payday_loans_triennial_report_sep_23_2013.pdf.

Ramirez, S.R. and Harger, K. (2020) 'Identifying border effects of payday-lending regulations', *Journal of Applied Economics*, 23(1): 539–59.

Ramsay, I. (2000) 'Access to credit in the alternative consumer credit market', Government of Canada [online], Available from: https://publications.gc.ca/site/eng/9.674187/publication.html.

Ramsay, I. (2012) 'Consumer credit regulation after the fall: international dimensions', *Journal of European Consumer and Market Law*, 1(1): 24–34.

Romm, T. (2023) 'Payday lenders aim to evade federal probes as borrowers plead for help', *Washington Post* [online] 28 October, Available from: https://www.washingtonpost.com/business/2023/10/28/payday-lending-supreme-court-lobbying/.

Rowlingson, K., Appleyard, L., and Gardner, J. (2016) 'Payday lending in the UK: the regul(aris)ation of a necessary evil?', *Journal of Social Policy*, 45(3): 527–43.

Schwartz, M.S. and Robinson, C. (2018) 'A corporate social responsibility analysis of payday lending', *Business and Society Review*, 123(3): 387–413.

Stegman, M.A. and Faris, R. (2003) 'Payday lending: a business model that encourages chronic borrowing', *Economic Development Quarterly*, 17(1): 8–32.

Strickland, S. (2022) 'Newfoundland and Labrador's payday loan rate to become lowest in the country', *VOCM* [online] 2 October, Available from: https://vocm.com/2022/10/02/newfoundland-and-labradors-payday-loan-rate-to-become-lowest-in-the-country/.

Wilson, T., Howlett, N., and Sheehan, G. (2009) 'Protecting the most vulnerable in consumer credit transactions', *Journal of Consumer Policy*, 32(2): 117–40.

Wolff, S.D. (2015) *The Cumulative Costs of Predatory Practices*, Durham, NC: Center for Responsible Lending.

Zinman, J. (2008) 'Restricting consumer credit access: household survey evidence on effects around the oregon rate cap', Working Paper No. 08-32, Philadelphia: Federal Reserve Bank of Philadelphia [online], Available from: http://www.philadelphiafed.org/researchand-data/publications/working-papers/2008/wp08-32.pdf.

PART III

The bad impacts of ineffective policies

12

Bad policies and the erosion of trust in comparative perspective

David Jesuit and Thomas Greitens

Introduction

Beginning in the 1970s, neoliberal policy changes to governments, their bureaucracies, and their economies helped the transition of many developing and developed economies to greater cycles of economic growth over time (Osborne and Gaebler, 1993; Larner, 2003).[1] Additionally, such policy changes became linked to the spread of more democratic governments across the world, at least according to the views of many media sources and policy makers (Yergin and Stanislaw, 2002). However, the patterns of economic growth from these changes were not equal. As early as the initial implementation phase in the 1970s, the labor market for high and low skilled positions diverged, quite dramatically, and helped to quicken the socioeconomic divide observed in modern economies (Harrison and Bluestone 1988; Atkinson et al, 1995; Mahler and Jesuit, 2006). As these countries entered the 2000s, such effects intensified and increasingly led to a bifurcation in prosperity, with higher income groups receiving more types of policy benefits than middle and lower income groups, and overall poverty levels generally rising across many parts of developed economies (OECD, 2001).

Arguably, such impacts indirectly contributed to ineffective policies and the continuing challenges of financial and technical regulations, sustainable development, climate action, and economic growth (as explored in the preceding chapters). Barring any significant changes and the continued advancement of ineffective policies with contested goals and those yielding more negative outcomes, such impacts will persist into the future. This will lead to corresponding increases in polarization in terms of income, social status, and democratic participation, as policy problems remain unaddressed across a variety of policy issues. Given this future, many scholars and good governance projects have attempted to analyze how such effects will influence the processes of democratic governance, and perhaps more importantly, what governments can do to help negate the ultimate effects of such realities in terms of policy outcomes. Typically, the key discussion in such analyses revolves around the idea of trust (OECD, 2001).

The importance of trust to policy outcomes

In the US, as well as several other developed economies, the public's trust in government seems to be deteriorating over time (Alford, 2001; Van de Walle et al, 2008). For example, the US has experienced a substantial decline in the public's trust in government since the early 1960s. In 1965, the public's trust in the government of the US hovered near 78 percent, while in 2017 it was barely at 20 percent, near a historic low (Pew Research Center, 2017).[2] According to Pew's data, a severe deterioration in the public's trust started in the late 1960s and accelerated in later decades with modest increases in trust in the 1980s and early 2000s inadequate to offset a significant overall downward trendline measured over six decades (Pew Research Center, 2017). Similar declines in the public's trust toward their government and their elected officials have also been discovered in many developed countries, especially democracies (Dalton, 2008).

Such declines are noteworthy for a number of reasons. First and perhaps most importantly, governments depend on trust from the public in order to solve prescient policy challenges. As explored in this book, when such challenges are solved, effective policies emerge with the generation of positive externalities with limited (or none) negative externalities. When such challenges are addressed, but not completely solved, moderately effective policies occur with negative externalities that can be corrected over time. When they are solved in ways that generate negative externalities that can be mitigated with future policies, moderately ineffective policies occur. And when they are left unaddressed, or even made worse via an additional policy, ineffective policies occur which generate significant negative externalities that produce harm. When they are left unaddressed or solved in ways that generate negative externalities, the opposite outcomes occur. Complicating matters, when ineffective policy outcomes occur, trust in government further declines in a feedback loop that leads to more declines in public trust in government and degradations in the perception of how government operates. This then leads to more policy arenas descending from effective policy outcomes to ineffective ones. As the harm from ineffective policies persists, an eventual bad policy outcome is produced with serious, negative implications for the public.

With public trust already in decline, governments are no longer able to accurately judge the extent of policy challenges and how policy solutions impact the public. This often occurs as various types of public engagement and public accountability processes degrade as the public loses trust in their government to solve policy challenges. Without such trust from the public, the ability of governments to effectively solve policy challenges erodes, generating a feedback loop for which more policy outcomes slide from effective to ineffective to bad over time.

For example, the Organisation for Economic Co-operation and Development (OECD) has noted the significant role of public trust in meeting 21st century policy challenges (OECD, 2001). The United Nations Educational, Scientific, and Cultural Organization (UNESCO) has emphasized the role of trust in implementing fact-based solutions to policy challenges in a knowledge-based society (Mansell and Tremblay, 2013). Additionally, many practitioners and academics also acknowledge the vital role played by the public's trust in their government when solving the wicked policy challenges that will confront most governments in the 2020s and beyond. In these studies, trust forms the basis of any collaborative governance arrangement, and those types of collaborations can help solve wicked policy problems (Bardach, 1998; Head and Alford, 2015). Without such trust, governments will not be able to engage their public on the implementation of complex policy solutions to wicked problems that require significant compromises on values and preferences from the public. Given this, it is not unreasonable to expect future governments failing to solve substantial policy challenges into the future when public trust is low.

Declines in public trust also erode the public's accountability over their governments, especially perceptions of fairness in the government's bureaucratic processes. Furthermore, such erosion in accountability decreases the bureaucracy's ability to effectively and efficiently implement services for their public. Such findings are a mainstay within the public administration literature (Balla and Gormley, 2017) and indeed may be one of the primary reasons for bureaucratic pathologies that led to neoliberal reforms in the 1970s in the first place (Niskanen, 1968). Additionally, a case can be made that erosions in public accountability help to accelerate the multiple accountability disorder (MAD).

In the MAD, bureaucrats become preoccupied with responding to paradoxical pressures from internal policy makers and external pressure groups rather than actual performance demands linked to the implementation of their services (Schillemans and Bovens, 2011). Consequently, ineffective policies occur as bureaucrats become consumed with conforming to the demands of their external support groups and policy makers rather than implementing effective policies (Romzek and Dubnick, 1987). Such effects may already be occurring as research into governmental responsiveness indicates that economic inequality is associated with differential governmental responses in terms of policy; wealthier groups receiving more benefits in terms of policy outcomes than other income groups (Bartels, 2008; Hager, 2009). Given the difficult policy decisions regarding the environment, public debt, a rapidly aging workforce, migration, immigration, nationalistic leanings, and the role of international organizations that may confront most developed economies into the future, the lack of public accountability over government has a real chance to result in repeated negative policy outcomes that will further erode public trust in their government and eventually transform ineffective policies into bad policy outcomes.

Finally, declines in public trust may reflect widening gaps in developed economies between wealthy and non-wealthy individuals. Inequality increasingly defines the public's reality in many developed economies. The impact of such inequality is systemic, spreading from economic differences to education to quality of life to health. For instance, socioeconomic status often positively correlates with measures of health, with individuals with higher measures of income, wealth, education, and occupation having better measures of general health (Wilkinson and Pickett, 2009; Evans et al, 2012). At a more macroscopic level, greater levels of inequality measured at the country level have negative consequences in terms of health (Rodgers, 1979). While inequality can often influence violence and mortality (and help explain some of this negative effect) (Hsieh and Pugh, 1993), newer research suggests that inequality itself may play an even greater role in negative health outcomes controlling for such variables (Pickett and Wilkinson, 2015). Overall, this suggests a complex relationship between socioeconomic variables, inequality, public trust, and ineffective policies. That relationship becomes even more dynamic and complex when measures of governmental performance are considered.

A key element of neoliberal policy is the notion of performance and how the reporting of performance data to the public can help rebuild the public's trust in their government (Osborne and Gaebler, 1993; Knack, 2002; Holzer and Zhang, 2004; Radin, 2006; Bouckaert, 2008). However, as governments adopted the performance reporting agenda suggested by neoliberal policies like New Public Management, significant challenges and problems with the implementation of performance reporting occurred. These included the subjectivity of performance measures and how such measures are often politicized (Gilmour and Lewis, 2006; Greitens and Joaquin, 2010); which types of performance reporting systems are best suited for government (Skogstad, 2003; Frederickson and Frederickson, 2006; Moynihan, 2008; Van Ryzin, 2011); how such systems may link back to trust (Yang and Holzer, 2006; Rothstein, 2011); and perhaps most impressively, whether performance reporting even has value given that it rarely leads to any type of public accountability (Dubnick, 2005; Joaquin and Greitens, 2011). Thus, the flawed implementation of performance reporting in many governments could even further degrade the public's trust in their government. This furthers the likelihood of ineffective policies and the eventual generation of bad policy outcomes.

Methodological approach

In this chapter, we use multilevel models to evaluate the complex relationship between citizen trust in public servants measured at the individual level, individual perceptions of governmental outcomes and processes, as well as national level variables related to governmental outcomes and processes, which can be linked back to ineffective policy outcomes. Multilevel efforts have numerous advantages given our data types.[3] Specifically, by using multilevel approaches we can control for individual perceptions regarding the success of governmental policy outcomes (level 1, subscript i) while concurrently determining whether national level (level 2, subscript j) measures of governmental processes influence trust at the individual level. Recursive dimensions of this relationship are also possible and such an approach allows for the control of individual satisfaction while testing for national level variations in policy outcomes.

All the variables measured at the individual level in this study come from the International Social Survey Program's (ISSP) 2016 Module on the 'Role of Government V.' Our dataset included a total of 20,235 observations nested within 20 countries. This was done in order to construct weights for each country at level 2, which were weighted by the inverse of their sample-size and normalized so that the mean level-2 weight equals one. The Graubard and Korn (1996) method was used in weighting the multilevel models in the results that follow. Using this method 'second-level weights are set to the cluster averages of the products of the weights at both levels, and first-level weights are then set equal to one' (StataCorp, 2011, p 305).

Dependent variable: trust in public servants

The dependent variable in this study measures trust in civil servants with a five-point ordinal-based question that examines whether 'most civil servants can be trusted to do what is best for the country'.[4] Mean levels of trust for the 20 countries included in our analysis are included in Figure 12.1, ranked from high to low levels of trust.[5] Generally, these data points indicate that individuals have low feelings of trust regarding their civil servants with the lowest levels reported in Spain, Lithuania, Japan, Chile, and France. The highest levels of trust in civil servants were in Switzerland, Norway, Finland, and Denmark.

In this survey, respondents were also asked a series of questions that reveal attributes about the quality of bureaucratic processes, including the impartiality and corruptness of government officials (see http://www.issp.org). Unfortunately, the questions included in the 2016 survey are not identical to the ones asked in 2006, which formed the basis for our current investigation. In 2016, the questions we chose to examine include the following:

- In general, how often do you think that the tax authorities in [country] treat everyone in accordance with the law, regardless of their contacts or position in society?
- How many public officials were involved in corruption?

Figure 12.1: Mean trust in public officials (2016) ranked from high to low

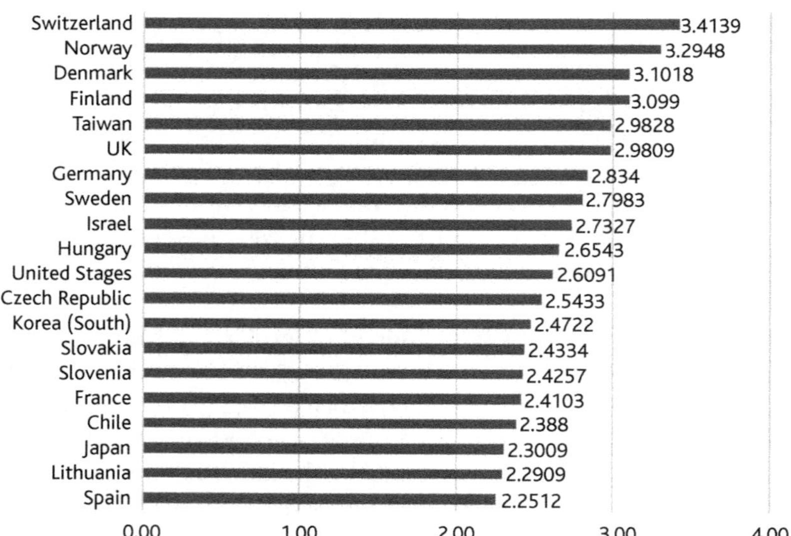

Table 12.1 reports mean values on these variables for each of the countries. As shown in the table, which also includes the values for the national level measures of government bureaucratic performance from the WGI, there is a good deal of variation in the countries' perceived level of fairness by their citizens. Spain and Chile have the lowest levels of impartiality by tax authorities, while Finland, Switzerland, and Norway are perceived to be the most fair, with a whole level and a half separating Spain and Norway. With respect to observed corruption of public officials, we once again see a wide range of values. In this case, the variable is coded in the opposite direction so that higher values indicate more corruption. Denmark and Switzerland report the lowest levels of observed corruption by public officials by their citizens while Lithuania and Chile report the highest levels.

The ISSP also surveyed respondents on individual satisfaction levels with governmental performance in terms of policy outcomes. Unfortunately, the policy satisfaction questions that were presented to all respondents in 2006, which inform previous research in this area, were only asked to respondents in a handful of countries in 2016, which required us to find an alternative approach. Specifically, we measure policy satisfaction in 2016 by coding responses to a question about levels of government spending. Those respondents who answered 'spend the same as now' to the question 'whether you would like to see more or less government spending' in each

Table 12.1: Mean measures of the quality of bureaucratic processes at the individual and national levels

	ISSP 2016		Worldwide Governance Indicators (WGI)		
Country	Tax authorities treat everyone in accordance with the law, regardless of their contacts or position in society?	How many public officials are involved in corruption?	Voice and accountability	Rule of law	Control of corruption
Chile	2.07	4.17	1.00	1.13	1.14
Czech Republic	2.40	3.48	1.04	1.02	0.54
Denmark	2.65	2.55	1.54	1.91	2.23
Finland	3.04	3.31	1.53	2.02	2.24
France	2.51	3.21	1.14	1.41	1.40
Germany	2.88	3.22	1.36	1.62	1.84
Hungary	2.50	4.06	0.40	0.42	0.10
Israel	2.40	3.75	0.79	1.07	1.19
Japan	2.58	3.14	0.99	1.42	1.52
Korea (South)	2.09	3.34	0.64	1.16	0.46
Lithuania	2.55	4.16	1.00	1.03	0.71
Norway	3.23	3.01	1.66	2.04	2.20
Slovakia	2.43	4.06	0.96	0.65	0.23
Slovenia	2.08	3.68	1.01	1.08	0.82
Spain	1.76	3.64	1.04	0.98	0.52
Sweden	2.86	3.21	1.56	2.02	2.19
Switzerland	3.09	2.70	1.53	1.95	1.99
Taiwan	2.50	2.88	1.01	1.14	0.88
UK	2.54	3.12	1.29	1.69	1.90
US	2.62	3.28	1.11	1.62	1.37

Notes: ISSP 2016: 1 = 'Almost never'; 4 = 'Almost always'; 1 = 'Almost none'; 5 = 'Almost all'. WGI index ranges from –2.5 to 2.5, with 2.5 signifying good governance.

of the following eight policy areas were coded as one, while all other valid responses were coded 'zero.' Thus, we consider the response to 'spend the same as now' as being satisfied with policy performance. In addition to each of these areas, we include a simple additive index in the multilevel analyses. These policy areas are:

- The environment
- Health
- The police and law enforcement
- Education
- The military and defense
- Old age pensions
- Unemployment benefits
- Culture and the arts

Demographic control variables

The ISSP 2016 survey also includes a number of demographic questions including age. Age is included in this analysis because previous research indicates generational effects regarding government with increasing levels of skepticism about government being found in younger populations (Dalton, 2005). Given the distribution of this variable, our analysis operationalizes this generational impact by squaring the age variable in a quadratic function. Consequently, all level-1 data (also known as individual level data) originate from this survey instrument.

Second-level data come from measures of national-level governmental processes and policy outcomes (such as poverty, unemployment, income). Multiple measures from the World Bank's Worldwide Governance Indicators (WGI) data set from 2016 are used to estimate national level governance processes (World Bank, n.d.a). Additionally, second-level data from the World Bank's World Development Indicators data set and the Luxembourg Income Study (LIS) Data Center are used in measures of national policy outcomes (Luxembourg Income Study, n.d.; World Bank, n.d.b). Overall, these data sources are used to analyze the relationship between individual perceptions of trust; individual satisfaction with governmental performance; national level policy outcomes related to poverty, unemployment, and income; as well as national level measures associated with the rule of law and corruption.

National measures of governmental outcomes and processes

A variety of data sources for national levels of policy outcomes and processes are used in this analysis. Building on previous research, data on unemployment, poverty, and Gini coefficients of inequality are included as national level variables for this analysis (see Table 12.2).

Data on inequality and poverty come from the LIS Data Center. LIS data have been collected from a multitude of countries over a period of decades and allows research to calculate multiple measures of inequality and poverty, with the most common calculation being the Gini coefficient (whereas 0 equates to everyone receiving the same income to 1 where one

Table 12.2: Mean responding 'spend the same as now' for each policy area (20 countries)

Country	The environment	Health	The police and law enforcement	Education	The military and defence	Old age pensions	Unemployment benefits	Culture and the arts
Chile	0.27	0.06	0.36	0.10	0.38	0.08	0.21	0.36
Czech Republic	0.56	0.29	0.48	0.41	0.46	0.28	0.42	0.55
Denmark	0.44	0.24	0.39	0.40	0.37	0.55	0.51	0.32
Finland	0.49	0.35	0.36	0.40	0.49	0.45	0.49	0.38
France	0.43	0.32	0.47	0.36	0.49	0.42	0.40	0.42
Germany	0.34	0.26	0.23	0.12	0.38	0.31	0.54	0.47
Hungary	0.35	0.04	0.41	0.17	0.38	0.22	0.36	0.46
Israel	0.34	0.12	0.33	0.12	0.38	0.14	0.37	0.46
Japan	0.41	0.33	0.62	0.34	0.44	0.41	0.55	0.54
Korea (South)	0.30	0.30	0.31	0.35	0.44	0.37	0.44	0.59
Lithuania	0.52	0.17	0.39	0.28	0.38	0.15	0.33	0.49
Norway	0.43	0.26	0.39	0.42	0.38	0.57	0.61	0.44
Slovakia	0.37	0.13	0.47	0.25	0.44	0.17	0.33	0.48
Slovenia	0.35	0.19	0.27	0.29	0.41	0.20	0.38	0.50
Spain	0.32	0.10	0.39	0.08	0.41	0.20	0.28	0.42
Sweden	0.44	0.14	0.23	0.30	0.37	0.28	0.55	0.48
Switzerland	0.49	0.50	0.49	0.48	0.47	0.49	0.48	0.50
Taiwan	0.18	0.25	0.28	0.22	0.31	0.32	0.32	0.35
UK	0.50	0.35	0.49	0.44	0.49	0.49	0.50	0.49
US	0.48	0.41	0.49	0.37	0.47	0.46	0.50	0.50

Source: Authors' calculation using ISSP (2016)

recipient receives all of the income). Measures of poverty also originate from the LIS Data Center and are calculated employing the relative approach (Brady, 2003). In our analysis, this results in poverty being calculated as the percentage of the population falling below half a nation's median income.[6]

Lastly, the WGI dataset includes variables on governance outcomes for a number of countries from 2013 to 2016. Based on previous research (Van Ryzin, 2011), three variables from that dataset were included in this analysis. These include: voice and accountability, rule of law, and control of corruption (see Table 12.1 for mean scores for each of these variables by country). The World Bank defines these as:

> Voice and Accountability, which captures perceptions of the extent to which a country's citizens are able to participate in selecting their government, as well as freedom of expression, freedom of association, and a free media. (World Bank, n.d.a)

> Rule of Law, which captures perceptions of the extent to which agents have confidence in and abide by the rules of society, and in particular the quality of contract enforcement, property rights, the police, and the courts, as well as the likelihood of crime and violence. (World Bank, n.d.a)

> Control of Corruption, which captures perceptions of the extent to which public power is exercised for private gain, including both petty and grand forms of corruption, as well as 'capture' of the state by elites and private interests. (World Bank, n.d.a)

Multilevel results

Results are included in Tables 12.3, 12.4, and 12.5. Table 12.3 reports the models that include only the level-1 control variables (that is, individual level data), age and its squared value, and our level-2 variables of interest. Examining column 1, we can see that there are clearly generational events that affect individual trust in public servants, as both age and age-squared are significant predictors of trust.[7] The negative sign for age and positive sign for its squared value indicates that trust in civil servants is lower for older citizens up until a certain age, at which time trust levels are higher. This implies that some event or scandal occurred in each country that affected individuals' trust in the bureaucracy, supporting Dalton's (2005) finding that there is a generational effect with respect to trust in government.

The more interesting results included in Table 12.3 are found in the remaining columns, as they include our level-2 variables. First, in columns 1 to 4 we analyze national levels of policy outcomes: unemployment, income

Table 12.3: Multilevel models for trust in public officials with demographic controls and level-2 variables

	1	2	3	4	5	6	7	8
Age	***−0.008	***−0.008	***−0.008	***−0.008	***−0.008	***−0.008	***−0.008	***−0.008
	0.003	0.003	0.003	0.003	0.003	0.003	0.003	0.003
Age sq.	***0.000	***0.000	***0.000	***0.000	***0.000	***0.000	***0.000	***0.000
	0.000	0.000	0.000	0.000	0.000	0.000	0.000	0.000
Intercept	***2.762	***3.014	***3.333	***3.127	***2.012	***2.099	***2.332	***2.157
	0.073	0.124	0.349	0.175	0.326	0.242	0.138	0.214
Unemployment		**−0.038						
		0.017						
Income ineq. (Gini)			*−1.926					
			1.050					
Poverty				**−0.036				
				0.015				
Voice and accountability					***0.660			
					0.253			
Rule of law						***0.483		
						0.155		
Control of corruption							***0.332	
							0.085	
Process sum (World Bank)								***0.159
								0.048

Notes: n=20,235, *** p<0.01, ** p<0.05, * p<0.10, two-tailed test. Top number is the estimate; bottom number is the s.e./s.d. (variances).

inequality, and poverty. In these models, all three are associated with trust in public servants, as higher levels of unemployment, income inequality, and poverty are all related to lower levels of individual trust in government. The Gini index, however, which measures income inequality, is only statistically significant at the $p<0.10$ level, while the other two variables attain significance at the $p<0.05$ level. The negative relationship between trust and unemployment confirms previous research (Jesuit, 2014), but the finding that inequality and poverty are associated with trust in government is new; previous research has shown such a relationship with generalized trust, but not trust in government.[8]

Columns 5 to 8 report the results of the models including the three components of the WGI we previously described and a simple additive index of them. In each case, the measure of the quality of national level government processes is statistically significant at the $p<0.01$ level, indicating that national level variables of governance performance influence trust when controlling for generational effects within each country. This is also consistent with previous findings. Nonetheless, as will be shown, such conclusions relying on the 2016 ISSP are tenuous.

Table 12.4 reports results of the models including the level-1 variables measuring government performance, both in terms of process and policy, as well as the individual-level controls. There is clear evidence that the quality of bureaucracy matters for trust. Specifically, the impartiality of tax authorities is associated with higher levels of trust in government and individuals' perceptions about more corrupt officials lowers trust. We will see that these findings are consistent throughout and significant at the $p<0.01$ level. As for policy outcomes, individual satisfaction with the policy effort in five of the eight areas we examine are statistically significant: health, law enforcement, pensions, unemployment benefits, and the arts. These latter two variables are statistically significant at the $p<0.05$ levels, while the others are significant at $p<0.01$. The simple additive index of these eight areas is also positive and significant ($p<0.01$), indicating that good policy performance, or more precisely individuals' perception of good policy performance, promotes trust in government.

Our final table combines all our level-1 and level-2 variables, with the exception of including only the additive indices we have created rather than their individual components. As we can see, none of the level-2 variables remain statistically significant when we control for individual level satisfaction with policy spending levels and perceptions about the impartiality and level of corruption within the civil service. On the one hand, these results cast some doubt on the findings reported in Table 12.3, which suggested that national policy outcomes such as unemployment and poverty depress trust in government, while national level measures of the signifying good quality of the bureaucracy promote trust. On the other hand, the relationship of such factors measured at the individual level to trust in government receive greater

Table 12.4: Multilevel models for trust in public officials with demographic controls and level-1 variables

	1	2	3
Age	***0.008	***0.007	***0.008
	0.003	0.003	0.003
Age sq.	***0.000	***0.000	***0.000
	0.000	0.000	0.000
Intercept	***2.762	***3.104	***3.115
	0.0.73	0.166	0.117
Tax impartiality	***0.222	***0.218	
	0.022	0.021	
How many corrupt	***–0.337	***–0.328	
	0.023	0.023	
Policy satisfaction index			***0.030
			0.007
The environment		–0.017	
		0.017	
Health		***0.063	
		0.022	
The police and law enforcement		***0.046	
		0.012	
Education		–0.019	
		0.024	
The military and defence		0.015	
		0.015	
Old age pensions		***0.073	
		0.024	
Unemployment benefits		**0.028	
		0.014	
Culture and the arts		**0.051	
		0.023	

Notes: n=20,235, *** p<0.01, ** p<0.05, * p<0.10, two-tailed test. Top number is the estimate; bottom number is the s.e./s.d. (variances).

Table 12.5: Multilevel models for trust in public officials with level-1 and level-2 variables

	1	2	3	4
Age	***0.007	***0.008	***0.008	***0.007
	0.003	0.003	0.003	0.003
Age sq.	***0.000	***0.000	***0.000	***0.000
	0.000	0.000	0.000	0.000
Intercept	***3.208	***2.969	***3.120	***3.000
	0.137	0.195	0.142	0.172
Tax impartiality	***0.219	***0.219	***0.219	***0.219
	0.021	0.021	0.021	0.021
How many corrupt	***–0.330	***–0.330	***–0.330	***–0.330
	0.023	0.023	0.023	0.023
Policy satisfaction index	***0.030	***0.030	***0.030	***0.030
	0.007	0.007	0.007	0.007
Unemployment	–0.014			
	–0.014			
Income ineq. (Gini)		0.495		
		0.531		
Poverty			–0.001*	
			0.009	
WGI Index				0.030
				0.029

Notes: n=20,235, *** p<0.01, ** p<0.05, * p<0.10, two-tailed test. Top number is the estimate; bottom number is the s.e./s.d. (variances).

support. In sum, this study confirms previous findings at the individual level of analysis and calls for further research examining these relationships at the national-level.

Conclusion

Trust is a complex phenomenon and the formation and maintenance of it remains vital to the understanding of modern governance structures and the generation of bad policies. In this chapter, we have explored how individual and national-level effects regarding perceptions of policy outcomes might influence trust, especially trust in an individual's national government. Our results confirm existing research on the determinants of individual trust and suggest that additional research should be conducted on how national level variables, especially broadly construed policy variables related to inequality, economic development, and bureaucratic performance, influence trust in government and the generation of ineffective policies which eventually generate bad policy outcomes.

Of particular interest to research on ineffective policies, the findings of this chapter suggest that perceptions of policy outcomes influence the public's trust in government. Consequently, when the public perceives ineffective policies, their trust in government declines. That finding, when supplemented with previous research on trust and policy outcomes examined in this chapter, suggests the true significance of ineffective policies. Namely, ineffective policies generate declines in trust, which then further degrades the policy process and increases the likelihood of more ineffective policies into the future. Since they do not effectively solve policy problems, ineffective policies degrade trust. That degradation of trust then leads to bad policy outcomes that make the existing policy problems, unaddressed by ineffective policies, worse in terms of harm and negative impacts. When bad policy outcomes are linked back to public perceptions of policy fairness and inequality levels (as shown in this chapter), such a process can show why inequality and polarization have increased since the implementation of the neoliberal reforms since the 1970s.

Such findings suggest that good governance groups like the World Bank, OECD, and UN should expand the data collection regarding national level policy outcomes, specifically variables linked to policy satisfaction and the quality of bureaucratic processes. If future surveys consistently focused on such national level concerns and expanded their data collection to more countries, then more rigorous research could be conducted to determine if such national level outcomes related to the satisfaction and performance of bureaucracy influence trust in government, and if such outcomes are then linked back to bad policy outcomes (as measured by public policy satisfaction).

In many ways, trust in government seems to be under threat as individuals in a variety of economically developed and developing countries embrace alternative approaches to governance that run counter to notions of good governance promoted in the latter half of the 20th century. At the same time, many international organizations have experienced stress as citizens in member countries lose faith in the value of membership and the ability of the organization to respond to current governance challenges. Given that the 21st century will bring forth a variety of wicked policy problems related to the environment, public health, inequality, public debt levels, international trade, immigration, and national security, the understanding of how notions of bureaucratic performance and national policy outcomes influence trust in government, and the generation of ineffective policies and bad policy outcomes. With a better understanding of this phenomenon, new governance structures and processes that consider the interplay between trust and effective policy solutions can be developed. Without this understanding, governance systems may start to erode and create a feedback cycle whereby lower levels of trust increasingly lead to additional ineffective policies, which in turn help to bring down individual trust in government even further, which in turn generate more bad policy outcomes into the future.

Notes

[1]   The neoliberal agenda also had numerous negative externalities, some of which are discussed in this chapter. The ultimate success of this agenda in terms of positive externalities remains controversial, see, for instance, Altvater (2009).

[2]   Pew's measure of trust is: 'How much of the time do you think you can trust the government in Washington to do what is right? Just about always, most of the time, or only some of the time?' The trust data reported reflects individuals that answered 'just about always' and 'most of the time'.

[3]   See Steenbergen (2012) for a good overview of the use of multilevel models, also known as hierarchical linear models, in political science.

[4]   Following Van Ryzin (2011), we recode the dependent variable so that 1=strongly disagree and 5=strongly agree.

[5]   Although more than 30 countries were included in this ISSP 2016 Module, measures of income inequality and poverty from the Luxembourg Income Study (LIS) are only available for 20 countries.

[6]   In measuring income we used the standard LIS methods for household size equivalization, top and bottom coding, treatment of zero income, income coverage, and so on. Those used in computing the widely used LIS 'key figures' are documented on the LIS website (http://www.lisdatacenter.org/data-access/key-figures/). Specifically, households are equivalized by the square root of the number of members and weighted by household size, and the standard LIS methods for top and bottom coding are used.

[7]   The results of the null or unconditional equation are available upon request.

[8]   Literature on the relationship between generalized trust and inequality is quite substantial. Among the most noteworthy are Uslaner (2002); Rothstein and Uslaner (2005); Rothstein (2011).

References

Alford, J.R. (2001) 'We're all in this together: the decline of trust in government 1958–1996', in J.R. Hibbing and E. Theiss-Morse (eds) *What Is It About Government that Americans Dislike*, Cambridge: Cambridge University Press, pp 28–46.

Altvater, E. (2009) 'Postneoliberalism or postcapitalism? The failure of neoliberalism in the financial market crisis', *Development Dialogue*, 51(1): 73–88.

Atkinson, A.B., Rainwater, L., and Smeeding, T.M. (1995) *Income Distribution in OECD Countries: Evidence from the Luxembourg Income Study (LIS)*, Paris: Organization for Economic Cooperation and Development.

Balla, S.J. and Gormley Jr., W.T. (2017) *Bureaucracy and Democracy: Accountability and Performance*, Washington: CQ Press.

Bardach, E. (1998) *Getting Agencies to Work Together: The Practice and Theory of Managerial Craftmanship*, Washington: Brookings Institution.

Bartels, L. (2008) *Unequal Democracy: The Political Economy of the New Gilded Age*, New York: Russell Sage Foundation.

Bouckaert, G. (2008) *Managing Performance: International Comparisons*, London: Routledge.

Brady, D. (2003) 'Rethinking the sociological measurement of poverty', *Social Forces*, 81(3): 715–52.

Dalton, R.J. (2005) 'The social transformation of trust in government', *International Review of Sociology*, 15(1): 133–54.

Dalton, R.J. (2008) *Citizen Politics: Public Opinion and Political Parties in Advanced Industrial Democracies* (5th edn), Washington: CQ Press.

Dubnick, M. (2005) 'Accountability and the promise of performance: in search of the mechanisms', *Public Performance & Management Review*, 28(3): 376–417.

Evans, W., Wolfe, B., and Adler, N. (2012) 'The SES and health gradient: a brief review of the literature', in B. Wolfe, W. Evans, and T.E. Seeman (eds) *The Biological Consequences of Socioeconomic Inequalities*, New York: Russell Sage Foundation, pp 1–37.

Frederickson, D.G. and Frederickson, H.G. (2006) *Measuring the Performance of the Hollow State*, Washington: Georgetown University Press.

Gilmour, J.B. and Lewis, D.E. (2006) 'Does performance budgeting work? An examination of the Office of Management and Budget's PART scores', *Public Administration Review*, 66(5): 742–52.

Graubard, B.I. and Korn, E.L. (1996) 'Modelling the sampling design in the analysis of health surveys', *Statistical Methods in Medical Research*, 5(3): 263–81.

Greitens, T.J. and Joaquin, M.E. (2010) 'Policy typology and performance measurement: results from the Program Assessment Rating Tool (PART)', *Public Performance & Management Review*, 33(4): 555–70.

Hager, N. (2009) *The Hollow Men: A Study in the Politics of Deception*, Nelson: Craig Potton Publishing.

Harrison, B. and Bluestone, B. (1988) *The Great U-turn: Corporate Restructuring and the Polarizing of America*, New York: Basic Books.

Head, B.W. and Alford, J. (2015) 'Wicked problems: implications for public policy and management', *Administration & Society*, 47(6): 711–39.

Holzer, M. and Mengzong Z. (2004) 'Trust, performance, and the pressures for productivity in the public sector', in M. Holzer and S. Lee (eds) *The Public Productivity Handbook* (2nd edn), New York: Marcel Dekker, pp 215–19.

Hsieh, C.C. and Pugh, M.D. (1993) 'Poverty, income inequality, and violent crime: a meta- analysis of recent aggregate data studies', *Criminal Justice Review*, 18(2): 182–202.

International Social Survey Program (ISSP) (2016) 'Role of government V', *International Social Survey Program* [online], Available from: http://www.issp.org.

Jesuit, D.K. (2014) 'Inequality, government performance, and trust in public managers', in C. Conteh, T.J. Greitens, D.K. Jesuit, and I. Roberge (eds) *Governance and Public Management: Strategic Foundations for Volatile Times*, New York: Routledge, pp 131–51.

Joaquin, M.E. and Greitens, T.J. (2011) 'The accountability performance link: an attempt at distilling some mechanisms in a management reform initiative', *Public Performance & Management Review*, 34(3): 323–49.

Knack, S. (2002) 'Social capital and the quality of government: evidence from the states', *American Journal of Political Science*, 46(4): 772–85.

Larner, W. (2003) 'Neoliberalism?' *Environment and Planning D: Society and Space*, 21: 509–12.

Luxembourg Income Study (n.d.) *LIS Database*, Luxembourg: LIS [online], Available from: http://www.lisdatacenter.org.

Mahler, V.A. and Jesuit, D.K. (2006) 'Fiscal redistribution in the developed countries: new insights from the Luxembourg Income Study', *Socio-Economic Review*, 4(3): 483–511.

Mansell, R. and Tremblay, G. (2013) *Renewing the Knowledge Societies Vision for Peace and Sustainable Development*, Paris: UNESCO.

Moynihan, D.P. (2008) *The Dynamics of Performance Management: Constructing Information and Reform*, Washington: Georgetown University Press.

Niskanen, W.A. (1968) 'The peculiar economics of bureaucracy', *American Economic Review*, 58(2): 293–305.

OECD (2001) *Governance in the 21st Century*, Paris: OECD Publishing.

Osborne, D. and Gaebler, T. (1993) *Reinventing Government: How the Entrepreneurial Spirit is Transforming the Public Sector*, New York: Plume.

Pew Research Center (2017) 'Public trust in government remains near historic lows as partisan attitudes shift', Pew Research Center for the People and the Press [online] 3 May, Available from: https://www.pewresearch.org/politics/2017/05/03/public-trust-in-government-remains-near-historic-lows-as-partisan-attitudes-shift/.

Pickett, K.E. and Wilkinson, R.G. (2015) 'Income inequality and health: a causal review', *Social Science & Medicine,* 128: 316–26.

Radin, B.A. (2006) *Challenging the Performance Movement: Accountability, Complexity, and Democratic Values*, Washington: Georgetown University Press.

Rodgers, G.B. (1979) 'Income and inequality as determinants of mortality: an international cross-section analysis', *Population Studies*, 33(2): 343–51.

Romzek, B.S. and Dubnick, M.J. (1987) 'Accountability in the public sector: lessons from the Challenger tragedy', *Public Administration Review*, 47(3): 227–38.

Rothstein, B. (2011) *The Quality of Government: Corruption, Social Trust, and Inequality in International Perspective*, Chicago: University of Chicago Press.

Rothstein, B. and Uslaner, E. (2005) 'All for all: equality, corruption and social trust', *World Politics*, 58(3): 41–73.

Schillemans, T. and Bovens, M (2011) 'The challenge of multiple accountability: does redundancy lead to overload?', in M.J. Dubnick and H.G. Frederickson (eds) *Accountable Governance: Problems and Promises*, Armonk: M.E. Sharpe, pp 3–21.

Skogstad, G. (2003) 'Legitimacy and/or policy effectiveness? Network governance and GMO regulation in the European Union', *Journal of European Public Policy*, 10(3): 321–38.

StataCorp (2011) *Stata Longitudinal-Data/Panel-Data Reference Manual* (release 12), College Station: StataCorp LP.

Steenbergen, M.R. (2012) 'Hierarchical linear models for electoral research: a worked example in stata', *ELECDEM,* Available from: https://www.exe ter.ac.uk/media/universityofexeter/elecdem/pdfs/istanbulwkspjan2012/ Hierarchical_Linear_Models_for_Electoral_Research_A_worked_examp le_in_Stata.pdf.

Uslaner, E. (2002) *The Moral Foundations of Trust*, New York: Cambridge University Press.

Van de Walle, S., Van Roosbroek, S., and Bouckaert, G. (2008) 'Trust in the public sector: is there any evidence for a long-term decline?', *International Review of Administrative Sciences*, 74: 45–62.

Van Ryzin, G. (2011) 'Outcomes, process and trust of civil servants', *Journal of Public Administration Research and Theory*, 21(4): 745–60.

Wilkinson, R., and Pickett, K. (2009) *The Spirit Level*, New York: Bloomsbury Press.

World Bank (n.d.a) 'Worldwide governance indicators' [online], Available from: http://data.worldbank.org/data-catalog/worldwide-governance-ind icators.

World Bank (n.d.b) 'World development indicators' [online], Available from: http://databank.worldbank.org/data/home.aspx.

Yang, K. and Holzer, M. (2006) 'The performance-trust link: implications for performance measurement', *Public Administration Review*, 66(1): 114–26.

Yergin, D. and Stanislaw, J. (2002) *The Commanding Heights: The Battle for the World Economy*, New York: Free Press.

13

The path forward: addressing bad policy for the sake of good policy

Ian Roberge

This book is among the first efforts to understand what constitutes ineffective policy, to explain its commonness, and to consider ways to reverse it and attain if not good policy at least fewer ineffective policies. Its genesis was a simple observation: governments across jurisdictions have adopted, implemented, and sustained policies that are known to be ineffective and undesirable, if not outright bad. The policy analysis/evaluation process suggests that when a policy is found to be lacking or has failed, governments should take corrective measures to remedy the situation. Within this idealized and somewhat linear self-correcting model, policy is assumed to perpetually improve over time. Nevertheless, there is plenty of evidence that suggests otherwise. As the various chapters of this volume demonstrate, policy makers may prefer ineffective policy over better solutions in varying circumstances and for many different reasons. Ineffective policy can also become locked in, with policy makers unwilling or unable to reverse themselves.

This concluding chapter addresses the question of policy makers' intent: why and under what circumstances do policy makers prefer ineffective policy over better policy options? What constraints and limitations do policy makers face in attempting to reverse bad policy? In responding, we draw on the lessons learned from the cases in this volume and emphasize some of the observations made in Chapter 2 by Roberge and Wijermars in their analysis of the relationship between ineffective policy and democratic regression. The takeaway argument is that a better understanding of the intent behind policies is essential for making sense of policy making in general, and especially of ineffective policy. Ineffective policy is not accidental, nor is it necessarily rare. Ineffective policy results from deliberate decisions. Since part of the purpose of studying ineffective policies is to reduce their occurrence, it is essential to understand why policy makers sometimes prefer ineffective policies and the conditions under which these decisions are made. This understanding can then inform policy reversal and the creation of better policies. Contributors to this book have not directly addressed the issue of intent. Yet, because the issue is central to the study of ineffective policy, it warrants greater development and reflection in this chapter and future research.

The remainder of this conclusion is structured in three sections. The first section identifies the major lessons about ineffective policy that can be identified across the cases. Based on the observation that policy making is deliberate, the second section considers the question of intent and why ineffective policy is selected instead of better policy. The final section presents paths for future research. This volume aims to open the door to important future inquiries on ineffective, bad, and undesirable policy. The focus is also on constructing much-needed opportunities for researching and developing more effective, good, and desirable policy for a stronger democratic life.

What did we learn?

This section denotes the major lessons that can be drawn from the many cases considered in this book. As noted in the introduction, each chapter in this volume presents cases of ineffective policy and considers their implications, as well as to tease out key implications from a research and/or practical perspective. Three interrelated lessons emerged from the analysis: the relevance of the policy ineffectiveness concept, the coverage and scope of policy ineffectiveness, as well as the deliberate nature of the policy-making process. Each of these observations is addressed sequentially in this chapter.

First, policy ineffectiveness is a significant real-world problem that is worth investigating. Although simple on the surface, policy ineffectiveness is a challenging concept to approach. Policy ineffectiveness is more than a policy failure. The latter refers, at its most simple, to a policy that does not work or is not meeting its stated objectives. Policies that are undesirable and bad – because, for instance, they risk causing harm – may be successful, or framed as successful and effective, if they meet their explicit goals. These policies cannot be considered to have failed, yet due to their negative impact, they need to be understood as ineffective. Policy ineffectiveness not only accounts for policy failures but it also goes further in assessing the desirability of a policy as well as recognizing its negative consequences, even outright harm. Policy successes are, among different factors used, identified by their positive outcomes ('t Hart and Compton, 2019). Policy ineffectiveness, in the same way, is recognizable because it is damaging. The study of policy ineffectiveness raises, in this regard, thorny methodological considerations, particularly because it must be explicitly normative. Measuring impacts and denoting harm ultimately requires rendering judgment, which presents challenges similar to those in standard policy analysis and evaluation, where assessments are carried out regarding what works and what does not. Judgment about policy is subject to political interpretations, preferences, and values. Policies described as ineffective in this book may be interpreted by others as not meeting the threshold for ineffectiveness or subject to disagreement on how undesirable they are. Debates over their designation and desirableness should take place in democratic societies. While grounded in evidence, identifying policy ineffectiveness is an exercise in judgment that needs acknowledgment of biases and preferences. Each chapter in this volume addressed the normative foundations of policy ineffectiveness in different ways illustrating the concept's versatility and usefulness.

The second major conclusion of this book is that the scope and the impacts of what is ineffective policy vary. This is most evident when we compare cases presented in this book across both North America and Europe, and within the policy areas of environment, finance, and technology. The different cases demonstrate that there are levels of gravity to ineffective policy. At one end, there are ineffective policies that are more circumscribed in impact over time. Chapter 6 by Tusikov addresses an ineffective policy that in a way reflects an error in judgment on the part of policy makers. The consequences could have been serious, but the policy was quickly terminated, and the city moved on. At the other end, there are policies where the harm, or the prospects of harm, is deeper and longer lasting, where policies are likely to be entrenched, and where reversal or changes are unlikely. Chapter 5 by Campbell-Verduyn addressing the United States government's chosen silence on the birth of Bitcoin is a good example of a non-decision with long-lasting and serious consequences. This industry, shunned by many countries, including China, established itself in the US. It is well-recognized that governments' unwillingness or inability to act early can leave private sector actors to define the field, leaving governments without any other option than to accept a fait-accompli. Chapter 8 by Hasselbalch highlights the long temporal aspect of harm, explaining how the EU's policy choices around its plastics strategy shifted, naturalizing the conditions of 'toxic growth'. There are also policies where the level of the impact is not as clear, or that fall somewhere between those two extremes. Determining not just whether a policy is ineffective, but the extent of its ineffectiveness – its level of gravity – is something that future research should give greater consideration to.

The third major lesson is that ineffective policy reflects patterns of conscious decision making, not simply unexpected consequences. There are multiple decisions and inflexion points in general policy making that make ineffective policy not accidental. For all cases in this book, policy makers made conscious decisions about how to proceed. As an example, the Ontario government's support for developers in its housing policy, as described by Winfield and Stirling in Chapter 9, is deliberate. Viewing ineffective policy as the result of conscious and purposeful decisions requires coming back to the question about policy makers' intent and the reasons why they prefer ineffective, undesirable, and bad policy over better policy. Finally, the three lessons can be understood as interwoven. Scholars must not shy away from labeling policy as ineffective, particularly given policy makers' preference for ineffective options over better alternatives. This is crucial when considering the concept's significance, including its negative outcomes and its broader implications for democratic practices.

Intent and ineffective policy

The question of policy makers' intent is tricky because, from a research perspective, there is limited access to information beyond what is made publicly available regarding the logic and thought process behind a policy decision. At the same time, policy making, as just noted, is deliberate, meaning that policy makers have options and can opt for another 'better' policy. Why do policy makers adopt a policy that they know, or ought to know based on much available evidence, will not work, and may even cause harm in worst-case scenarios?

There are many possible answers to this question as outlined across the chapters in this book. Thomas Dye (1972) long ago defined public policy as anything a government chooses to do or not to do. Policy making cannot be discussed or analyzed without properly considering the matter of choice and why policy makers act in the way that they do. The consideration of intent does not rule out that many policy makers have chosen a career path that allows them to serve the public so as to do good. Politicians often enter democratic politics to address a problem of specific concern to them; public servants are imbued with the public service ethos. There are undoubtedly numerous circumstances in which policy makers know and would like to reverse ineffective policy, but for whatever reason it becomes difficult if not impossible to do so. We stress intent to make clear that policy is the result of deliberate action. Policy making is purposeful in that it is the result of many decisions made over the life cycle of a policy. Framing policy as deliberate means that other decisions could have been preferred. It thus becomes important to understand why certain choices have been made as opposed to others. In sum, we suggest that it is legitimate to ask, and to research more fully in the future, when policy makers have options, why do they, too often, get them so wrong? It is fair to assume that policy makers serve for many other reasons than just for the betterment of their democratic community. Motives relating to power, status, or even wealth are equally important to consider. In pursuit of professional and personal objectives, they may prefer a policy that serves them such as obtaining and retaining power. This preference may lead them to prioritize policies that do not necessarily serve the public's interests, even if those policies may not be effective. The relationship between intent, the exercise of political power, and ineffective policy is complicated, and worth detailing further. Three explanations are developed in this section expanding on the analysis in Chapter 2 by Roberge and Wijermars as well as drawing on evidence from the various cases in this book. Our list of considerations is representative, though by no means exhaustive, underscoring once more the need for greater research that is more specific to ineffective policy.

(In)competence and ignorance

The first possible explanation for why ineffective policy is preferred to better policies is that policy makers are ultimately incompetent, if not ignorant. For the latter, it is important to remember that decision making is mired in uncertainty and ambiguity (Best, 2016) and policies are developed without full information. Policy makers may equally not be able to make sense of the evidence with which they are presented, or simply they may prefer to ignore it. Williams (2021), for instance, argues that ignorance is rational because it reflects the anticipated costs of acquiring and possessing knowledge. He states, 'whether a given case of motivated ignorance is instrumentally rational depends on whether it is sufficiently responsive to the agent's interests as manifest in the evidence that she has at her disposal' (2021, p 7818). While Williams applies this reflection to the behaviors of citizens regarding climate change, the argument equally holds for policy makers. They may simply prefer not knowing or even ignoring the effects of a policy because to know would compel them to take actions that they would prefer not to take. At a more satirical level, the comedian Andy Borowitz (2022) wrote a book titled, *Profiles in Ignorance: How America's Politicians Got Dumb and Dumber*. While this is not a form of argument that we will explore further in this chapter, the return of populism coincides with a shift targeting intellectualism and expertise. Politicians may, indeed, prefer to appear ignorant to be electable.

The chapters in this book substantiate a version of this first explanation for ineffective policy. As previously noted, the chapters highlight the extent to which policy makers may prefer a select policy because they are blind to alternatives and simply cannot envision other solutions. This argument is most forcefully made by Haggart's review of the development of the COVID-19 app in Chapter 7. He points out that searching for technological solutions to misunderstood problems is bound to lead to ill-fated policies. In Canadian COVID-19 responses, policy makers not only sold a policy that was unlikely to succeed, but they also never considered how a technical solution was not appropriate for the multifaceted and fast-changing set of problems that they needed to address. In a particularly salient example of combined incompetence and ignorance, Tusikov's account in Chapter 6 of Toronto's experiment with the development of a 'smart city', policy makers' initial enthusiasm for novelty and uniqueness completely failed to detect the myriads of problems inherent to the project – policy makers did not need a crystal ball to identify the deficiencies in the project from the very beginning, but they were blind to them. The policy makers' frame of reference in both cases was so narrow that it could not provide for the very real limits of the adopted policies. Chapter 3 by Kranke, on green growth versus post-growth in its analysis of the German Federal Ministry for Economic Affairs and Climate Action provides yet another example of how policy makers may prefer to play the ostrich rather than engage in a substantive debate.

Complexity and legitimate policy debate

The second consideration when it comes to intent is policy complexity. The 'better' or much less the 'best' policy is not always easy to identify. 'Wicked' policy problems are by their very nature complex and have no easy solution (Head, 2022). We would suggest that this does not mean that some policies will not perform better than others. If there were easy solutions to complex problems, one must assume that they would have been found and adopted already. The literature on policy formulation deals with questions about policy design and mixes (Howlett and Mukherjee, 2018). The interwoven nature of policy problems, workable solutions and available policy instruments, previously existing policies, as well as the unknowns means that there are few, if any, simple solutions assuming the problem itself can neatly be determined. As we noted earlier, public policy is subject to legitimate debate on how best to address a problem in society. There is also no guarantee within such a debate that the 'best' policy will be selected. This is part of the problem, as mentioned earlier, of studying ineffective policy; such research must reflect good science but will ultimately rest on preferences and judgment. Furthermore, not all debates are legitimate; the use of discourse, rhetoric, misleading science and data, to make claims has been well-documented (Michaels, 2020). Policy ineffectiveness within this realm of thought is the result of the messiness of the world, its complexity and uncertainty.

The cases in this book substantiate this second perspective. Chapter 4 by Asquer elaborates both theoretically in terms of the multiplicity of options from good to bad, as well as empirically accounting for the different perspectives regarding offshore wind farm policies. Chapter 11 by McKeen-Edwards also makes clear that complete ineffectiveness or undesirability is difficult to discern. There is enough of an argument justifying the existence of payday loans in Canada and the US, despite the harm that is caused by the industry, making their practice not easy to dismiss, and the policies not easy to dismantle. There are also constitutional constraints in federal states that make reform challenging, as well as pressure and lobbying by many self-interested private sector actors.

Ill-intent

The third consideration is ill-intent, where power is exercised and policy is developed in a self-interested way. There are multiple versions of this argument from regulatory capture (OECD, 2017) to policy deceptions (Baines et al, 2020) and deceptive public policy (Schneider and Ingram, 2019) to hidden agendas (McConnell, 2018), and outright corruption. Policy and regulatory capture, policy deceptions and corruption all accentuate the likelihood of ineffective policy, though as is the pursuit of political self-interest, they are not predictors of it. The intent of policy makers in adopting select measures is unlikely to be to harm per se, or harm may be justified as desirable, or may even be seen as an acceptable outcome because the policy maker is pursuing other objectives, whether framed as in the greater good or simply personal. This category openly acknowledges that policy makers have vested interests – that they work to their benefit – that they carry through in their policy work.

The question surrounding the framing and presentation of policy serves as a good reminder that judging intent is challenging. Policy makers rarely, if ever, admit to ill-intent and provide justifications for their policy preferences, referring, as noted earlier, to legitimate policy debates. As such, judging intent once more raises questions of subjectivity and normativity in assessing evidence.

The ill-intent of policy makers is something the policy literature is often reluctant to tackle openly, while it is done somewhat more openly in other fields such as political science and international relations, or economics. Each chapter of this volume has been careful not to make exaggerated claims. Campbell-Verduyn's chapter on the Bitcoin white paper (Chapter 5) comes the closest to openly thinking about ill-intent in arguing that the US government's failure to act did not fully consider the public interest. In Chapter 9, Winfield and Stirling's discussion of Ontario's housing policy and its spillover to the environment references the very close connection between the Premier and his entourage with developers. There would be value in thinking more completely about the impact of ill-intent on ineffective policy, and policy making more generally because the consequences are significant. As mentioned previously in this volume, whether real or imagined, popular perceptions that governments are no longer working in the interest of the people is part of what has fueled citizens' distrust of public authorities – Chapter 12 by Jesuit and Greitens expands on that point and clearly shows that ineffective policy is damaging. If policy makers have negative intent, policy change in the hopes of better policy becomes much more difficult.

Intent in context

The institutionalist literature reminds us that policy makers act within a broader set of parameters that must be accounted for. These parameters affect the full policy cycle by determining what is on the agenda, the available options, decision-making processes, and implementation. Even when well-intentioned, policy makers may not always be able to pursue 'good' policies, or the obstacles to doing so may be too onerous. While the impediments to reform can be legitimate, they can also serve as an excuse to justify the status quo or preference for an ineffective policy. Institutional constraints do not replace or eliminate intent, though they must be considered since they affect the available possible solutions to a policy problem.

There are different ways to think about these limitations. For instance, the lack of capacity in government and dysfunctions in the public service hamper the development of 'good' public policy and foster an environment that is rife for developing ineffective policy. The shift to governance and the centralization of authority alongside lessening capacity is, in some cases, a reasonable explanation for policy ineffectiveness. Government restructuring, processes linked to austerity, and public misconceptions about government bureaucracy all partly explain why the public service can no longer deliver the goods. Public sector officials at all levels are overwhelmed and under tremendous pressure from multiple sources whether from other parts of government or societal actors making the practice of public administration a lost art form. At the highest level, policy makers ought to know but they do not have the energy or the time to work through policy problems and solutions. They rely on the advice received and the quality of that advice varies and may well be partial as bureaucrats pursue their own interests or have fallen prey to external pressures. Savoie (2018), for instance, argues that Canada and the United Kingdom have moved to court government where important decisions are made by a few powerful individuals reflecting their political calculus and where less important decisions are subject to a cumbersome and slow process elsewhere in government. In other words, accounting for governance arrangements, it may now be ever more difficult to deliver quality policy making.

The various cases in this book substantiate versions of this argument. Most significantly, and without surprise, the case studies highlight the risks and consequences of the involvement of private sector actors in policy making. Chapter 9 by Winfield and Stirling on housing policy and its spillover into the environment presents a salient example of court government and bureaucratic dysfunction in Ontario, as well as the access and influence of developers in the process. Chapter 10 by Lockwood on the Volcker rule is another straightforward example of the influence of private sector actors in policy making, potentially resulting in outright regulatory capture. The debates surrounding the Volcker rule reinforce the idea that complex technical fields are often subject to intense behind-the-scenes lobbying getting in the way of good policy making. Chapter 3 by Kranke further suggests that even a Green Minister is hard-pressed to see beyond green growth to a post-growth agenda. Questions of capacity and dysfunctions represent plausible reasons why policy ineffectiveness is preferred.

A second aspect is the limitation that comes from lock-ins and inertia, as well as the reality that circumstances and perspectives change over time. There are situations where the status quo may indeed be preferable to any of the alternatives, even when the current situation is undesirable and bad. There are many circumstances, however, where policy makers are unwilling or unable to enact change. In addressing broader governance issues, institutionalist theories (Peters, 2016) provide varied explanations to explain incremental change. In this volume, Chapter 8 by Hasselbalch on the EU Plastics Strategy is a prime example of a policy that starts with the right intentions and turns bad over the years. Although the policy was well-intentioned, it resulted in an entrenched ineffective policy. As the definition of ineffective policy in this book makes clear, these types of policies can also generate unwanted and unintended consequences. Policy makers, obviously, are not always able to forecast the various effects of a policy; policy spillovers in which the effects of a policy are felt in other policy areas also need to be considered. Chapter 9 by Winfield and Stirling demonstrates that the Ontario government housing policy on its merit is bad, though its spillover into environmental policy amplifies its ineffectiveness and undesirability. Ultimately, addressing policy ineffectiveness requires determining how best to overcome institutional constraints and resistance to change and react with greater flexibility when there are unintended consequences.

Furthermore, there is a need to consider changing perspectives over time. This temporal issue is partially addressed in Chapter 2 by Roberge and Wijermars when they analyze the relationship between democratic regression and ineffective policy. Part of the argument is that something that was considered good at one time may turn undesirable and bad later. This is most evident in Chapter 3 by Kranke, discussing the green economy. The deconstruction of the concept of the green economy outlines changing perspectives around economic growth, alternative forms of economic arrangements, and different plausible futures. The initial movement to green growth was seen to reconcile economic growth with the need to ensure environmental sustainability – that was deemed a much-needed and desirable change. Over time, though, the very idea of green growth has come to be questioned and what was once perceived as good and desirable could now be said to represent an idea that, in fact, impedes the change that is truly required.

Lock-ins and changing perspectives over time illustrate that the discussion on intent exists in context. Policy makers may well understand that, and in some cases, they may want to develop a policy or enact change, but they are unable to bring it about; alternatively, they may indeed prefer inaction or the semblance of action, even when a policy is bad. Campbell-Verduyn in Chapter 5 considers the challenges, if not the outright inability, of policy makers to reconcile conflicting policy preferences and objectives in the context of the development of blockchain technology and Bitcoin. Lockwood, in Chapter 10 on the Volcker rule underscores a policy that has been stripped down, appearing more as a façade and proving ineffective in practice. The cost of change, whether in political capital or other, may outweigh the perceived benefits of a new policy or of fixing existing ones. While policy makers may prefer an alternative, they may also not believe that it is worthwhile to pursue. There is, as such, a permanence to ineffective policy.

Future research

The rest of this chapter builds on findings across the various chapters to consider how to take the research for this book forward. The objective of doing so, we stress, is to foster conditions for better policy making and better policies.

The first possible area of research involves investigating more case studies, especially in policy fields beyond those considered in this volume. As the bibliometric analysis in our introductory chapter shows, references to bad policy are common in fields such as health and law. This book considered the financial services sector, the environment, and technologies, reflecting the knowledge and interest of those involved in its creation. There is, however, much to learn from other policy fields. In many Western countries, the health sector, for instance, is under serious stress. How did we get here? What ineffective policies led to this situation? The cases in this volume are from Europe and North America. Extending the research to other parts of the world, such as Asia, or even to international organizations, would be valuable. Scholars interested in policy successes have put forward examples from around the world. There is a need for equivalence when it comes to ineffective policy. One of this book's main findings is the varying levels of gravity, or scope, of policy effectiveness. Adding to the select number of cases across policy fields presented here will provide greater insights into the causes, conditions, and impacts resulting from differing levels of ineffectiveness. In short, we need a fuller picture: more observations can productively be garnered by increasing the number of case studies from a broader range of policy fields.

The purpose of cases and observations is to provide a more precise understanding of ineffective policy through the development of theories, or at least models. Asquer in Chapter 4 directly considers questions of conceptual clarity and begins the development of a theoretical framework that could be expanded upon for a better understanding of ineffective policy. Roberge and Wijermars, in Chapter 2, considered the relationship between democratic decline and policy ineffectiveness though some of their propositions require further testing. There is a need to conduct such work in greater depth. For instance, what type of institutional design is more likely to lead to ineffective policy? How do different political systems generate ineffective policy? What are the conditions that can lead to a policy reversal or a change for a better option? What is the role of courts in addressing ineffective policy? The public policy literature through its different theories, models, and instruments provides opportunities to address these questions. For instance, Perl et al (2018) ask whether policy models can cope with politicized evidence and willful ignorance. There is a need to make use of these while focusing specifically on ineffective policy. Furthermore, there is literature to build on that has considered, for instance, bad ideas and how they have translated into ineffective policy (Oren and Blyth, 2019). It is equally possible to think that considerations on policy ineffectiveness can shed new light on existing public policy questions.

As stated throughout this volume, ineffective policy also runs the risk of causing harm. This is another area that is worth studying more in-depth. Questions of impact and harm go beyond the simple idea that policy automatically generates winners and losers to substantially account for its differentiated effects. The study of policy ineffectiveness needs to be clear on the negative impacts of a policy, whether harm is generated and specifically how it is incurred and by whom. Hasselbach in Chapter 8, for example, provides an important temporal link to harm in that the unrealistic expectations in the plastics policy leave key elements of climate change unaddressed for the future. It is also important to recognize the intersectional nature of harm, which implicitly or even explicitly reinforces larger systemic inequalities. The understanding of harm here is not necessarily universally felt. In essence, ineffective policy harms groups and segments of society, with important repercussions on the whole population, which others may fail to acknowledge or see. Policies and practices that reinforce systemic racism exemplify this type of policy. In this book, McKeen-Edwards in Chapter 11 addresses harm in this way because ultimately payday loans represent a service that is utilized disproportionately by marginalized communities and in some cases to cover necessary life expenses like shelter. Future research on ineffective policy will need to be precise on the harm caused to whom and the implications. It will also provide a potential space to connect with diverse sources of knowledge and voice, explicitly engaging with underlying sources of privilege.

This book claims that studying ineffective policy is necessary to bring about better policy. However, we admittedly have not fully laid out the mechanisms by which this is possible. Therefore, further research should examine, if ineffective policy is the result of intent, how can policy makers' preferences be shifted to favor better options? We suggest that investigating this question offers an opportunity to revisit the source of policy studies, where policy making was seen as problem solving, and to reconsider how policies can be used to make things better. To view public policy as problem resolution is to anchor policy work in sound, honest, and credible social science research. The concept of evidence-based policy (Baron, 2018) is seen as desirable and is often referenced by politicians, policy makers, and even scholars. Yet, when the practice is critically assessed, evidence-based policy seems irrelevant because it is unrealistic and undermined by many other considerations, especially of a political nature. At the same time, policy effectiveness and ineffectiveness must be evidence-based. How can good science influence policy making? As is the case with many other institutions, science has become less trusted than in the past. Working to rebuild trust in science generally is essential to better policy making. Moving from ineffective to effective policy requires a collective effort to sustain the scientific enterprise by recognizing how it can contribute to a better society, as well as pushing beyond existing limits to knowledge. At the same time, policy makers will need to be convinced that it is worthwhile for them to support better policies. Translating scientific knowledge in all its forms to policy makers is critical to reversing bad policy. A possible avenue to explore when these dynamics work well and poorly lies in a focus on how narrative and storytelling can bring about change (Davidson, 2017). What stories about ineffective policy need telling to bring about change? The objective of studying ineffective policy is to identify what does not work so that better options can be considered. Doing so requires that we think more carefully, not just about how knowledge is created, but also about how knowledge is transferred and used in the policy process.

Final thoughts

This book demonstrated that studying ineffective policy – and taking explicit ownership of 'bad' policy making – is necessary work from which policy scholars ought not to turn away. As scholars invested in public policy, whether from the policy studies field per se or other disciplines, as well as citizens, we all have a role to play in more meaningfully addressing the malaise that is afflicting many Western democracies. Focusing on ineffective policy is not just another critique of governments; rather, it is about helping to find real solutions to problems for which scholars have much expertise to share and build on in engaging with democratic deliberations across various issue areas.

This book has demonstrated that ineffective policy is costly on many levels. Policy problems are misaddressed, or not addressed at all. This can be seen in environmental policy making and governments' silence on the effects of technology. The consequences can be much worse if ineffective policy generates emergencies and crises. Problems fester and become more acute than they might otherwise be. There are times when the effects of an ineffective policy may be hidden and not easily identifiable, yet still be significant. Ineffective policy in one field can snowball, affecting other policies and exacerbating other problems, making them more difficult to address or amplifying them. It may also prevent other plausible solutions to existing and emerging problems from being considered. Policy ineffectiveness is more than mistakes, blunders, or even fiascos and catastrophes. Policy ineffectiveness refers to a broader governmental inability to address problems in society. The effects of ineffective policy, succinctly, are not benign.

Wrapping up this book we return to the fundamental questions raised in Chapter 2 by Roberge and Wijermars regarding the relationship between ineffective policy and democratic regression. A key takeaway from their contribution to this volume is that there is a cycle in which democratic regression leads to and sustains ineffective policy, which in turn is an indicator of and reinforces shortcomings in the exercise of democracy. This book has considered why governments adopt and implement ineffective policy; the other side of the coin has, admittedly, not fully been addressed. Why do citizens accept and tolerate ineffective policy? We know that citizens in democracies no longer trust the government in the way that they used to, as addressed by Jesuit and Greitens in Chapter 12. This is once again far from a straightforward relationship. Policy ineffectiveness can decrease trust. That lack of trust tends to widen the gap between government and citizens. Policy makers, on the other hand, should see declining trust as an incentive to do better, though admittedly there is scant evidence to that effect. Hence the need to investigate how to make sense of the relationship between policy makers and citizens in periods of democratic regression. When it comes to ineffective policy, do citizens push politicians and policy makers to look for simple solutions to complex problems that cannot possibly work? Put differently, do citizens (in)directly demand ineffective policy? Could it be that citizens no longer expect public institutions to work for them, and as citizens turn away, public institutions fulfill this prophecy and no longer work in the public interest? Answers to these questions are urgently needed as governments must work or at least be seen to work, to perform and be effective, to address issues that matter to people to ensure legitimacy. Ultimately, ineffective policy undermines the relationship between governments and citizens. This book provides hope that better, if not outright good policies, are possible to help shape a brighter future.

References

Baines, D., Brewer, S., and Kay, A. (2020) 'Political, process and programme failures in the Brexit fiasco: exploring the role of policy deception', *Journal of European Public Policy*, 27(5): 742–60.

Baron, J. (2018) 'A brief history of evidence-based policy', *The Annals*, 678(July): 40–50.

Best, J. (ed) (2016) 'Bureaucratic ambiguity', *An Introduction to the Sociology of Ignorance*, London: Routledge, pp 84–106.

Borowitz, A. (2022) *Profiles in Ignorance: How America's Politicians Got Dumb and Dumber*, Avid Reader, p 320.

Davidson, B. (2017) 'Storytelling and evidence-based policy: lessons from the grey literature', *Palgrave Communications*, 3(1).

Dye, T.R. (1972) *Understanding Public Policy*, Englewood Cliffs, NJ: Prentice-Hall.

Head, B.W. (2022) *Wicked Problems in Public Policy: Understanding and Responding to Complex Challenges*, Cham: Springer Nature.

Howlett, M. and Mukherjee, I. (2018) 'Introduction: the importance of policy design: effective processes, tools and outcomes', in: M. Howlett and I. Mukherjee (eds), *Routledge Handbook of Policy Design*, Boca Raton, Florida: Taylor and Francis.

McConnell, A. (2018) 'Hidden agendas: shining a light on the dark side of public policy', *Journal of European Public Policy*, 25(12): 1739–58.

Michaels, D. (2020) *The Triumph of Doubt: Dark Money and the Science of Deception*, Oxford: Oxford University Press.

Oren, T. and Blyth, M. (2019) 'From big bang to big crash: the early origins of the UK's finance-led growth model and the persistence of bad policy ideas', *New Political Economy*, 24(5): 605–22.

Organization for Economic Development and Cooperation (OECD) (2017) *Preventing Policy Capture Integrity in Public Decision Making*, Paris: OECD Publishing.

Perl, A., Howlett, M., and Ramesh, M. (2018) 'Policy-making and truthiness: can existing policy models cope with politicized evidence and willful ignorance in a 'post-fact' world?', *Policy Sciences*, 51(4): 581–600.

Peters, G.B. (2016) 'Institutional theory', in: C. Ansell and J. Torfing (eds) *Handbook on Theories of Governance*, Cheltenham: Edward Elgar Publishing.

Savoie, D. (2018) *Court Government and the Collapse of Accountability in Canada and the United Kingdom*, Toronto: University of Toronto Press.

Schneider, A.L. and Ingram, H.M. (2019) 'Social constructions, anticipatory feedback strategies, and deceptive public policy', *Policy Studies Journal*, 47(2): 206–36.

't Hart, P. and Compton, M. (eds) (2019) *Great Policy Successes*, Oxford: Oxford University Press.

Williams, D. (2021) 'Motivated ignorance, rationality, and democratic politics', *Synthese*, 198: 7807–27.

Index

Note: References to figures appear in *italic* type; those in **bold** refer to tables